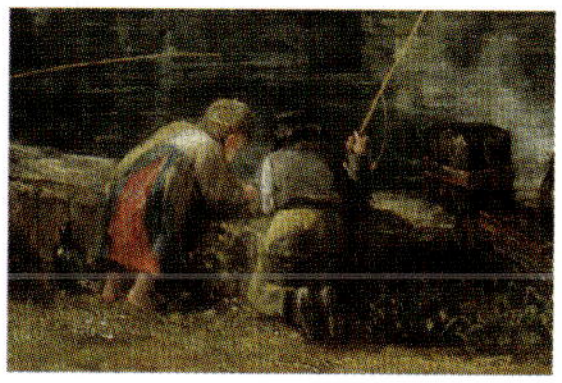

Letters of
John Constable

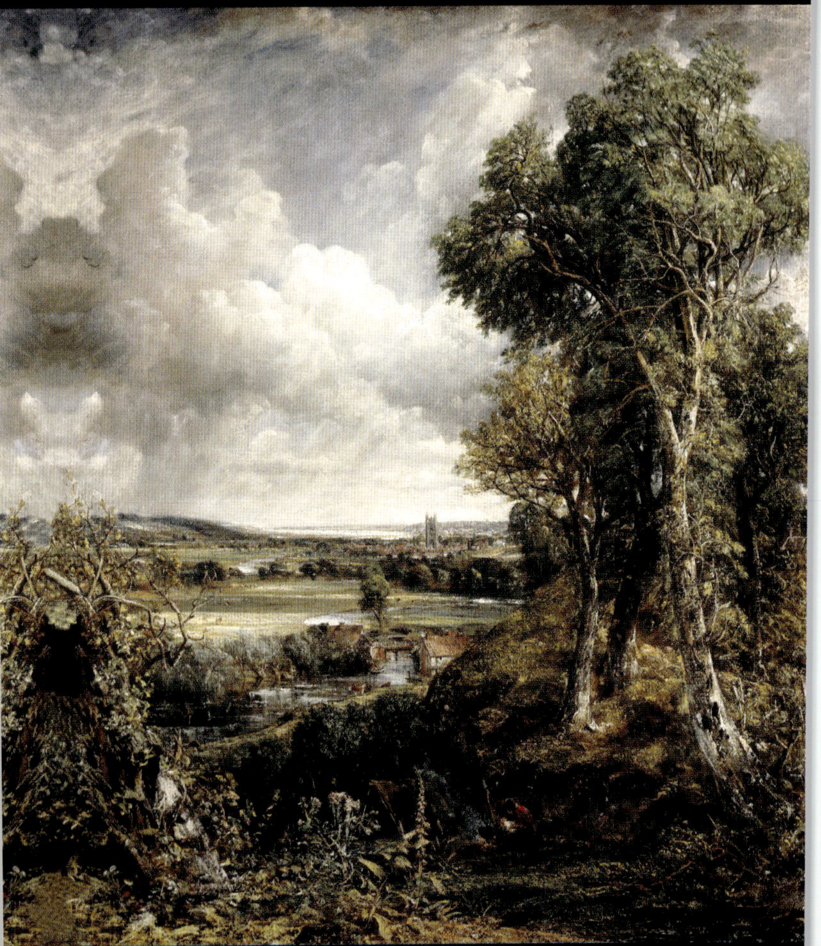

LETTERS OF JOHN CONSTABLE

A selection chosen, edited and introduced by
ANNE LYLES

PALLAS ATHENE

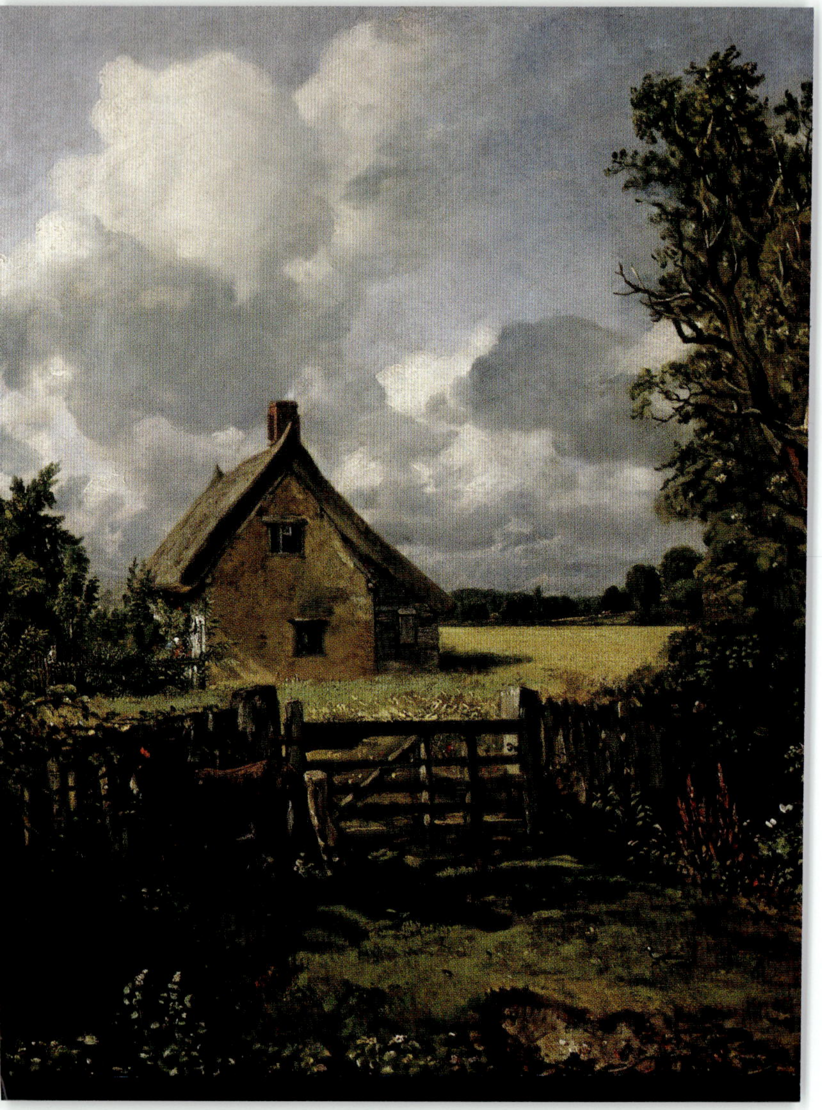

CONTENTS

Fronstispiece: The Vale of Dedham, 1828
Opposite: Cottage in a Cornfield, c. 1815, finished 1833
Overleaf: Coast scene near Brighton, 1824-8

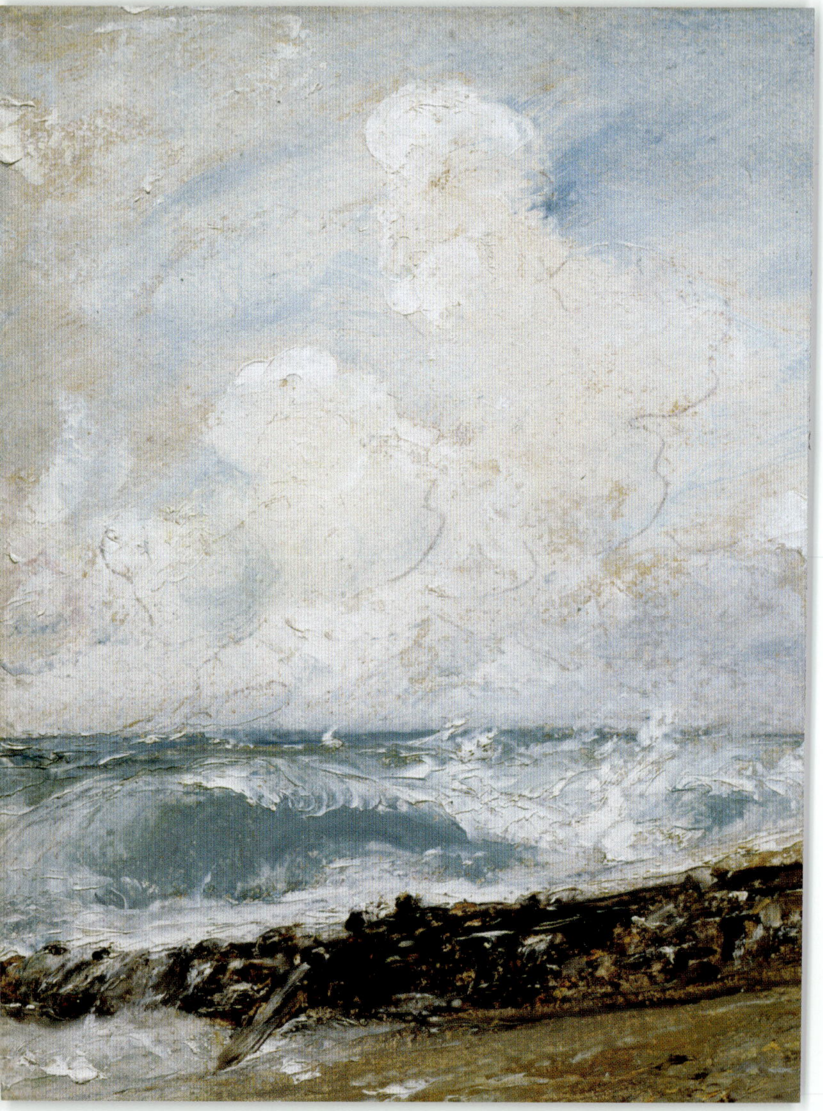

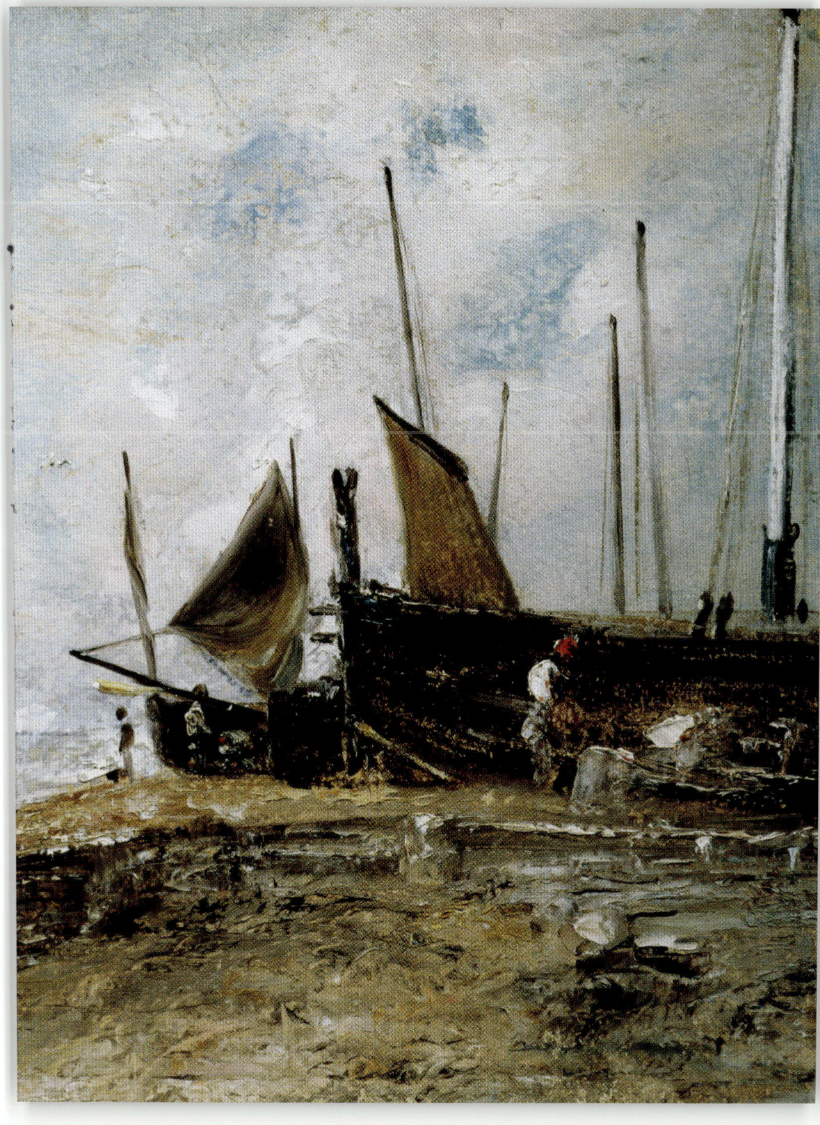

CHRONOLOGY

1764 Golding Constable inherits Flatford Mill
1767 Golding Constable marries Ann Watts
1776 Birth of John Constable
***c.* 1792** JC begins to work for his father
1795 JC introduced to Sir George Beaumont, whose mother lives at Dedham
1796 or 1797 Meets Canon Fisher, later Bishop of Salisbury
1799 Obtains consent from parents to study art in London. Admitted probationer at Royal Academy Schools. Begins friendship with Richard Ramsay Reinagle
1800 Admitted to Life Academy
1801 Tour of Derbyshire with Daniel Whalley, his cousin
1802 Turns down post of drawing master at Marlow Military Academy, returning to East Bergholt in the summer to made studies from nature. Father buys him a studio in East Bergholt
1803 Spends one month travelling along Thames estuary on a voyage on an East Indiaman, making sketches of shipping, including of the *Victory* moored at Chatham
1804 Paints portraits in Suffolk, mainly local farmers
1806 Tour to Lake District

1807 Exhibits views of Lake District at RA. Introduced to Lord Dysart and commissioned by him to make copies of family portraits

1810 Lord Dysart buys a landscape by JC from the RA exhibition

1811 First visit to Salisbury, to stay with Bishop Fisher and his wife. Meets the Bishop's nephew John Fisher (later Archdeacon) who was to become his closest friend. Takes lodgings at 63 Charlotte Street

1813 Sits next to Turner at RA banquet, admiring his 'wonderful range of mind'

1815 Death of Ann Constable, JC's mother, in spring. In summer paints a great deal outdoors in very fine weather. Stays at East Bergholt into the autumn to be close to his father whose health is failing

1816 Enclosure of East Bergholt Common. Death of Golding Constable, JC's father. Visits Wivenhoe Park to paint views of the park for General Slater-Rebow. Marries Maria Bicknell in London in the autumn, then honeymoons in Dorset and Wiltshire

1817 Exhibits small portrait of John Fisher at the RA, also *Flatford Mill* (Tate).Takes house in Keppel St, Bloomsbury. Long summer holiday with Maria in Suffolk. Birth of first child, John Charles

1819 John Fisher installed as Prebendary, moves into Leadenhall in Salisbury Cathedral Close. JC exhibits *White*

Horse (Frick), the first of his River Stour 'six-footers', at RA; it is bought by Fisher, who hangs it at Leadenhall the following year. Birth of second child, Maria Louisa. Elected Associate Royal Academician

1820 Exhibits second Stour 'six-footer', *Stratford Mill* (National Gallery, London) at RA. Long summer visit with Maria and family to stay with the Fishers

1821 Birth of Charles Golding Constable, third child. Exhibits third Stour 'six-footer', *The Hay Wain* (National Gallery, London) at the RA. Starts painting sky studies in oils in Hampstead

1822 Exhibits fourth Stour 'six-footer', *View on the Stour near Dedham* (Huntington Library and Art Collections) at RA. Continues to paint cloud studies in Hampstead. Birth of Isabel Constable, their fourth child, in Hampstead. Moves from Keppel Street to 35 Charlotte Street (former house and studio of Joseph Farington who died the previous year)

1823 Exhibits *Salisbury Cathedral from the Bishop's Grounds* (V & A Museum, London) at RA. Extended stay with Sir George Beaumont at Coleorton in Leicestershire

1824 Exhibits fifth Stour 'six-footer', *The Lock* (private collection, formerly Thyssen Coll) at the RA. Sells on first day of the exhibition. Purchase for the nation of the picture collection of banker John Julius Angerstein, to be exhibited at his house, 100 Pall Mall, until a new building for the collections was to open in Trafalgar Square in 1837. JC installs family in lodgings in Brighton so Maria can benefit from sea air. *The Hay Wain* and *View on the Stour near Dedham* purchased by Anglo-French dealer John Arrowsmith and exhibited at the Paris Salon (at the Louvre). JC awarded a gold medal

1825 Exhibits sixth Stour 'six-footer', *The Leaping Horse*, at the RA exhibition. Birth of Emily, fifth child. Death of Bishop Fisher. Quarrels with Arrowsmith

1826 Exhibits *The Cornfield* (National Gallery, London) at the RA. Paints portrait of Mrs Treslove. Birth of Alfred Abram, sixth child

1827 Death of Sir George Beaumont. Exhibits *The Chain Pier, Brighton* (Tate Britain, London) at the RA. Takes a permanent residence for the family in Hampstead, at 6 Well Walk. Takes two eldest children on a visit to Flatford, where the young John Constable enjoys fishing

1828 January, Birth of Lionel Bicknell Constable, seventh child, at Well Walk. Exhibits *Dedham Vale* (National Gallery, Scotland) at RA. November, death of Maria Constable in Hampstead

1829 February, elected Royal Academician. Exhibits *Hadleigh Castle* (Yale Center for British Art, New Haven) at RA. Stays with John Fisher in Salisbury twice. Starts working on print series, *English Landscape*, with engraver David Lucas

1830 Serves on Hanging Committee for the forthcoming exhibition at RA. Exhibits *Helmingham Dell* (Nelson Atkins Museum of Art, Kansas City) at RA

1831 Visitor at RA Schools. Serves for a second time on the RA hanging committee. Exhibits *Salisbury Cathedral from the Meadows* (Tate Britain and partners) at RA. Attends coronation of William IV in Westminster Abbey. Ill towards end of year with rheumatic fever

1832 Exhibits *The Opening of Waterloo Bridge* (Tate Britain) at RA. Summer; fifth and final part of *English Landscape* published. Death of John Fisher. Death of assistant Johnny Dunthorne

1833 June: delivers first lecture on landscape painting to the Literary and Scientific Society of Hampstead. JC's friend and future biographer C. R. Leslie leaves for America to take up a teaching post at West Point

1834 Ill again with rheumatic fever. C. R. Leslie and his family return to England. Exhibits only watercolours at RA exhibition, including *The Mound of the City of Old Sarum* (V & A, London). July: leaves Well Walk permanently. Stays with brewer George Constable (no relation) in Arundel, Sussex. September: joins C. R. Leslie and his family as guests of 3rd Earl of Egremont at Petworth

1835 Sells *The Valley Farm* (Tate Britain) to collector Robert Vernon before showing it at the Royal Academy exhibition. June: delivers second lecture on landscape to

Literary and Scientific Society at Hampstead. Stays with George Constable in Arundel, Sussex. Son Charles Golding starts as midshipman

1836 Exhibits *The Cenotaph* (National Gallery, London) at the RA, and *Stonehenge* (watercolour, V & A , London), the last RA exhibition to take place at Somerset House before the move to a new building in Trafalgar Square. Delivers four lectures on landscape at the Royal Institution. Gives third (and final) lecture on landscape in Hampstead

1837 Working over the winter on *Arundel Mill and Castle* (Toledo Museum of Art). Visitor in Life Class at RA Schools. **1st April: dies** in Charlotte Street in early hours of the morning. *Arundel Mill* exhibited posthumously at the new RA premises in Trafalgar Square. *The Cornfield* given by subscribers to the National Gallery towards end of the year

1843 Publication of first edition of C. R. Leslie, *Memoirs of the Life of John Constable Esq, R.A.*

1845 Publication of second (revised) edition of Leslie's *Memoirs*

1888 Family collection including contents of JC's studio left to the V&A by his last surviving child, Isabel

Overleaf: Dedham from Langham, late 1820s

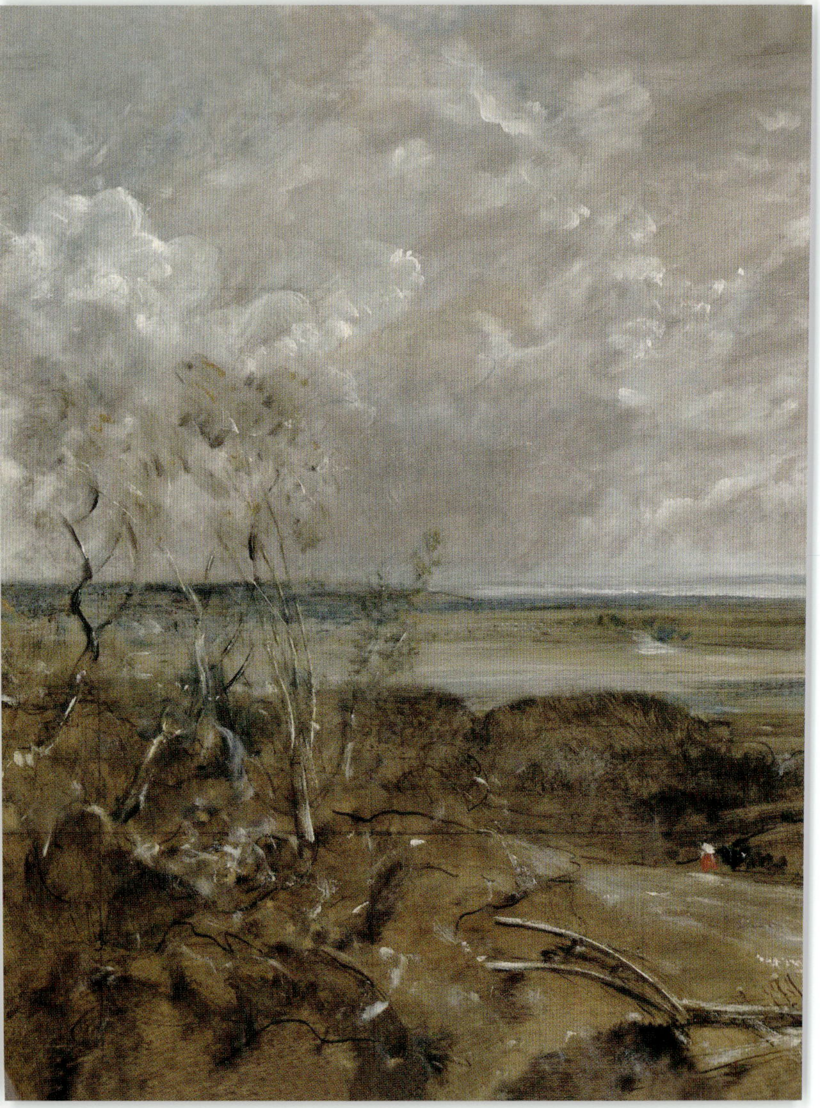

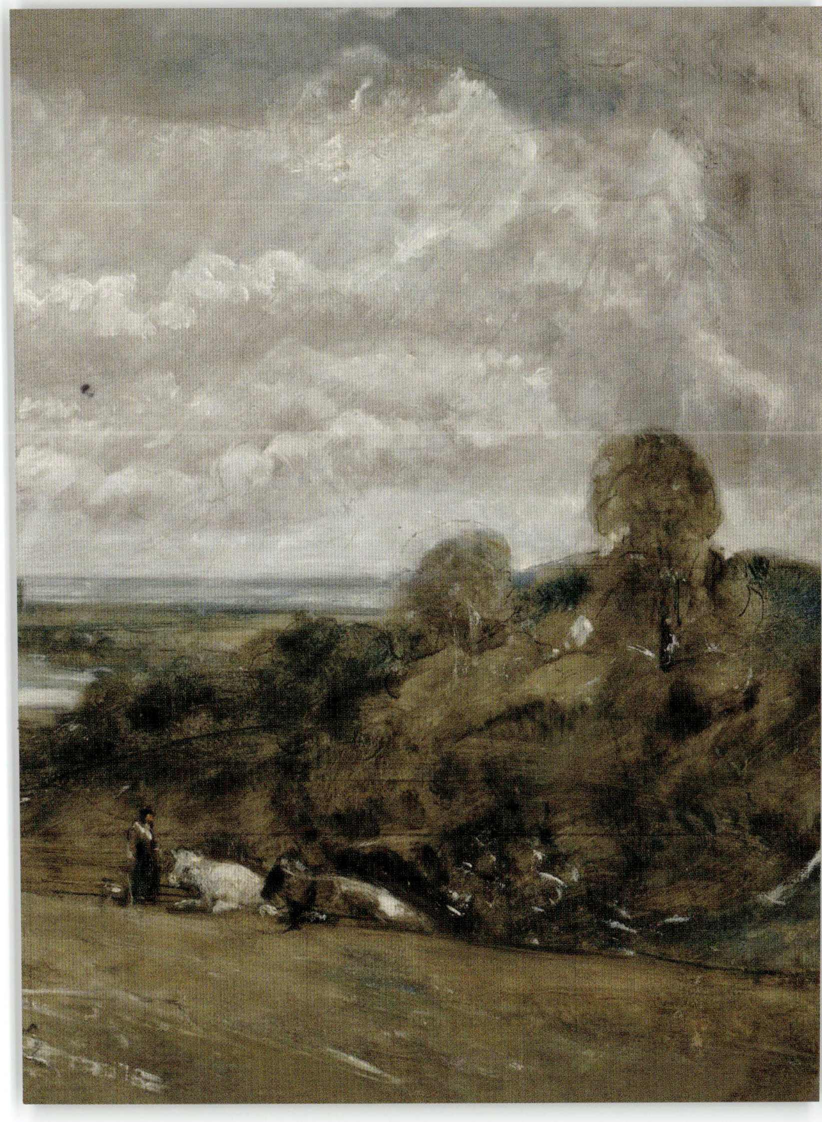

CAST OF CHARACTERS

SIR GEORGE BEAUMONT, BT. (1753–1827) Collector, patron, arbiter of taste and amateur artist (exhibited work at Royal Academy as 'Honorary Exhibitor'). Befriended JC in the latter's early years in London, having first been introduced to him at Dedham, Essex, *c.* 1795. JC stayed at Beaumont's country estate, Coleorton, Leicestershire, for six weeks in 1823, copying Old Masters (mainly Claude) and sketching in the landscaped grounds. Beaumont's collection of Old Masters and contemporary British art was bequeathed as an early foundation gift to the National Gallery, London. Although Beaumont gave JC much support, he never purchased one of his paintings.

ABRAM CONSTABLE (1783–1862) Younger brother of JC. Trained to succeed their father Golding Constable in running the family milling and farming business, thus freeing John to train as an artist in London. After Golding's death in 1816, moved with their sister, Mary (1781-1865) back to Flatford Mill where he continued to run the family business and thus provide his siblings with an income. Retired (and sold the family businesses) in 1846.

ANN CONSTABLE (1748–1815) Mother of JC. Born Ann Watts, daughter of a London cooper, married Golding Constable in 1767. JC was the fourth of their six children. A regular correspondent with her son, often sending him parcels of food or coal in the winter months, and encouraging him to work hard but to keep an eye on his health. Enabled introductions on her son's behalf to influential visitors to Suffolk or Essex, such as Sir George Beaumont (q.v.). Died of a stroke in 1815, which first came on when she was working in her newly planted flower garden at East Bergholt House.

GOLDING CONSTABLE (1739–1816) Father of JC. Inherited Flatford Mill, and much adjacent land, from a distant relation, and became a prosperous farmer and corn merchant. Owned a fleet of barges for transporting milled corn down the navigable river Stour for onward shipment, by sea, to London. In 1772–4 built substantial mansion, East Bergholt House, to house his growing family; JC born there in 1776. Originally opposed JC's hopes to study as an artist, but relented when a younger son, Abram (q.v.) became of age and showed suitable ability to be trained up in the family business instead.

MARIA CONSTABLE, *née* BICKNELL (1788–1828) Wife of JC. Daughter of Charles Bicknell, solicitor to the Prince

Regent and to the Admiralty. Met JC in Suffolk, probably as early as 1800 when still only twelve, on a visit to her maternal grandfather, the Revd Dr Durand Rhudde, Rector of East Bergholt-cum-Brantham. JC declared his love for Maria in 1809, but given the opposition of Dr Rhudde, the couple did not marry until autumn 1816, shortly after Golding Constable's death when JC came into his inheritance. Maria bore JC seven children. Her life was cut short at 41 following a long struggle with tuberculosis.

JOHN DUNTHORNE (*c.* 1770–1844) Plumber, painter, glazier and enthusiastic amateur artist. Lived next door to East Bergholt House, home of the Constable family, and became regular sketching companion of the young JC in Suffolk in the 1790s. Corresponded with JC in the latter's early years in London when training to become an artist at the RA schools. Their friendship was broken in 1816, but renewed again in the 1830s.

JOHN ('JOHNNY') DUNTHORNE (1798–1832) Son of John Dunthorne (q.v.). As a boy worked for JC in East Bergholt, grinding colours for him, and in the following years occasionally supplied drawings of local features for JC when the latter was working on Suffolk subjects in his London studio. From 1820 until about 1829 worked, at intervals, with JC as an assistant in his London studio, helping set his palette, 'squaring' or tracing compositions, drawing in outlines, even partially painting some of JC's second versions of compositions (both landscapes and portraits). From 1827 exhibited his own paintings at the RA, and by 1830 had established himself as a picture-cleaner and restorer. JC was greatly moved by Dunthorne's premature death in 1832, especially as it followed soon after that of his friend Archdeacon John Fisher (q.v.).

ARCHDEACON JOHN FISHER (1788–1832) JC's closest friend, with whom he had an extensive and remarkable correspondence, which affords important insights into the artist's character and aims as a painter. They probably first met in Salisbury in 1811, when JC was invited to stay at the Bishop's Palace by Bishop John Fisher (q.v.), the archdeacon's uncle. The younger John Fisher was ordained priest in 1812, and thanks to preferment from his uncle, obtained multiple livings, becoming vicar of Osmington in 1813, Archdeacon of Berkshire in 1817, and Canon Residentiary at Salisbury Cathedral in 1819. The latter position came with a house, Leadenhall, in the Cathedral Close, where JC spent extended stays in 1820 and 1829. The Archdeacon was an important patron to JC, buying *The White Horse* and *Salisbury Cathedral from the Bishop's Grounds*, both of which hung at Leadenhall. Died in 1832 in France.

BISHOP JOHN FISHER (1748–1825) From a well-connected clerical family. Appointed preceptor to fourth son of George III, Edward (later Duke of Kent), hence his nickname the 'King's Fisher'. Canon at Windsor in 1786, and later tutor to Princess Charlotte, daughter of Prince Regent. Appointed rector of Langham in Suffolk in 1790, meeting the young JC there a few years later, and giving him significant help in his early career. Bishop of Exeter in 1802 and Bishop of Salisbury in 1807. An amateur artist himself, commissioned paintings from JC, for which the artist always remained grateful, honouring the Bishop's memory shortly after the latter's death with a landscape, *The Glebe Farm*, 1826, featuring Langham Church.

CHARLES ROBERT LESLIE (1794–1859) Born in London to American parents. Raised in Philadelphia then returned to London to train as an artist, eventually becoming a Royal Academician. Specialised in mainly small, narrative pictures. Close friend to, and regular correspondent with, JC mainly in second half of latter's life. Wrote an important biography of JC in 1843, revised 1845 and often reprinted. Also liaised closely with JC's family on sorting the contents of his studio following his death, as well as with the engraver, David Lucas (q.v.), on publishing further, posthumous subjects from JC's paintings for *English Landscape*.

DAVID LUCAS (1802–1881) Mezzotint engraver, born in Northamptonshire and trained by printmaker S.W. Reynolds. Came to attention of JC in 1829, subsequently working in close collaboration with the painter in the preparation of 22 mezzotint plates for *English Landscape*, published in five parts between 1830 and 1832. An extensive correspondence survives between the two men, revealing how demanding JC could be of Lucas's translation of his paintings into mezzotint form, frequently requesting many corrections at proof stage. Two other, large single plates by Lucas, *The Lock* and *The Cornfield*, were also published in JC's lifetime. Lucas's artistic reputation rests chiefly on his successful collaboration with JC. He died in Fulham Union workhouse in 1881 and was buried in a pauper's grave nearby.

MRS SARAH SKEY, *née* BICKNELL (1775–1840) Elder half-sister of Maria Bicknell (later Maria Constable, q.v.), who often went to stay with her at Spring Grove, Bewdley, Worcestershire. Towards the end of 1811 Maria wrote from Spring Grove entreating JC to cease thinking of her. Instead, he jumped onto a coach to Worcester to persuade Maria to change her mind. Mrs Skey – effectively defying her father's wishes – welcomed him at Spring Grove, and the romance between JC and Maria was renewed at a critical stage in its early development.

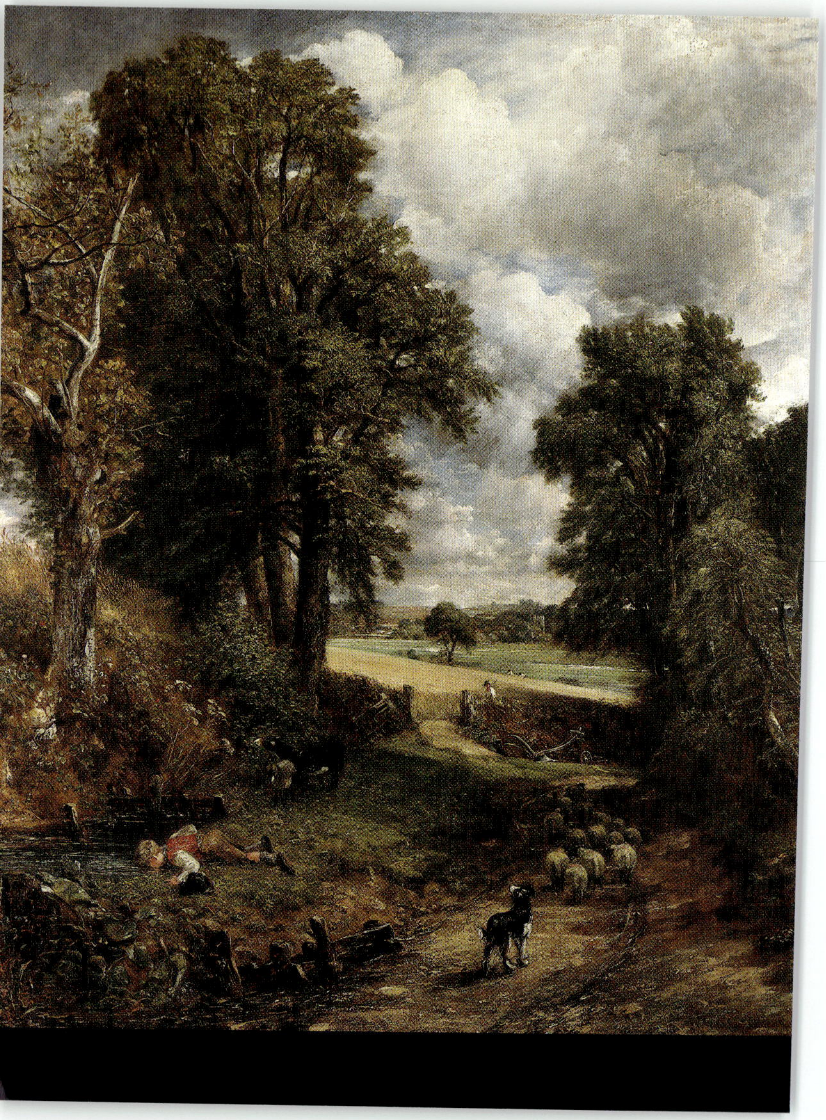

INTRODUCTION

The work of the British landscape painter John Constable (1776–1837) is today widely celebrated by a national audience (and, increasingly, an international one as well). Paintings such as *Flatford Mill*, 1817 (Tate Britain), or *The Haywain*, 1821 (National Gallery, London), have gained familiarity (if not overfamiliarity) through extensive reproduction on posters, mugs or tea towels. Showing scenes in Suffolk, where Constable had spent his childhood, these paintings are often idealized in the popular imagination as representing the quintessence of an English rural idyll. Together with his direct contemporary, and rival, J. M. W. Turner, John Constable is today a household name.

Constable did not, however, achieve this level of fame in his own lifetime. In the second half of his career his paintings certainly became more widely noticed, and appreciated, by British critics who indeed often compared them with those of Turner. Constable was also widely praised in Paris in 1824, when *The Haywain* was exhibited at the Louvre, and nearly acquired by the French nation.

Opposite: The Cornfield, 1826

This was a remarkable achievement given how much livelier, and more firmly established, the art community was in France than Britain at this date.

Such press interest in his own lifetime would not, however, have been enough to guarantee Constable's present-day fame. Artistic reputations notoriously wax and wane. Moreover, in the years following Constable's death in 1837, only one of his paintings, *The Cornfield*, 1826, was on public view in Britain, acquired by subscribers in 1837 in his memory for the National Gallery, London. But one of the most perceptive of Constable's obituarists (and the only one to remark on Constable's success in France), writing in *Bell's Weekly Messenger*, anticipated that the distinctiveness of Constable's style (which he called the artist's 'peculiarity') would 'render his works lasting and valuable in the eyes of all true judges of art, when many of the common-place productions of his contemporaries are sunk in oblivion'.

Little would this obituarist have known that a biographer was waiting in the wings to pen an influential memoir of Constable's life and work that would help this very prediction come to pass. This was the artist C. R. Leslie, a close friend towards the end of Constable's life. A Londoner by birth, but an American by ancestry, Leslie had first got to know Constable about 1820, a few years after the latter had settled permanently in London following his marriage to Maria Bicknell in 1816. At this point Constable was beginning to make a name for himself at the Royal Academy with his large-scale exhibition canvases of Suffolk subjects, known as 'six footers' (measuring approximately 6 feet, or 174 cm, in width). Indeed the first of these – *The White Horse*, 1819 (Frick Collection, New York) – effectively earned Constable his long-coveted election as an associate Royal Academician in 1819. Leslie, himself a painter (of mainly small-scale subject pictures), later claimed that it was because he so admired Constable's landscape art that he subsequently came to know him personally. The close bond between the two was cemented when both became fathers and, in ensuing years, godparents to each other's children. In writing his *Memoirs of the Life of John Constable*, Leslie decided to base them chiefly on his subject's letters and own writings, a not uncommon device at the time, serving to add an air of authenticity to such accounts. However there was also the advantage that Leslie had often been in correspondence with the artist himself, so knew what an impressive and engaging letter writer he was. Acting to some extent as a father figure to Constable's children in the years following their father's death, Leslie was given full access to Constable's papers, and able to select for citation in the

Overleaf: A Scene on the River Stour ('The White Horse'), 1819

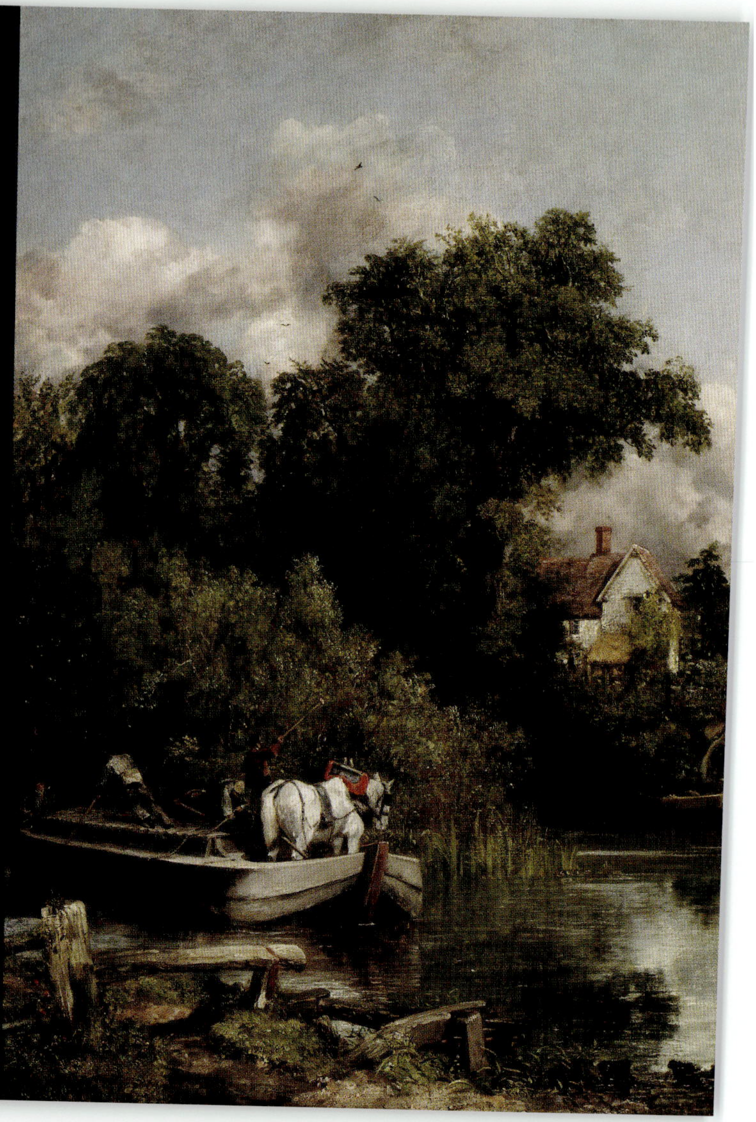

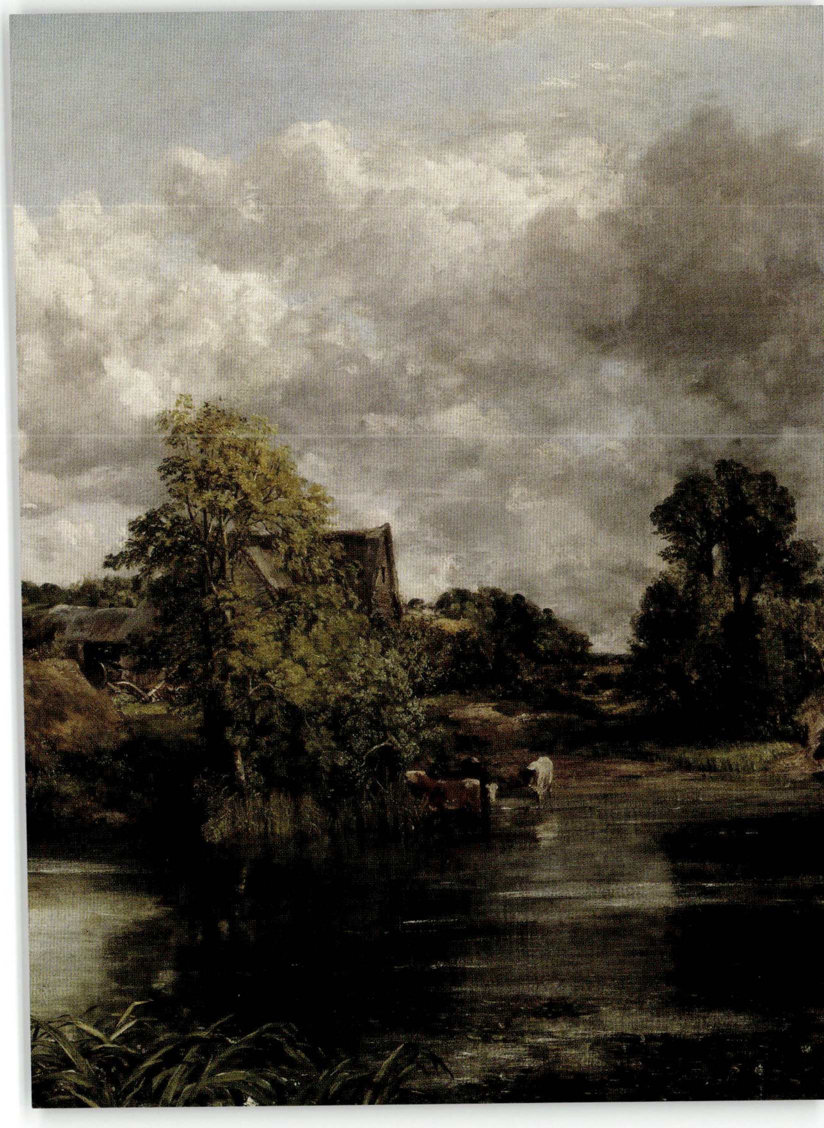

Memoirs interesting memoranda Constable had made, quotations from poetry or his thoughts on landscape. These latter included the important notes Constable had made for the Lectures on Landscape painting he delivered towards the end of his life at the Royal Institution, the Worcester Atheneum and at the Hampstead Literary and Scientific Society. Above all, Leslie had access – and cited extensive excerpts from – those remarkably insightful, and today especially celebrated, letters between Constable and his other most important friend, Archdeacon John Fisher.

Fisher and Constable seem to have first met around 1811 through the former's uncle, also John Fisher (who was Bishop of Salisbury at the time). Despite a considerable age difference, they soon became fast friends, and were to exchange in their letters personal news interlaced with thoughts about art, nature, literature, and religion, often leavened with gossip about characters or events in the clerical world. They were united in their firm support of the established Anglican Church, and it was to Fisher (as well as, sometimes, to Maria) that Constable would air his prejudices about Nonconformists (his particular targets being Baptists or Calvinists, p. 176). It was also to Fisher that Constable wrote perhaps his single most famous letter, from Hampstead in 1821, about his original inspiration in becoming a painter ('I should paint my own places best – Painting is but another word for feeling.

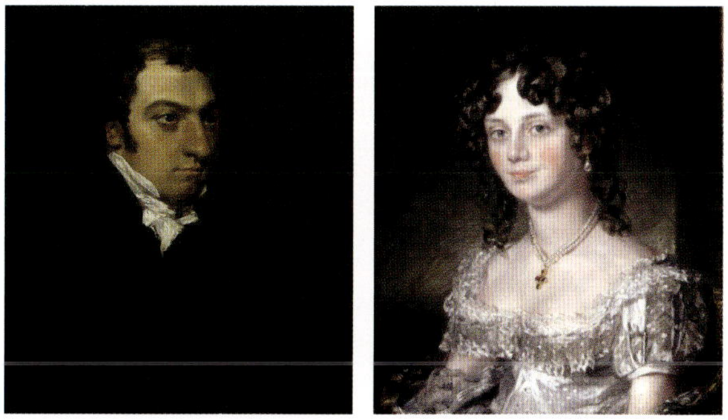

Archdeacon John Fisher and his wife Mary, 1816

I associate my "careless boyhood" to all that lies on the banks of the *Stour*'); and about his motives in making his cloud studies in oils in Hampstead around this date ('It will be difficult to name a class of landscape, in which the sky is not the "*key note*", the standard of "*Scale*", and the chief "*organ of sentiment*") (p. 125).

After Fisher's death in 1832, Constable wrote to Leslie saying how powerfully his friend's death had affected him as 'we …confided in each other entirely'. Leslie himself thenceforward became Constable's chief confidant. Leslie's *Memoirs* were first published in 1843, but became

Overleaf: Cloud Study, 1822. Inscribed: 'Augt 1 1822 11 o'clock A.M. Very hot with large climbing clouds under the sun. Wind westerly.'

more widely read from 1845 when a new, more affordable edition came out. It was to prove remarkably popular, and often reprinted. *The Memoirs* helped keep Constable's name in the public memory for the next half century.

This was especially important at a time when the critic John Ruskin was promoting the reputation of his artist hero J. M. W. Turner, more often than not at the expense of other artists. Indeed it seems to have been partly in response to the publication of Leslie's *Memoirs* that Ruskin went out of his way to denigrate Constable's art. In 1844, for example, just a year after the publication of the first edition of the *Memoirs*, Ruskin wrote in *Modern Painters* (first volume, second edition) that Constable's 'early education and associations… induced in him a morbid preference of subjects of a low order. I have never seen any work of his in which there were any signs of his being able to draw.'

Leslie, however, had also had an agenda in writing the *Memoirs*. He cast Constable as a sort of beleaguered artistic warrior, battling against the odds – against the conventions of the day – to succeed in his mission of transforming landscape painting into a more truthful and 'naturalistic' art. He described Constable as 'the most genuine painter of English landscape that has yet lived'. Whilst this interpretation of the artist is not entirely inaccurate, it is nevertheless misleading. Constable's earlier paintings and oil sketches, many of which were made in the open air – and are today highly praised for their spontaneity and expressiveness – are indeed more closely based on direct observation than those made by any of his artistic forebears. However most of the work Constable made in his later career (which Leslie liked less) was substantially produced in the studio, assembled either from existing, or purposely made, fresh material.

Furthermore, whilst Constable was indeed determined to produce a landscape art more evidently based on direct experience than on earlier artistic models, he was fundamentally an academic artist whose career was shaped by academic ambitions. He knew full well that there is no such thing as an 'innocent' eye. Rather, he was hugely knowledgeable about earlier landscape painting (as Leslie himself acknowledged). From his earliest years studying art in London, Constable had to teach himself oil painting (something the Academy itself did not teach at that date) by copying examples from the Old Masters, such as Ruisdael, Claude, Rubens or from eighteenth-century British painters, especially Richard Wilson. He also sought out examples of Old Master paintings in private collections, and in time was to become a collector himself (in particular of Old Master prints). He could hardly have

Overleaf: Malvern Hall, Warwickshire, 1809. This may be Constable's first painting to have been painted out of doors

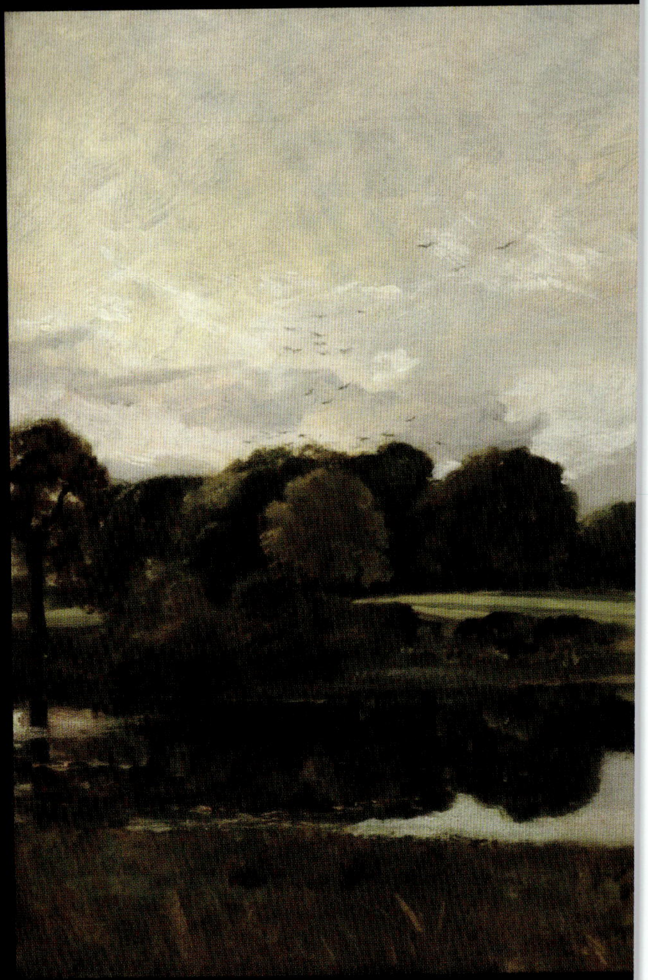

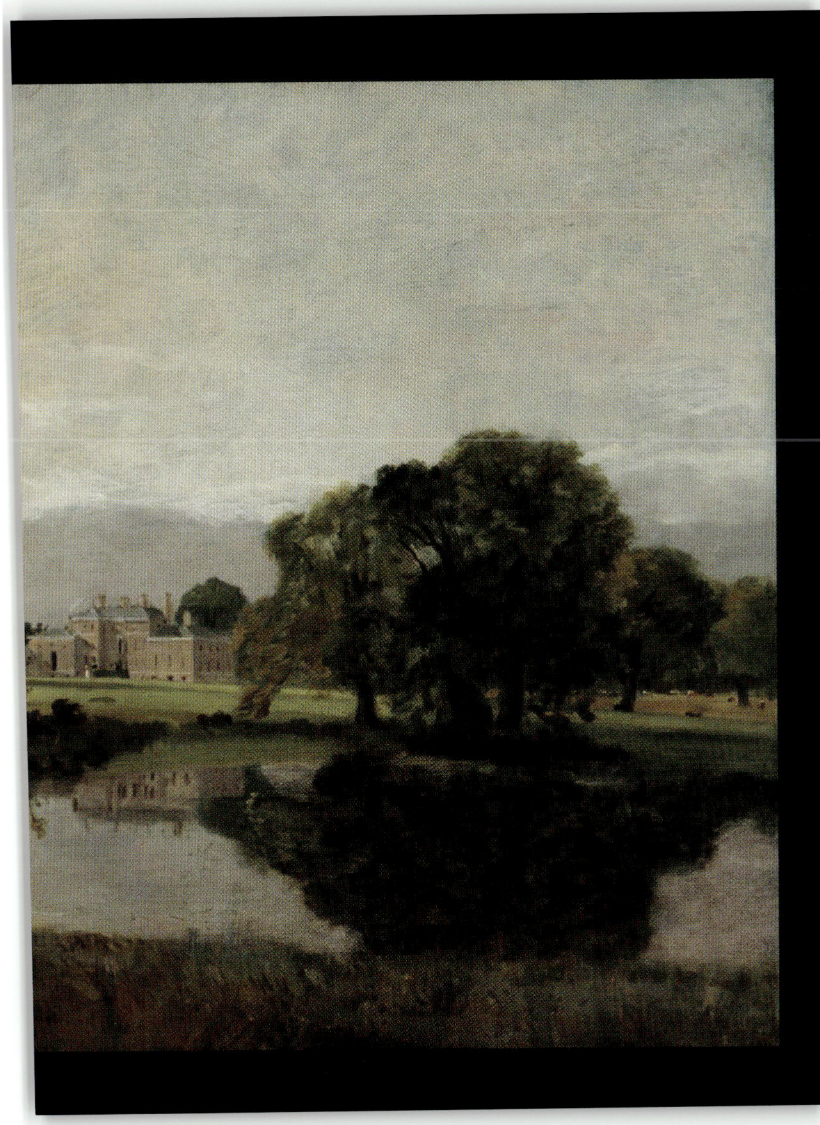

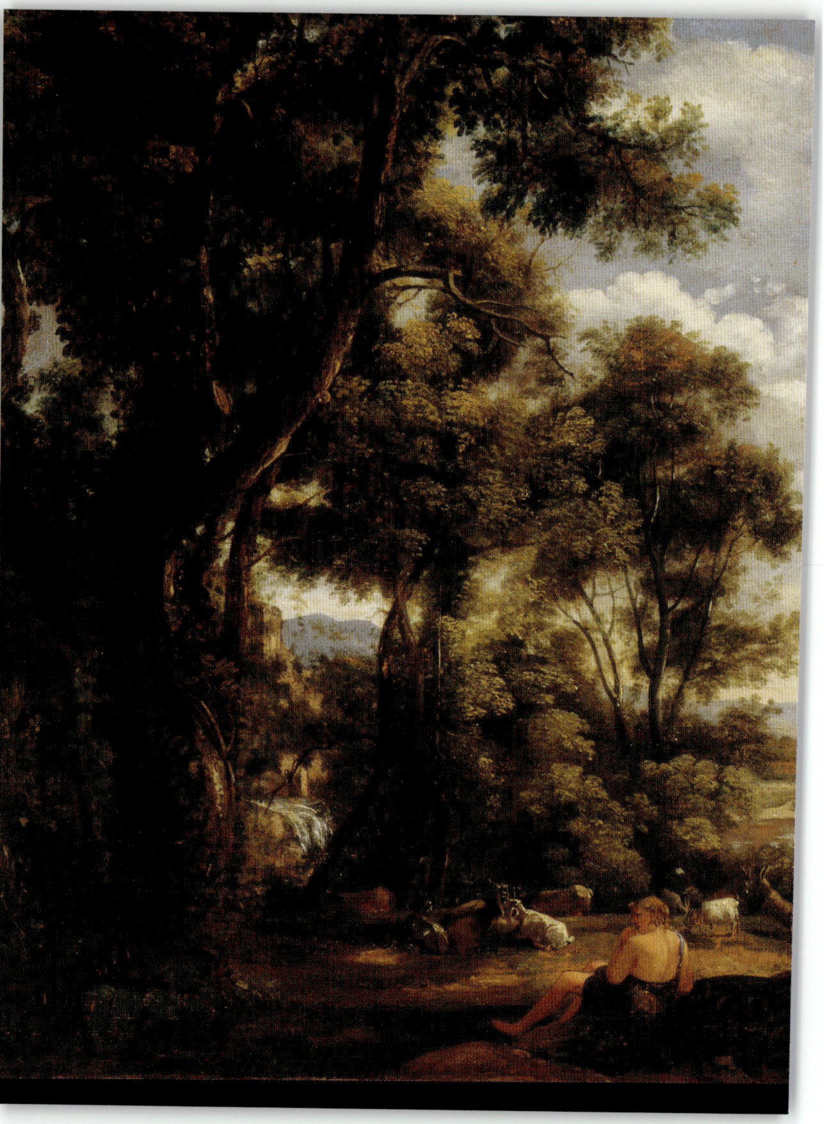

delivered such illuminating lectures on landscape painting in his late career without this sort of background knowledge. So it was clear that any artistic 'battle' Constable might choose to fight would have to be from within the Academy's own walls. Hence Constable's ambition to become a full Royal Academician.

It was, nevertheless, to prove a long journey, one narrated by Leslie in the *Memoirs* using extracts from Constable's correspondence dating from between 1799, when he was first admitted as a student in the Academy's Schools until 1829 when he was finally elected a full Academician. In 1799 Constable had written from London to John Dunthorne in East Bergholt (the local plumber, glazier and inn sign painter who had helped Constable experiment with oil painting in earlier years) explaining he was now admitted as a student at the Schools, having submitted a figure ('the Torso', presumably a copy from a plaster cast of the Belvedere Torso). Three years later Constable then told Dunthorne how much he was enjoying attending lectures on anatomy, which served to carry his mind to the 'Divine Architect' (p. 66).

When finally elected a full Academician in 1829 – thirty years after first being admitted as a student – Constable received a letter from Fisher hailing his victory a 'triumph...of patient moral integrity over bare chicanery'.

Opposite: Landscape with Goatherd and Goats (after Claude), 1823

Constable had mentioned to Fisher that Turner had called at his house and studio in Charlotte Street, Fitzrovia, to congratulate him on his success. This, Fisher said, was evidence of Turner claiming Constable 'as a brother labourer' (p. 193).

At the time when Leslie was writing his *Memoirs*, few of the open air sketches mentioned above were available for public viewing. This situation changed completely when, in 1888, Constable's last surviving child, Isabel Constable, gifted or bequeathed substantial numbers of paintings and drawings by her father to the National Gallery, the Victoria & Albert Museum, the British Museum and the Royal Academy. These gifts included (especially amongst the examples donated to the Victoria & Albert Museum) a large part of the remaining stock of Constable's studio, which had contained most of his working sketches, whether open air or studio studies. The public availability of this new material provided new insights into the artist's working methods and, accordingly, a further boost to the artist's reputation.

What was still lacking at this date, towards the end of the nineteenth century, was any further insight into Constable's life, activities or personality as revealed in his extensive correspondence. Although in the first half of the

Opposite: Study of the Trunk of an Elm Tree, c. 1821

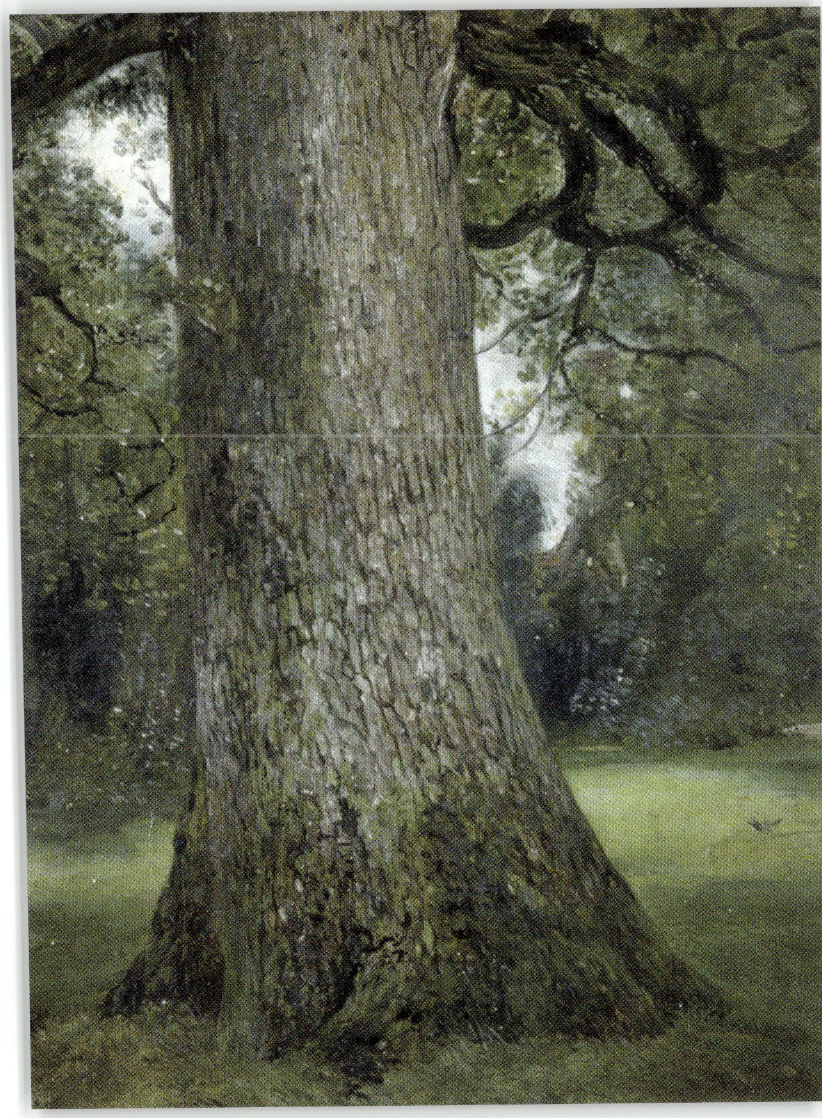

twentieth century some additional letters from or to Constable (not previously cited in Leslie's *Memoirs*) had occasionally been published, it was not until the 1960s that his entire correspondence was made available by the Suffolk Records Society. Six volumes of the letters appeared between 1962 and 1968, organised not in a chronological sequence but according to the individuals – friends, family and professional acquaintances – with whom Constable had corresponded. The volumes were transcribed and edited by Ronald Brymer Beckett, a retired lawyer with impeccable administrative and organisational skills who had worked for many years in the Indian Civil Service. Beckett also provided his own extensive, even exhaustive, explanatory notes which were set amongst the transcriptions of the letters themselves. A volume of Constable's *Discourses* followed in 1970, giving the full letterpress drafted by Constable to accompany some mezzotint engravings Constable had commissioned printmaker David Lucas to make after his paintings, known as *English Landscape*, published in the early 1830s. The *Discourses* volume also included fuller versions or variants (than those published in Leslie's *Memoirs*) of the notes Constable had made for his Lectures on Landscape. Then in 1975 the Suffolk Records Society issued a final volume, *Further Documents and Correspondence*, under different editors, to complete the series. This, as its title implies, mainly included letters omitted from the earlier volumes. However, it also contained a list of the contents of Constable's extensive library, covering not just art but also divinity, literature, natural philosophy and books of antiquarian and topographical interest. Only now could it be fully appreciated just how very well read Constable was.

The publication of Constable's entire correspondence was a phenomenal achievement, bearing in mind the lack of digital resources at the time and the fact that Beckett had to contend with the difficulty of deciphering Constable's handwriting. For Constable's letters had tended to be written towards the end the day, often by candlelight, when he was already tired after a long day's painting, or else in a hurry to catch the post. In October 1822, Fisher started his reply to a recent letter from Constable with the comment: 'I think you did quite right to lay down your palette for your pen; for if you were painting no better than you wrote your canvas would not be very intelligible'.

This particular letter was written from Osmington, Dorset, one of Fisher's many livings in an age of clerical pluralism. Some years before, in October 1816, Constable had been invited by Fisher to spend his honeymoon there with Maria. Theirs had been a long and arduous courtship lasting some seven years. They had first met in the Suffolk village of East Bergholt, where Constable had been born, and where his father operated as a corn and coal

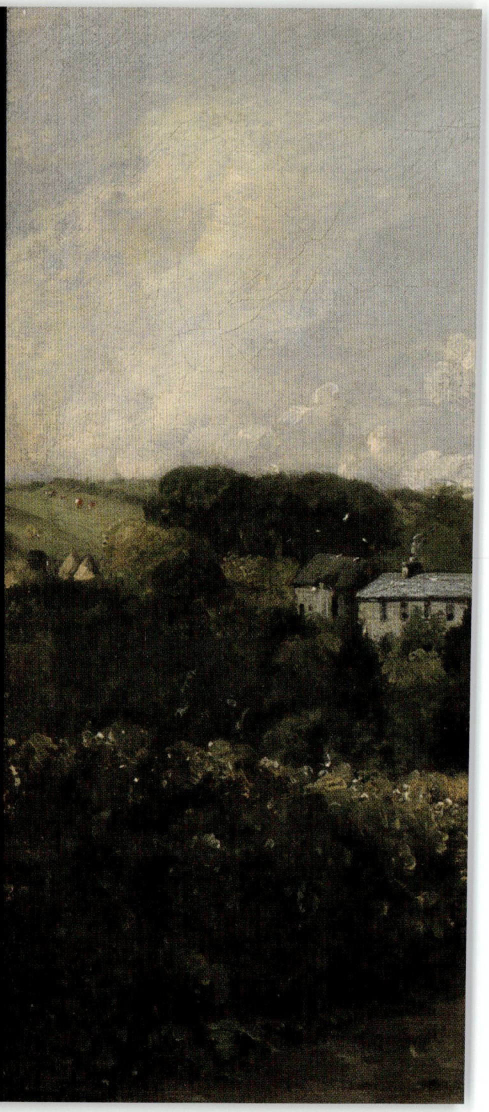

Osmington Village, 1816-17.
Given by Constable
to the Fishers.

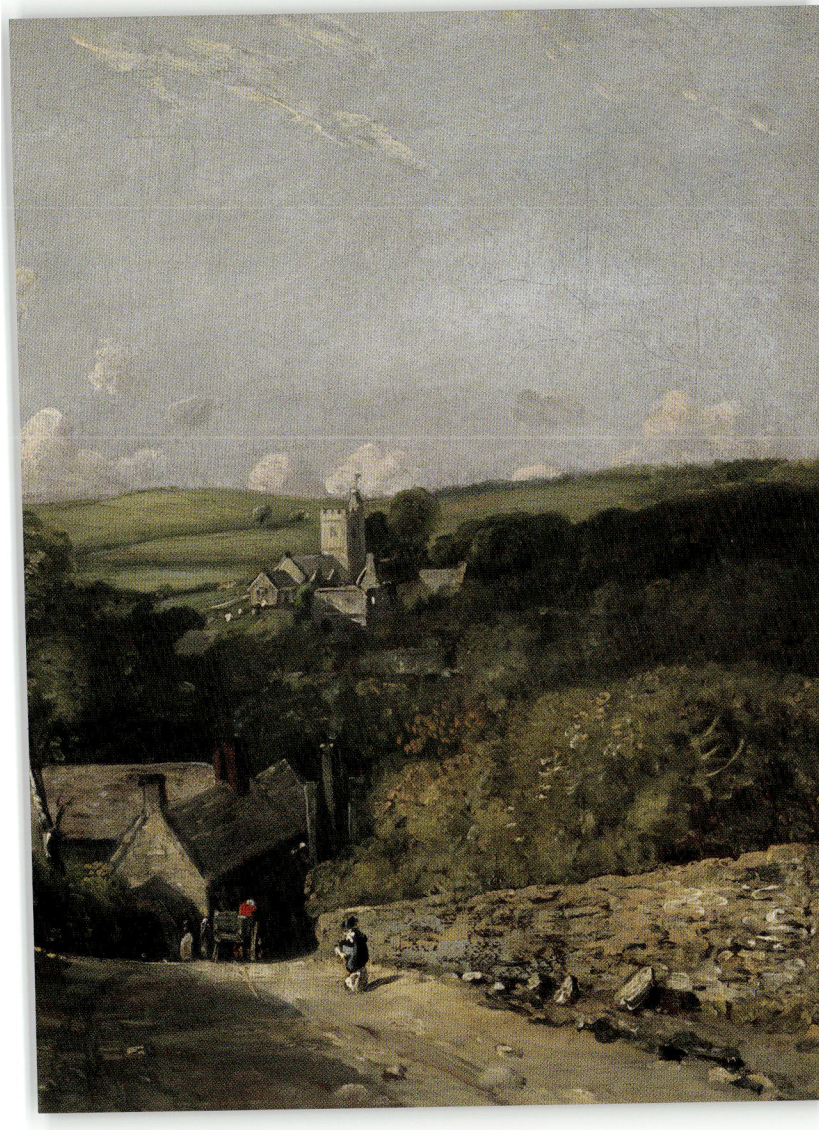

merchant. Maria's maternal grandfather, the Reverend Durand Rhudde, was rector at the church there, and it was on visits to the Rectory that Constable had first met Maria. By 1809 he had declared his love for her. However, the rector was opposed to the relationship, so Maria's father – Charles Bicknell, solicitor to the Admiralty in London (as well as to the Prince Regent) – intermittently forbade Constable to visit her at Spring Gardens in Whitehall where the family lived, or indeed even to write to her. Their correspondence charts the ups and downs of their courtship (given they did continue to exchange letters, often without permission). By temperament Constable was a deeply anxious person, and in Maria he had found someone who was intelligent, patient and who, like Fisher, knew how to calm the artist's nerves. If Maria was surely aware that Constable's commitment to painting always came first, she also knew that he was unwilling to give her up. Thus, when in 1816 he came into an inheritance following his parents' death, they decided to marry without her family's permission. It was John Fisher himself who performed the ceremony at her local parish church, St Martin in the Fields.

The marriage was an intensely happy one, and Constable proved a devoted husband and father to their seven children. However Maria's health was fragile – tuberculosis ran in the family. As her condition began to

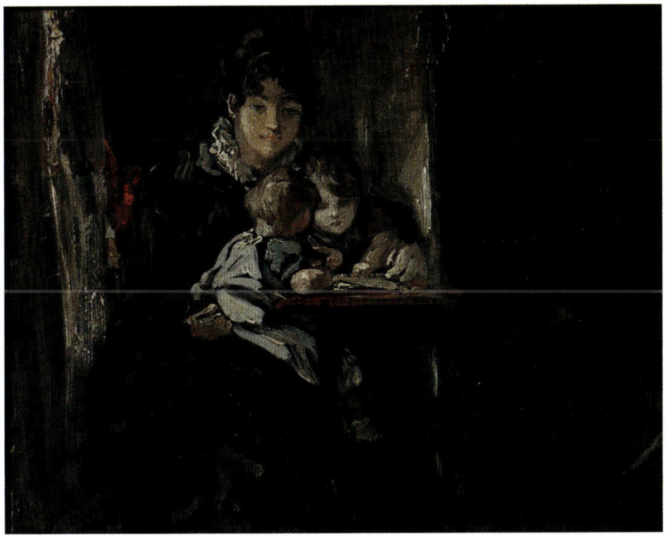

Maria Constable and two of her children, c. 1820

deteriorate, Constable found temporary lodgings during the summer in locations with better air than that of polluted central London – both for her benefit and that of their children. He found accommodation in Hampstead from 1819, and – for its sea air – in Brighton between 1824 and 1828 (and, shortly after arriving there in 1824, wrote to Fisher saying how much he disliked the resort,

p. 163). All this added greatly to his expenses, already stretched by the increasing size of his family, and in the letter which Fisher writes to Constable from Osmington in 1822 he offers to lend the artist money. Three years later Constable was confiding to a new patron, Francis Darby of Coalbrookdale – whom he barely knew but was corresponding with in connection with the latter's wish to buy two of his Hampstead paintings – about his near constant state of anxiety. 'My life is a struggle between my "social affections"', he told Darby, 'and my "love of art". I daily feel the remark of Lord Bacon's that "single men are the best servants of the public"' (p. 179). Maria for her own part, usually stoical in the face of her husband's time away from home owing to professional commitments, knew when to put her foot down. In the autumn of 1823 she wrote to tell him that she was 'heartily sick' of his long absence in Leicestershire – where Constable had been extending his stay with his patron Sir George Beaumont at Coleorton Hall, happily immersed in copying one of the latter's favourite paintings by Claude. She meanwhile was holding the family fort and having to put up with some of Constable's most unwelcome visitors, whom she dubbed 'your loungers'. She suggested he should not even contemplate showing her his copy after Sir George's Claude on his return or she would be tempted to throw it out of the window (p. 145).

Inevitably the tone – and level of formality – in Constable's letters varies according to the recipient or with his increasing level of intimacy with them. In his correspondence with Maria, his form of address evolves over time from 'Miss Bicknell', via 'my dear Maria', and 'my dearest Maria' to his fond nickname for her, 'Fish'. The letters he writes to her before their marriage, when not referring to the difficulties of their courtship, often speak of his progress in painting (in the early years this might also concern portrait painting, which he had taken up reluctantly as it paid well and thus in theory would improve their prospects to marry). He might also tell her of the beauty of the countryside near East Bergholt – or of events or people in the village she would have remembered from earlier visits there herself (in 1814 he tells her 'there is a very grand match nearly ready at Old Hall', p. 98). More occasionally Constable might mention what he had been reading, once citing the Rev Archibald Alison's *Principles of Taste* and its uplifting message that the author considers us 'endowed with minds capable of comprehending the "beauty and sublimity of the material world" [...] as the means of leading us to *religious sentiment*' (p. 99).

After their marriage, if they were apart and needed to correspond – as arose in the 1820s when Maria and the

Overleaf: Fen Lane, East Bergholt, 1817

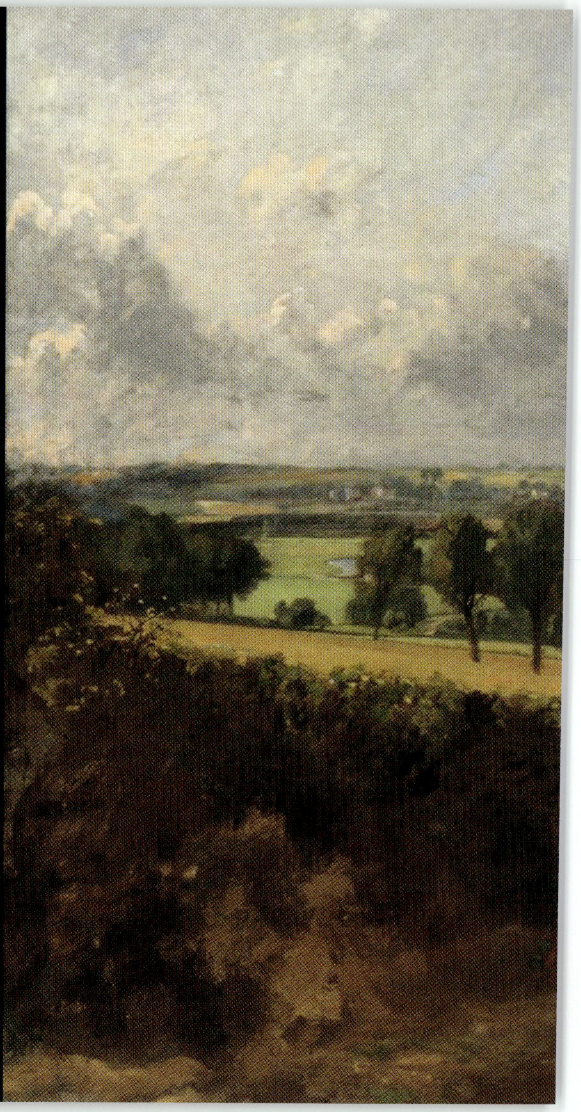

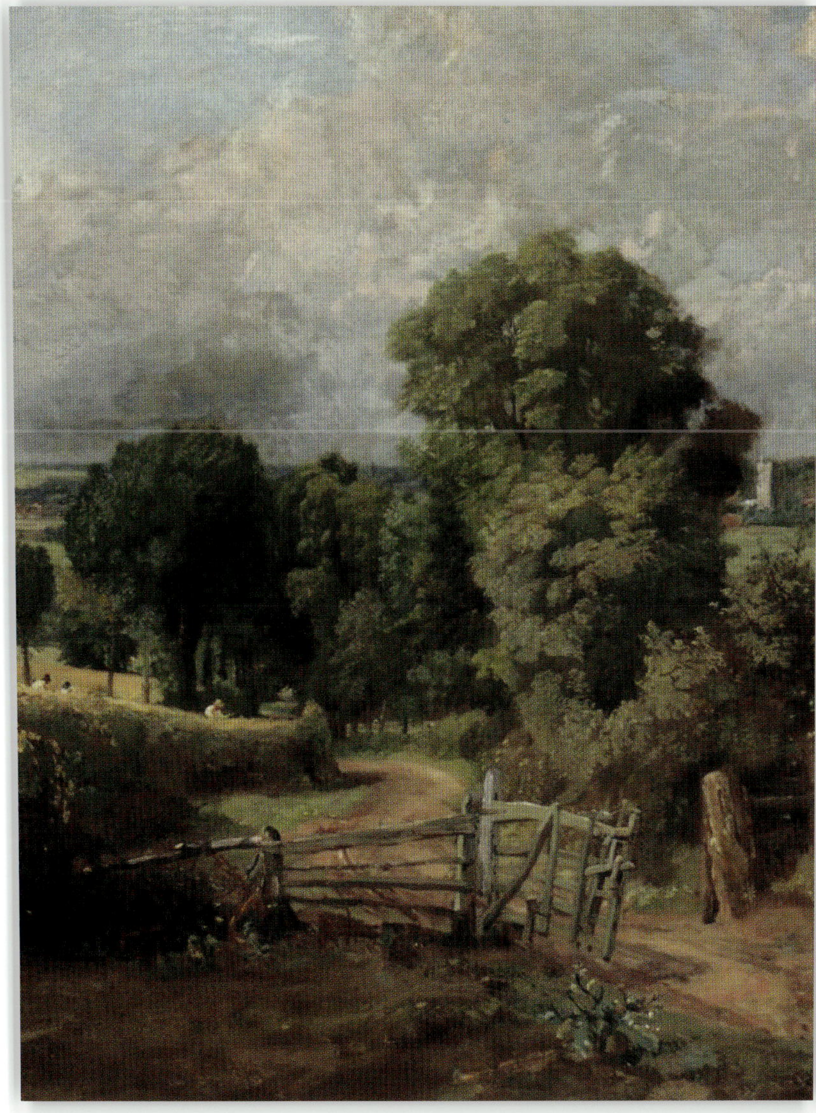

children were in Brighton and when Constable would return, at intervals, to his studio in London to work on his large exhibition pictures – their exchanges would tend to refer to domestic matters as much as to his painting. Constable decided to keep a journal during the weeks he spent apart from his family in 1824 and 1825, pages of which could be hand delivered to Maria by friends making the journey to Brighton to save on postage, paid at this date by the recipient. His journal entries might concern his health, the behaviour of the servants, his meals, his visitors, his art or his own frequent outings, in no particular order of priority. Thus his sighting of a hot air balloon or else, inside the house, a cat trapped on a ledge, the appearance of goldfinches, robins or a mouse – might be recorded by him in the same day's entry as, say, his telling Maria about the favourable reception of his paintings in Paris (p. 154). It was when in company with John Fisher – by this date living in Salisbury as Canon Residentiary but also frequently in London – that the two men had spotted the hot air balloon from the top of the Haymarket, on their return from looking at paintings at the British Institution (a rival exhibiting body to the Royal Academy) and at Christie's.

Not only did Constable and Fisher often look at, or exchange views about, pictures together, Fisher had long seen himself as chief 'advisor' to Constable about the latter's own work – indeed he could sometimes be as frank in this regard as Maria was in berating her husband for an overlong absence. When Constable was embarking on his sixth large painting of yet another view on the navigable section of the River Stour, *The Leaping Horse*, 1825 (Royal Academy, London), Fisher suggested Constable might this time 'diversify his subject as to time of day', p. 171 (the artist generally preferred to set his landscapes in the summer, and usually – as so perceptively observed by Richard and Samuel Redgrave – with the sun sited directly overhead). Constable's reply to Fisher was typically unflinching. He would not vary his landscapes simply 'to keep the public in good humour ...I imagine myself driving a nail. I have driven it some way by persevering with this nail I may drive it home' (p. 173).

As it happens, shortly afterwards Constable did decide to diversify his art, if not as to time of day then certainly as to subject. He began to concentrate on inland Suffolk scenery instead – it was around this time he painted *The Cornfield*, 1826, and embarked on variants of his Hampstead views. He even decided to paint a large picture of *The Chain Pier, Brighton*, 1827 (Tate, London). Fisher no doubt felt he had every right to advise Constable on matters relating to the latter's painting. He had purchased *The White Horse* from Constable; he had also purchased, and given to a Salisbury neighbour, the artist's second

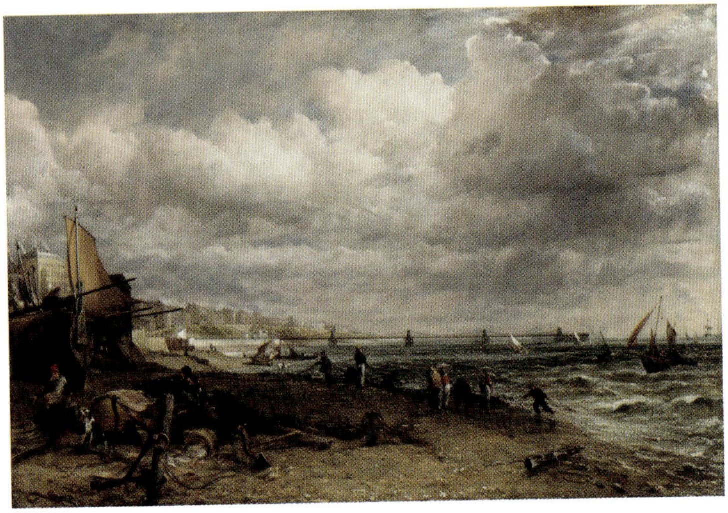

The Chain Pier, Brighton, 1827

six-footer *Stratford Mill*; and when Fisher's uncle, the Bishop, objected to the '*dark cloud*' in Constable's specially commissioned view of *Salisbury from the Bishop's Grounds* (Victoria & Albert Museum, London) – an objection Constable had anticipated (p. 135) – the younger Fisher ended up acquiring the picture himself whilst Constable chose to paint an entirely new version for the uncle.

After Maria's death at the end of 1828, which was followed by that of Archdeacon Fisher in 1832, life became increasingly difficult for Constable. He had charge of seven children, and he also began to suffer bouts of ill health himself, specifically it seems episodes of rheumatic fever which caused him acute pain. In 1831 he confessed to David Lucas, now working on the mezzotint engravings for *English Landscape*, that 'my indisposition sadly worries me and makes me think (perhaps too darkly) on almost every subject' (p. 196). Constable then proceeded to unburden himself in the same letter to his talented, hard-working and long-suffering engraver as to his worries about the long duration of the project, '*its expense, its hopelessness of reumuneration*'. He did though add that he meant not to blame Lucas himself for any of this (and ended the letter by asking after the health of Lucas's wife).

Sometimes Constable's illness forced him take to his bed. In January 1832, it was from 'My bed. Charlotte Street' that he wrote a letter to C. R. Leslie thanking him for so evocatively describing some of the pictures the latter had recently seen on a visit to Petworth House, Sussex, home of the 3rd Earl of Egremont (p. 208). Leslie had suggested, no doubt with a view to distract Constable from worrying about his health, that perhaps the artist might like to join him (Leslie was already a regular guest at Petworth) on a future visit. Constable's initial instinct was to reject Leslie's offer: 'As to meeting you in these grand scenes, remember the great were not made for me, nor I for the great'. This sounds like special pleading. Constable had of course already enjoyed a long house stay with an aristocrat (Sir George Beaumont) nearly a decade before. It would seem that the real explanation here is less to do with his awkwardness over social status as his recalling the episode when, in 1824, the 3rd Earl – a keen collector of contemporary art (of Turner's work in particular) – had been shown one of Constable's Hampstead paintings but then failed to buy it.

As it happens, Constable did subsequently join Leslie at Petworth in September 1834, though the Earl never did buy one of his paintings. This interpretation of Constable's initial reluctance to visit Petworth is surely confirmed by his subsequent remark to Leslie – in the very next sentence – that 'My limited and abstracted art is to be found under every hedge, and in every lane, and therefore nobody thinks it worth picking up' (p. 211). Not even – it would seem – Lord Egremont.

Constable has a marvellous turn of phrase, and this one, about his 'limited and abstracted art' – like many of his other perceptive observations about painting and nature – is very memorable. However it is surely a mistake

Opposite: Hampstead Heath, c. 1820-30

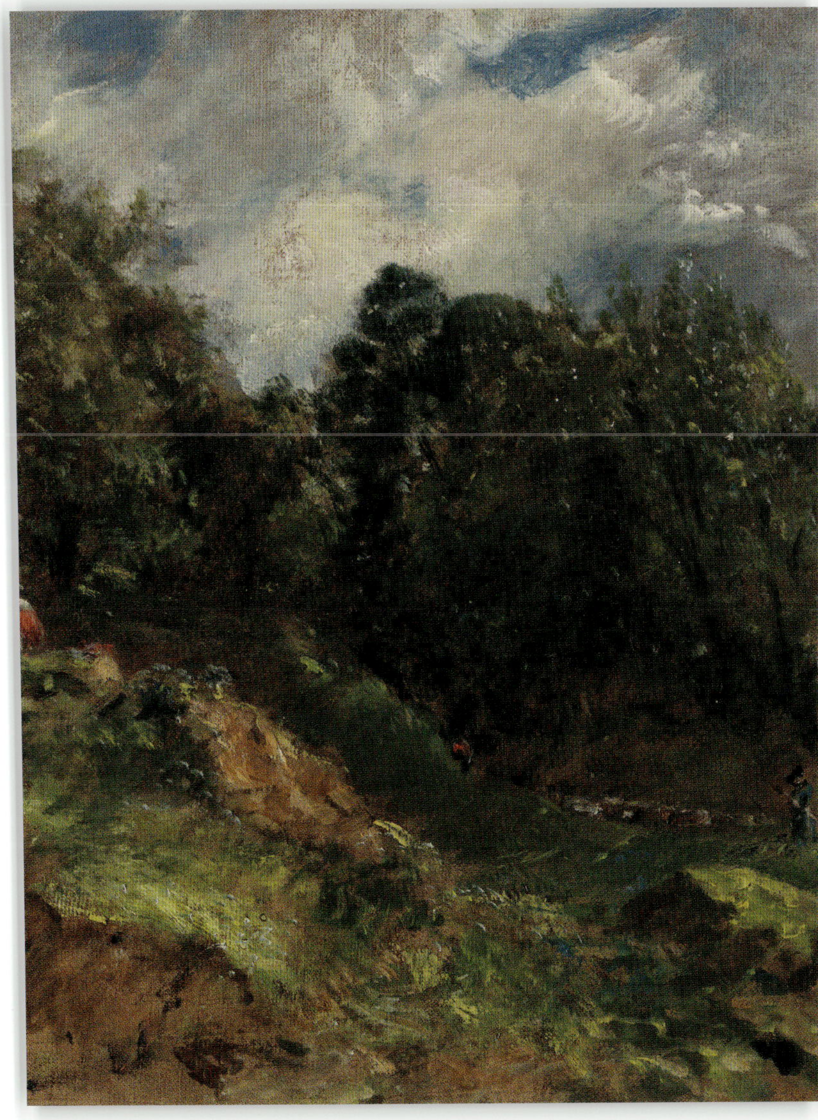

to cite it – as is so often done – shorn of its context. Had such a phrase been coined by Constable in, say, a letter to Maria written from East Bergholt around 1810 or 1811 when he had recently embarked on a campaign of open air sketching in the local lanes, one could perhaps take it more at face value. However by the time he wrote this letter to Leslie in 1832, his art had long moved in different directions. This was the year Constable painted his largest, and perhaps grandest, canvas, *The Opening of Waterloo Bridge* (Tate, London), a picture which owes more to eighteenth-century Italian painter Canaletto and his views of Venice than to any of Constable's own direct fieldwork in the Suffolk lanes.

Constable's letters should, then, ideally be assessed in the context of their exact date, addressee and his likely motives at the time he wrote them (or bearing in mind previous disappointments). Indeed, a careful reading of his correspondence reveals him to be a much more complex person than is often assumed – or certainly more complex than if judged purely by some of his more quotable sayings (taken out of context) or else by his artistic output alone. Moreover, as revealed in the letter the artist wrote to Lucas also cited above it is evident that (especially in later life) Constable was prone, particularly when feeling anxious or unwell, to unburden himself unguardedly of his prejudices or worries (especially worries about money) – unaware that one day such letters would be published. How many other artists might have felt or written similarly at the time, one wonders, but whose letters – unlike those by Constable – have no longer survived?

It is in this context, arguably, that some of Constable's more excessive utterances should be judged. He was a Tory, and believed in the time-honoured 'rightness' of the English countryside. A church tower, usually that of St Mary's Dedham, often provides a tiny feature punctuating the distant horizon of his Suffolk landscapes. As a supporter of the Anglican Church, he had opposed the Catholic Emancipation Act (1829), and was fearful of the implications of the Reform Bill (passed as the Reform Act in 1832) – mostly, it seems, concerned for the legacy he hoped to pass on to his children. The two members of the House of Lords he most disliked for their reforming tendencies were Joseph Hume and Henry Brougham. In September 1831, Constable found himself sitting immediately behind Brougham during the service for the coronation of William IV at Westminster Abbey (as a full Royal Academician, Constable had been invited to attend). He could not resist drawing Brougham in caricature, wearing over his huge wig a precariously placed coronet donned

Overleaf: The Opening of Waterloo Bridge ('Whitehall Stairs, June 18, 1817'), 1829-31

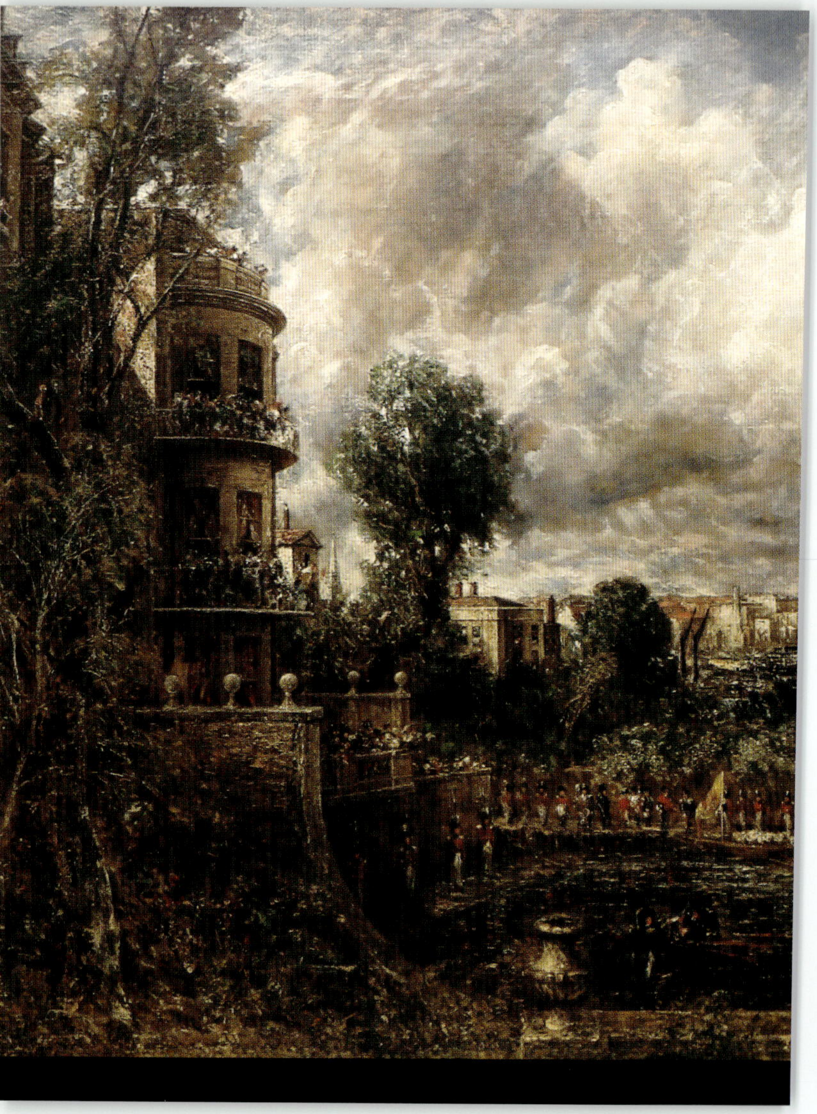

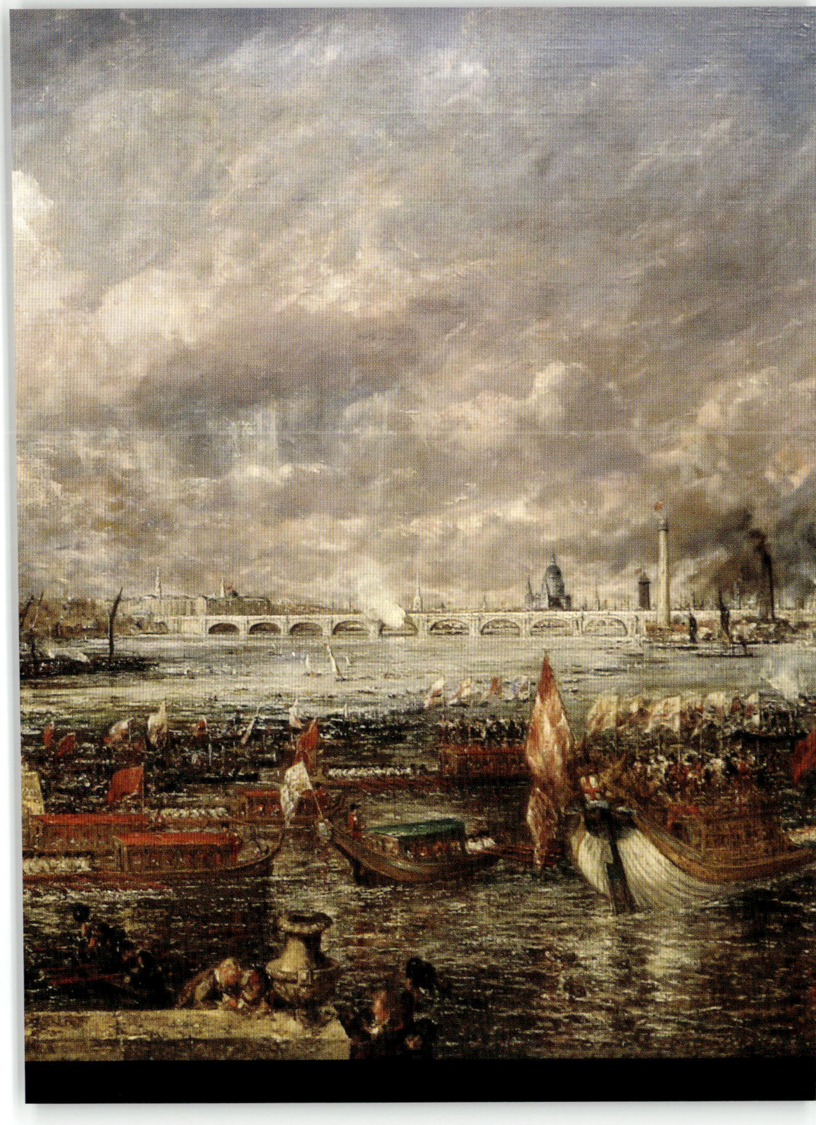

by the newly created peer towards the end of the ceremony (p. 201). Writing to Leslie in early November 1831, in the build up to the passing of the Reform Act and when Constable told him 'I am much worse [in health] than when you and Mrs Leslie were here', he seems to have worked himself into something of a frenzy about the Bill. He dreaded, he told Leslie, 'this tremendous attack on the constitution of the country' ... in which the government (a Whig government) was now in danger of falling into 'the hands of the rabble and dregs of the people, and the devil's agents on earth – the agitators' (p. 204). However, only three days later – when he told Leslie 'he was now perhaps quite well' – he wrote that he no longer had the 'least concern' about the Reform bill, whether it be '*dead* or *alive*' (p. 205).

The Redgrave brothers, writing in the later nineteenth century, believed Leslie in his *Memoirs* had presented the artist 'couleur de rose'. Whilst Leslie did in fact publish this particular exchange of correspondence in the *Memoirs*, it is true that he omitted other letters (or parts of letters) which demonstrated Constable's more sarcastic or scatological side. When (to use Fisher's phrase), Constable lay down his palette for his pen, it has been seen how this talented letter writer would often weave the private and personal with the public and the professional. This, surely, is what makes his letters so remarkable, and often so endearing, to the specialist and general reader alike. The correspondence – as well as being, in its entirety, a remarkable historical resource – gives us fascinating insights into Constable's art and his personality. We see him sometimes anxious, at other times relaxed (when in sympathetic company); 'quick in detecting cant and quackery' in others (as Leslie observed), but just as quick to cast himself as a victim within the art world of his day; thoughtful and generous to others but often carelessly out-spoken or deeply sarcastic. The fully published correspondence – and this small volume only gives a small cross-section – reveals the artist 'warts and all' rather than 'couleur de rose'.

The twentieth-century poet and writer Geoffrey Grigson once described Constable's correspondence with John Fisher as 'an English classic of universal human relevance' – something one might perhaps claim for Constable's correspondence as a whole. What cannot be doubted is that to read the correspondence is not only rewarding in itself, but also serves to direct one back again to the paintings, however many times one might have seen them in reproduction.

EDITORIAL NOTE

When Ronald Beckett transcribed and edited John Constable's extensive correspondence in the 1960s, he decided to organize it by the correspondents themselves, the better to achieve a sense of an unfolding dialogue between sender and recipient. This selection, by contrast, incorporates a wide range of correspondents in a single volume and has been arranged in chronological order so as to create a coherent narrative. It aims to capture some of the key moments in Constable's life and career, charting its various twists and turns, and including insights into his professional ambitions alongside demanding family commitments.

We are grateful to the Suffolk Records Society for permission to republish the letters selected here, their transcripts closely following those of Beckett except for some occasional modernisations of spelling and punctuation. Sometimes only excerpts from the letters have been selected, where other paragraphs seemed of less relevance or overly obscure. As with Beckett's volumes, footnotes are given in an attempt to clarify references to other artists or paintings cited in the letters. These either follow annotations made by Beckett himself, or else represent fresh suggestions from the editors.

AL & AFW

FURTHER READING

R. B. Beckett, ed., *John Constable's Correspondence*, Ipswich, six volumes, 1962–8: I. The Family at East Bergholt 1807-1837; II. Early Friends and Maria Bicknell (Mrs Constable); III. The Correspondence with C. R. Leslie; IV. Patrons, Dealers and Fellow Artists; V. Various Friends, with Charles Boner and the Artist's Children; VI. The Fishers

R. B. Beckett, ed., *John Constable's Discourses*, Ipswich, 1970

Gillian Forrester, *John Constable*, London, 2024

Martin Gayford and Anne Lyles, *Constable's Portraits*, London, 2009

James Hamilton, *Constable: A Portrait*, London, 2022

Richard Humphreys, *John Constable: The Leaping Horse,* London 2018

Nicola Moorby, *Turner and Constable: Art, Life, Landscape*, New Haven & London, 2025

C. R. Leslie, *Memoirs of the Life of John Constable, Esq. R.A.*, 1843, 1845; annotated edition by Jonathan Mayne, London, 1951

Susan Owens, *Constable's Year: an Artist in Changing Seasons*, London, 2026

L. Parris, C. Shields and I. Fleming-Williams, edd., *John Constable, Further Documents and Correspondence,* London & Ipswich, 1975

Richard and Samuel Redgrave, *A Century of Painters of the English School*, London, 2nd edition, 1890

William Vaughan, 'Constable's Englishness', *The Oxford Art Journal*, vol. 19, no. 2, 1996, pp. 17-27

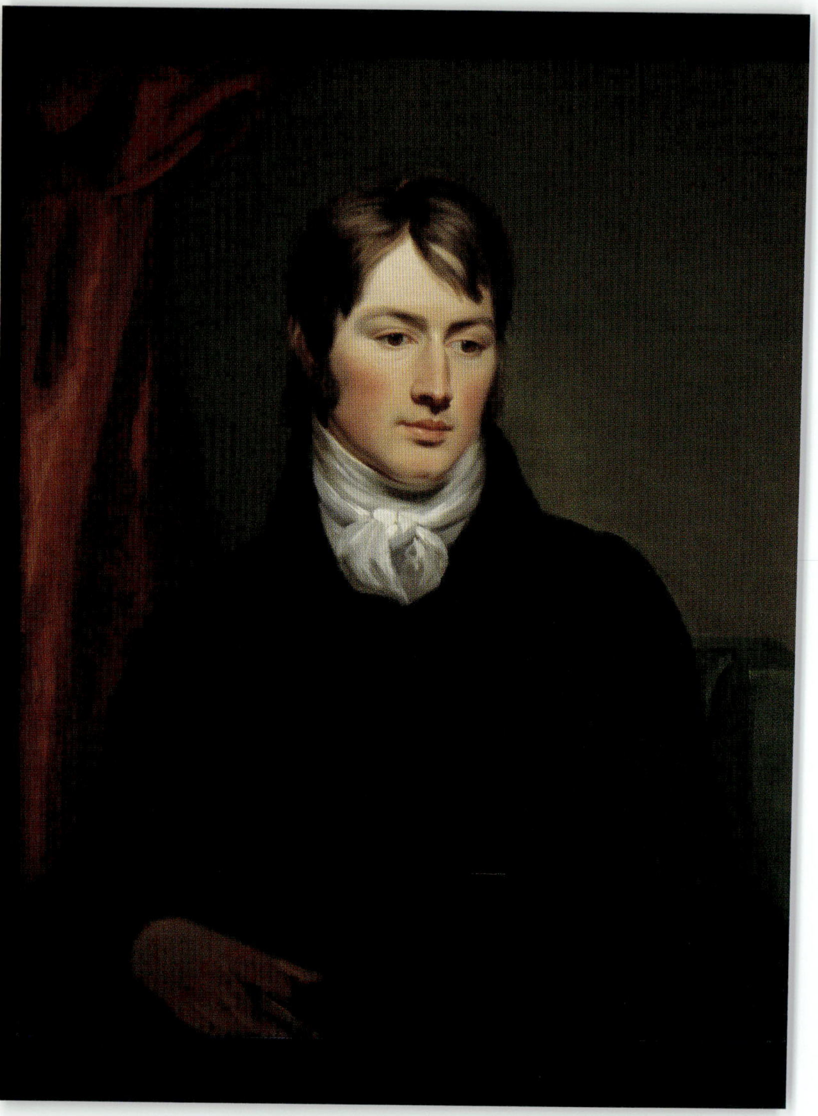

CONSTABLE TO JOHN DUNTHORNE
LONDON, 4 FEBRUARY 1799

Dear Dunthorne

I am this morning admitted a student at the Royal Academy; the figure which I drew for admittance was the Torso. I am now comfortably settled in Cecil Street, Strand, No. 23. I shall begin painting as soon as I have the loan of a sweet little picture by Jacob Ruisdael to copy. Since I have been in town I have seen some remarkably fine ones by him, indeed I never saw him before; yet don't think, by this, I am out of conceit with my own, of which I have seen a print, 'tis of the same size and reversed.

I shall not have much to show you on my return, as I find my time will be more taken up in *seeing* than in painting. I hope by the time the leaves are on the trees, I shall be better qualified to attack them than I was last summer. All the time that you can conveniently spare from your business may be happily spent in this way, perhaps profitably, at any rate innocently. …

Smith's friend Cranch has left off painting, at least for the present. His whole time and thoughts are occupied in exhibiting an old, rusty, fusty head, with a spike in it,

Opposite: Portrait of Constable by Ramsay Richard Reinagle, c. 1799. The two artists were at the Royal Academy Schools together and shared lodgings

which he declares to be the real embalmed head of Oliver Cromwell!* Where he got it I know not; 'tis to be seen in Bond Street, at half a crown admittance.

How goes on the lay figure? I hope to see it finished when I return, together with some drawings of your own from nature. ...

John Constable

CONSTABLE TO JOHN DUNTHORNE
RATHBONE PLACE, LONDON, 8 JANUARY 1802

Dear Dunthorne

... About a fortnight back, I was so fully in the hope of making an immediate visit to Bergholt that I deferred writing. I then knew nothing of the anatomical lectures which I am at present attending, and which will be over in about a week or ten days.

I am so much more interested in the study than I expected, and feel my mind so generally enlarged by it, that I congratulate myself on being so fortunate as to have attended these lectures. Excepting astronomy, and that I know little of, I believe no study is really so sublime, or goes more to carry the mind to the Divine Architect. Indeed the whole machine which it has pleased God to form for the accommodation of the real man, the mind,

* Now buried in the garden of Sidney Sussex College, Cambridge

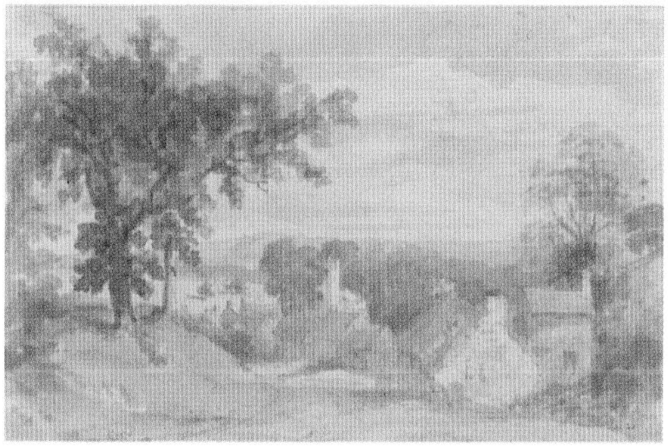

The entrance to the village of Edensor, Derbyshire, August 1801

during its probation in this vale of tears, is as wonderful as the contemplation of it is affecting. I see, however, many instances of the truth, and a melancholy truth it is, that a knowledge of the things created does not always lead to a veneration of the Creator. Many of the young men in this theatre are reprobates.

I have done little in the painting art since I have been in town yet. A copy of a portrait and a background to an ox for Miss Linwood is all.* I have not time to say half I could wish about my Derbyshire excursion, therefore, I will say nothing… .

John Constable

* Mary Linwood (1755–1845) embroidery artist

CONSTABLE TO JOHN DUNTHORNE
LONDON, 29 MAY 1802

My dear Dunthorne,

I hope I have done with the business that brought me to town with Dr. Fisher. It is needless now to detail any particulars as we will make them the subject of some future conversation – but it is sufficient to say that had I accepted the situation offered* it would have been a death blow to all my prospects of perfection in the Art I love.

For these few weeks past I believe I have thought more seriously on my profession than at any other time of my life – that is, which is the surest way to real excellence. And this morning I am the more inclined to mention the subject having just returned from a visit to Sir G. Beaumont's pictures. – I am returned with a deep conviction of the truth of Sir Joshua Reynolds's observation that 'there is no *easy* way of becoming a good painter.' It can only be obtained by long contemplation and incessant labour in the executive part.

And however one's mind may be elevated, and kept up to what is excellent, by the works of the Great Masters – still Nature is the fountain's head, the source from whence

* Of drawing master at the newly-founded Marlow Military Academy, precursor to Sandhurst.

all originality must spring – and should an artist continue his practice without referring to nature he must soon form a *manner*, & be reduced to the same deplorable situation as the French painter mentioned by Sir J. Reynolds, who told him that he had long ceased to look at nature for she only put him out.

For these two years past I have been running after pictures and seeking the truth at second hand. I have not endeavoured to represent nature with the same elevation of mind – but have neither endeavoured to make my performances look as if really *executed* by other men.

I am come to a determination to make no idle visits this summer or to give up my time to commonplace people. I shall shortly return to Bergholt where I shall make some laborious studies from nature – and I shall endeavour to get a pure and unaffected representation of the scenes that may employ me with respect to colour particularly and any thing else – drawing I am pretty well master of.

There is little or nothing in the exhibition worth looking up to – there is room enough for a natural painture. The great vice of the present day is *bravura*, an attempt at something beyond the truth. In endeavouring to do something better than well they do what in reality is good for nothing. *Fashion* always had, & will have its day – but *Truth* (in all things) only will last and can have just claims on posterity.

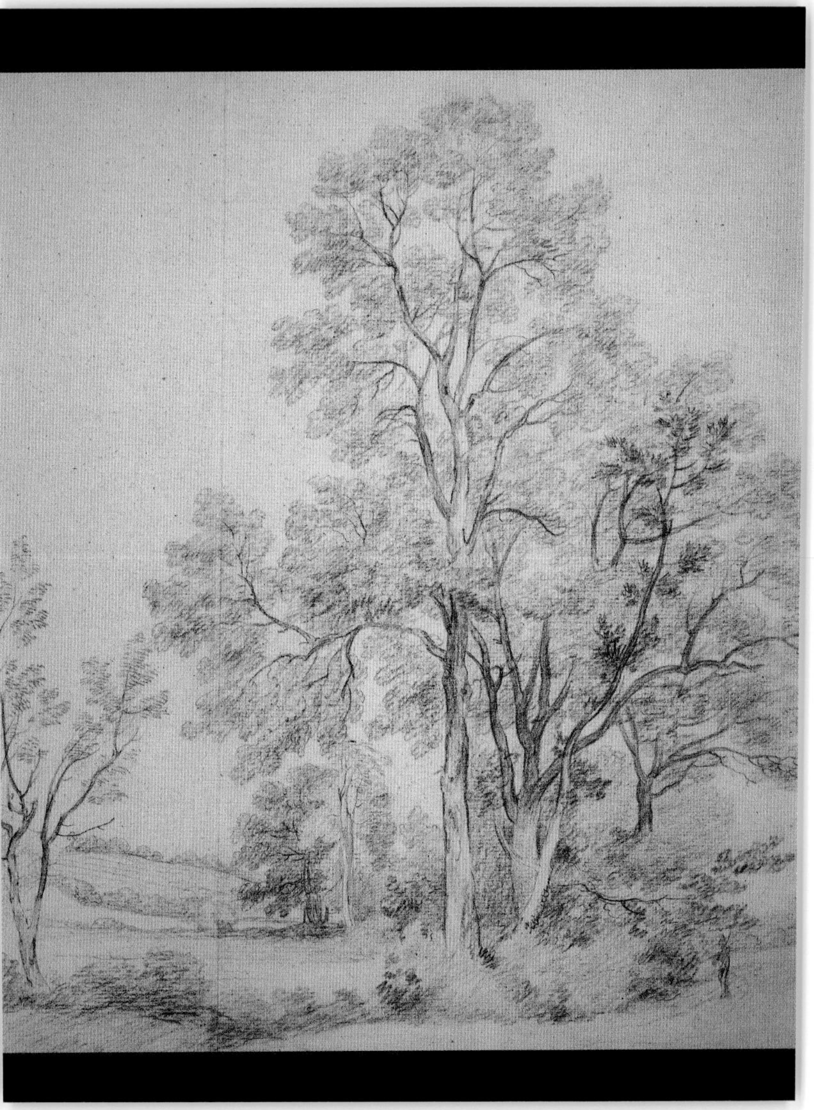

I have received considerable benefit from exhibiting – it shows me where I am, and in fact tells me what no body else could. There are in the exhibition fine pictures that bring nature to mind – and represent it with that truth that unprejudiced minds require.*

These are reflexions that at this time I should have written for my own use – but as I know that I could not write to you on a subject that would be more agreeable, I send you them as a letter.

And indeed I have had much ado to keep my mind together enough to write to be understood owing to a reumatick pain in one side of my head, particularly in my teeth and lower jaw, which has caused one cheek to swell very much. I believe I got cold at Windsor as I was there in the late severe weather.

Should you want any thing in the pencil† way &c let me know next week for I hope the next to leave London.

Remember me kindly to your wife & believe me
to be sincerely yours
John Constable

* Constable had just exhibited at the Royal Academy for the first time; the painting was a landscape, but is untraced. † 'Paintbrush'; the word does not usually mean a graphite pencil until after Constable's lifetime.

Opposite: A Stand of Elm Trees, c. 1802

Overleaf: Dedham Vale, 1802

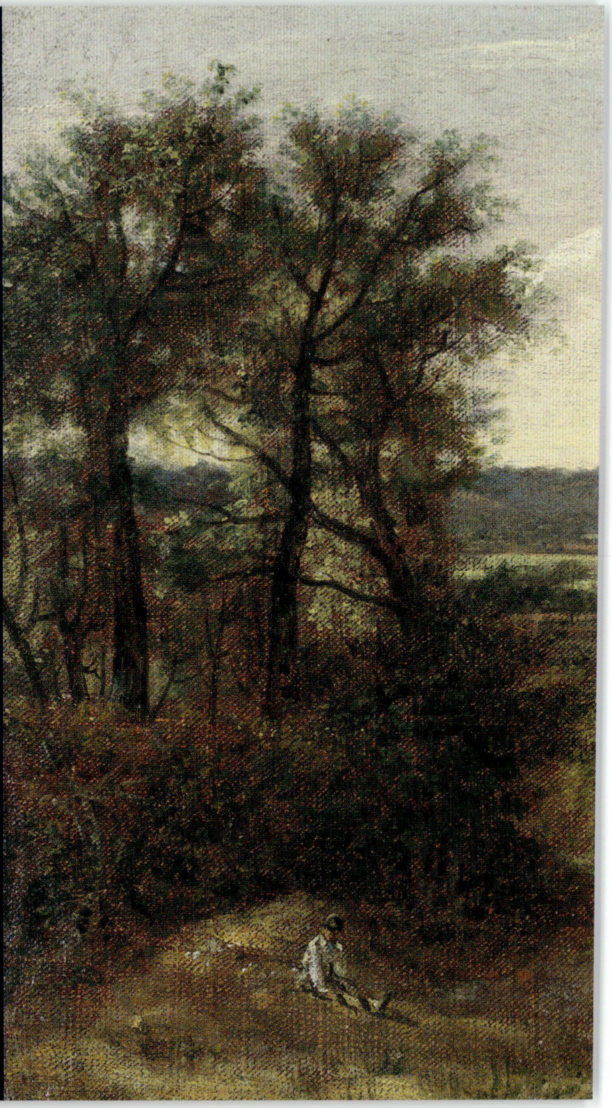

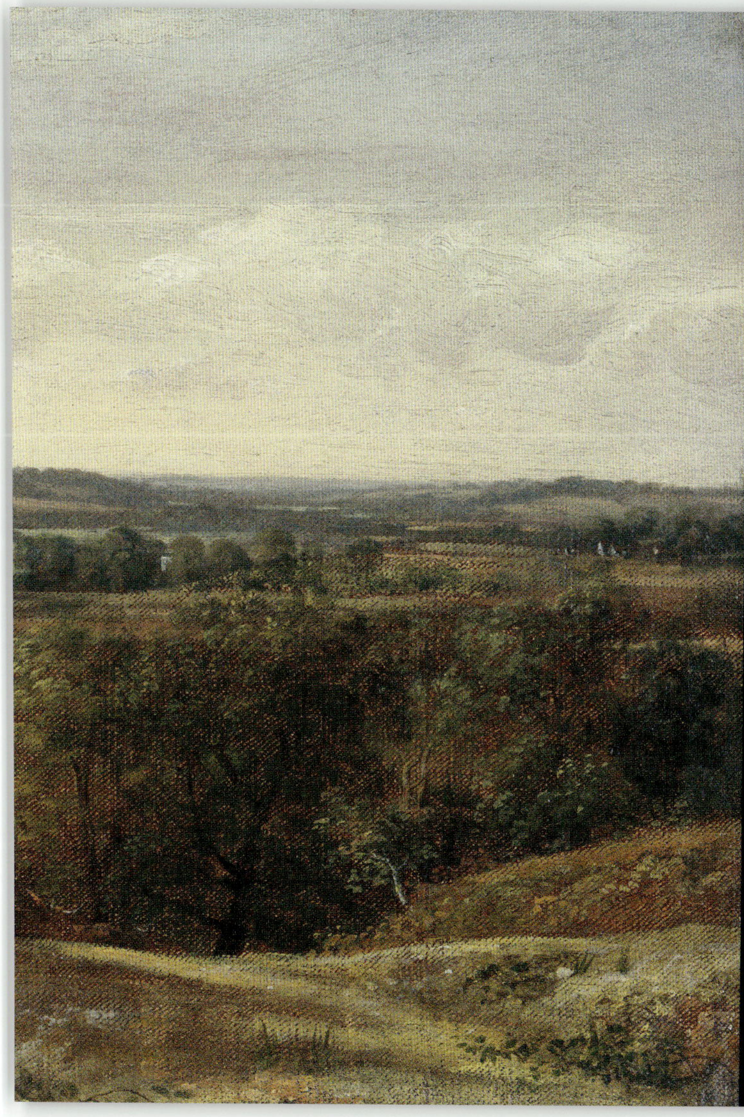

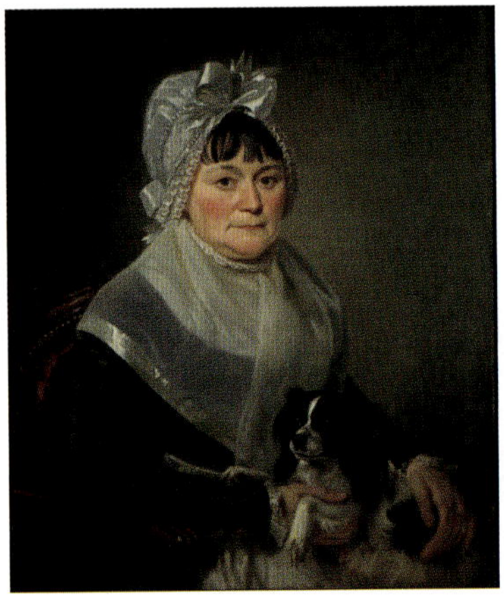
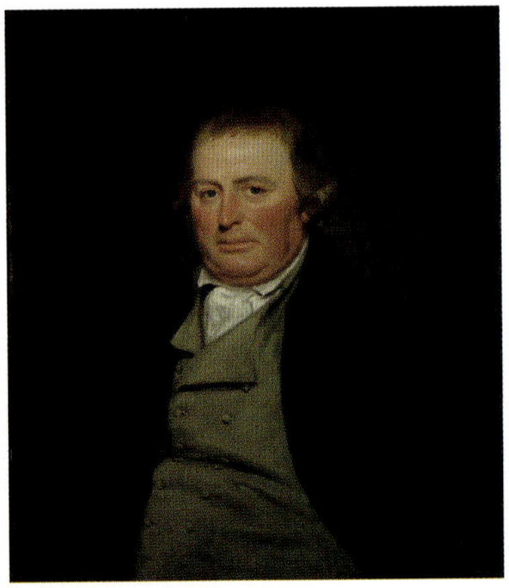

Constable's parents:
Ann and Golding Constable, c. 1815

ANN CONSTABLE TO CONSTABLE
EAST BERGHOLT, 7 JULY 1808

Dear John,

Your prompt acknowledgement of the safe arrival of the parcel, was more than I had hoped for, and as opportunity presents of forwarding this letter which perhaps may not come to your hands before Monday, yet I embrace it – to tell you how very satisfactory it is, that my endeavours & wishes are approved, and all anxiety as to safety removed.

[...] Miss Proby was who chiefly at the Cliff, fell out with her friend Mrs C[obbold], [...] – and took herself off, to London. However I hear Mrs Cobbold has written to her & told her she was welcome to come to the Cliff, till her mother's return from Yorkshire in October – if she could behave as she should do & not take too much upon her. Such is a life of dependence on the kindness of others – & yet parents & their asylum is not always valued according to its real worth.

Thank God your father's health is better, but his cough is very troublesome indeed, he is now gone to Flatford & I fear will be vexed, as upon spending yesterday at the new floodgates there appears to be some unlucky leakage, but I trust it can be rectified without taking up the new work or drawing off the water & detaining barges, gangs &c. which has been the case this last fortnight – & must have been longer but for the luck of fine weather.

This morning began to mow the town meadow, & harvest will then have to be thought of – Man was not intended for idleness – or at least incurred the punishment of Labour for disobedience. God bless you.

Ann Constable

[...] All much the same as usual and in the village. The

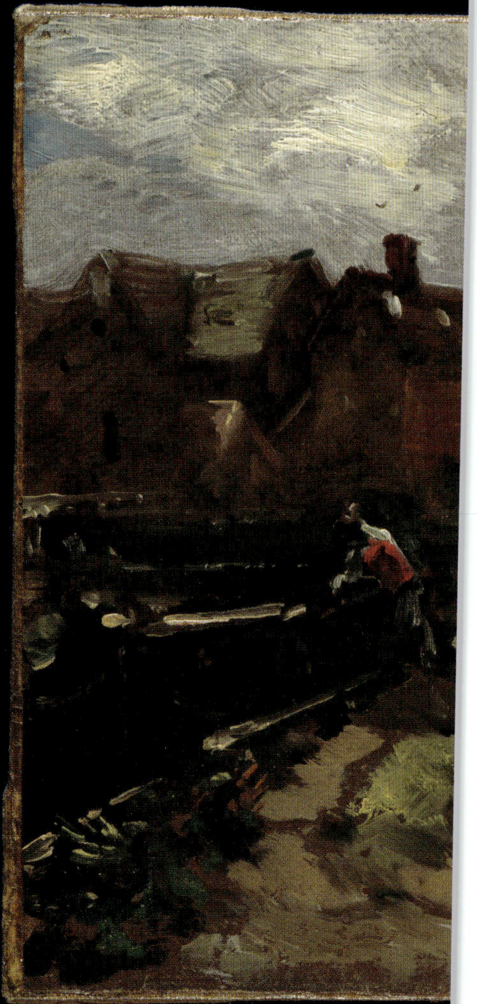

Flatford Mill from the lock, c. 1810

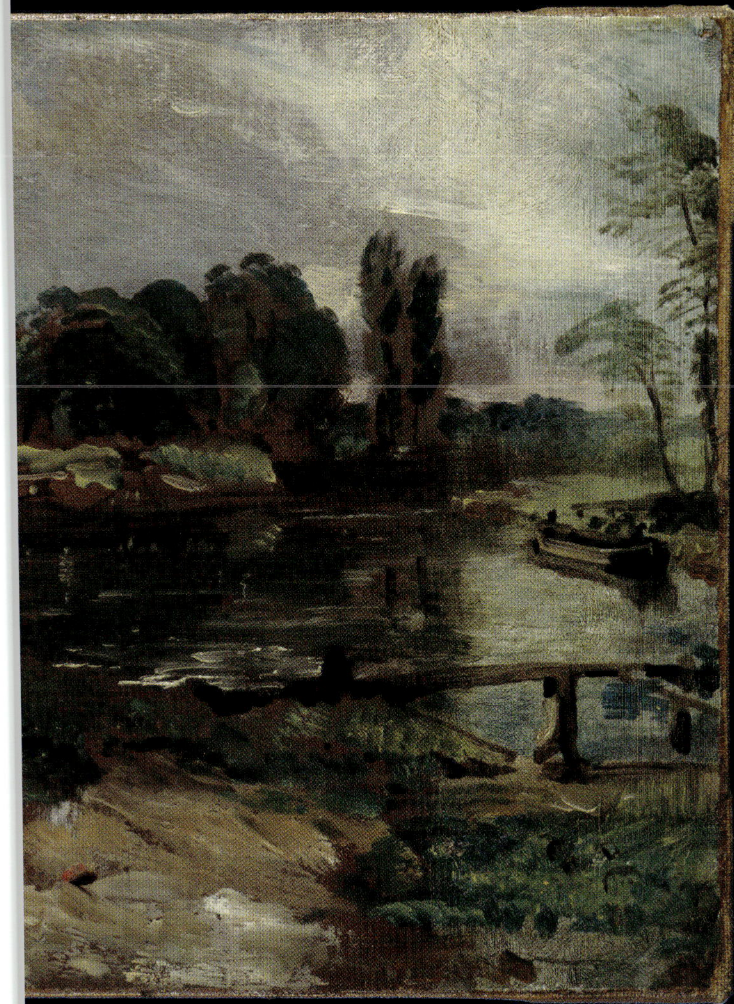

measles has prevailed very much – but proved fatal only to Mrs Barnard's little boy, which caused her great vexation – but the loss *appears* as if it would ere long be supplied.

ANN CONSTABLE TO CONSTABLE
EAST BERGHOLT, 15 MARCH 1810

My dear John,

By your kind sister Whalley I have the opportunity of sending your inkstand to E. Ham, and she will forward it. I ventured to put *ink* and *sand* into the glasses as you may find them useful though in a *small degree*. Thank God your father's health seems really as it were quite renovated. Mr Travis has attended him most skilfully and *friendly* – & all is well.

As to myself sickness has never before appeared to me in so serious a form – it was on the habit; but accelerated by anxiety & irritation. Repeated bleeding, blistering & great perspiration though essential to the great inflammation has brought me lower than I ever was before, but I yet hope, all will be well.

Your last letter in most parts pleased me because written with more energy than usual. You must exert yourself if you feel a desire to be independent – and you must also be wary how you engage in uniting yourself with a house mate, as well as in more serious & irrevocable yokes.

You are very seldom absent from the mind of your truly affectionate mother

Ann Constable

Be very careful of that precious blessing, health – and let us know when you are comfortably settled which I hope you will be – I am ready to assist with anything you may want of furniture.

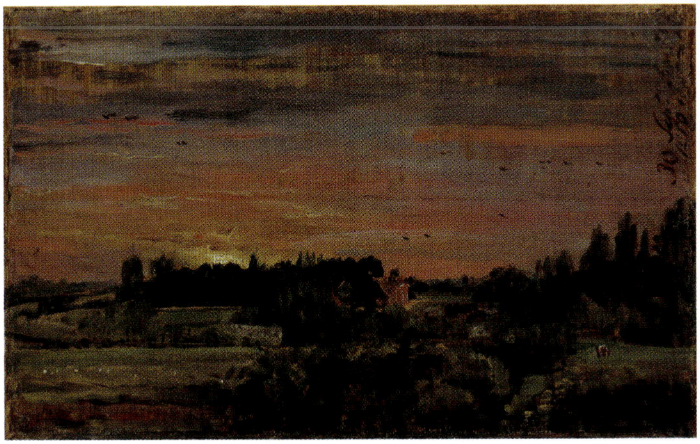

View toward the Rectory, East Bergholt
Inscribed '30 Sep. 1810 E. Bergholt Common'.
Constable wrote that it was while he was walking over these fields with Maria Bicknell that he fell in love with her

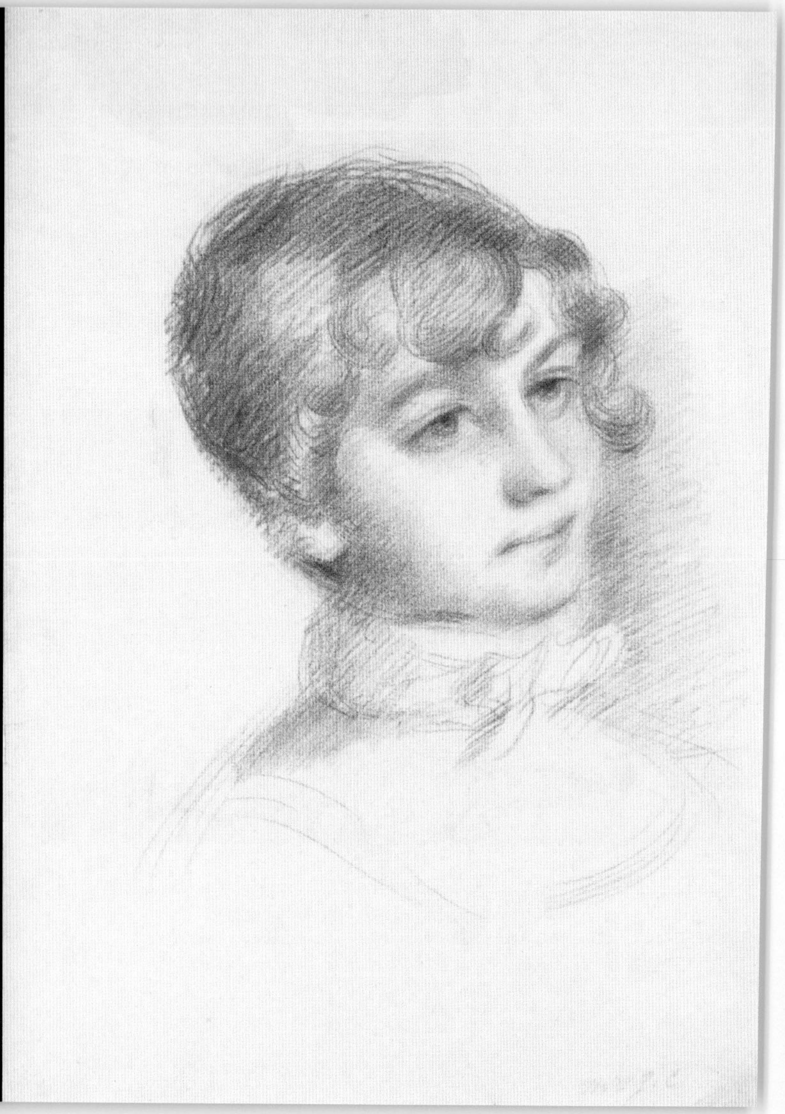

MARIA BICKNELL TO CONSTABLE
SPRING GROVE, BEWDLEY, WORCESTERSHIRE,
2 NOVEMBER 1811

My dear Sir,

You have grieved me much by the melancholy account you give of your health and I shall feel better satisfied when I know you are in Suffolk where I do not doubt that good air, nursing, and attention of your friends will go a great way towards your recovery.

I dare not suffer myself to think on your last letter. I am very impatient as you may imagine to hear from Papa on a subject so fraught with interest to us both – but was unwilling to delay writing to you as you would be ignorant of the cause of such seeming inattention. I hope you will not find that your kind partiality to me made you view what passed in Spring Gardens* too favourably, you know my sentiments, I shall be guided by my Father in every respect.

Should he acquiesce in my wishes I shall be happier than I can express, if not, I shall have the consolation of reflecting that I am doing my duty, a charm that will stifle every regret and in the end give the greatest satisfaction to

* The family address in London

Opposite: Maria Bicknell, c. 1805-09

my mind. I cannot write any more till the wished but fearfully dreaded letter arrives, with the most ardent wishes for your health.

believe me, dear Sir, your obliged friend
Maria E. Bicknell

CONSTABLE TO MARIA BICKNELL
LONDON, 4 NOVEMBER 1811

Dear Miss Bicknell

Can I ever sufficiently thank you for the happiness your letter this morning has given me. My health is so much better that I think I may consider myself nearly recovered.

I trust that I cannot have deceived myself as to a too favourable reception in Spring Gardens. Your father told me he should write to you, and that I should hear from him when he had your answer – let me hope that there will not be so much (as you imagine) depending on one letter alone from your Father, though it certainly must be of the greatest consequence.

Believe me, dear Miss Bicknell,
always most affectionately yours
John Constable

MARIA BICKNELL TO CONSTABLE
SPRING GROVE, BEWDLEY, 4 NOVEMBER 1811

My dear Sir,

I have received my Father's letter, it is precisely such a one as I expected, reasonable and kind. His only objection would be on the score of that necessary article Cash, what can we do? To live without it is impossible, it would be involving ourselves in misery instead of felicity, could we but find this golden treasure we might yet be happy, you say it is not impossible.

I wish I had it, but wishes are vain – we must be wise, and leave off a correspondence that is not calculated to make us think less of each other, we have many painful trials required of us in this life, and we must learn to bear them with resignation.

You will still be my friend, and I will be yours, then as such let me advise you to go into Suffolk, you cannot fail of being better there. I have written to Papa, though I do not in conscience think he can retract anything he has said. If so, I had better not write to you any more, at least *till I can coin*, we should both of us be bad subjects for poverty, should we not? Even Painting would go on badly, it could not survive in domestic worry.

I hope you have done a good deal this summer.

Salisbury I suppose has furnished some sketches. You are particularly fortunate in possessing the affectionate esteem of so kind and excellent a man as Mr Watts,* whose wishes you must consult in this most important and interesting point. Remember, dear sir, if you wish to oblige me and all your friends, it must be by taking care of your health.

Adieu, and think me always, sincerely yours,

M. E. Bicknell.

CONSTABLE TO MARIA BICKNELL
63 CHARLOTTE STREET, LONDON, 27 MAY 1812

I had left Town on Friday [...] or believe me my dear Maria your letter would not have remained so long unanswered. I was not well when I wrote to you, but I am now quite recovered – perhaps I had confined myself too much, or what is more likely have been over anxious ('Fame is the spur').

I am still looking towards Suffolk where I hope to pass the greater part of the summer, as much for the sake of pursuing my favourite study as for any other account. You know I have succeeded most with my native scenes. They have always charmed me & I hope they always will – I wish not to forget early impressions. I have now very distinctly marked out a path for myself, and I am desirous of pursuing it uninterruptedly.

* Constable's rich uncle

I am getting on with the pictures for Lady Heathcote – I shall be glad to get these disagreable sprawling things out of the house.[1] Lady Louisa Manners has got a wretched copy by Hoppner [after] Sir J. Reynolds which she wishes me to repaint[2] – so that I fear I must be at least a fortnight or three weeks before I can get into Suffolk. [...]

CONSTABLE TO MARIA BICKNELL
EAST BERGHOLT, 10 JULY 1812

[...] I will now endeavour to tell you how I employ myself and I hope account for my delay in writing to you. For more than this week past I have been wholly engaged on a portrait of Mr William Godfrey[3] which was just completed in time, as he set off the next day to embark for the West Indies – I believe they are quite pleased with it. I have a note from Mr G. expressive of his own and Mrs Godfrey's entire satisfaction. I think myself it is far the best I have done, for I was quite upon the spur – they having had their own portraits done in London a little time before.

I wish all they tell me about it could make me vain of

1. Lady Heathcote was the daughter of Lady Louisa Manners, *née* Tollemache, later 7th Countess of Dysart. The Tollemaches of Helmingham in Suffolk were long-term supporters of Constable, and Lady Dysart a lifelong friend. 2. Ham House, Richmond 3. Private collection

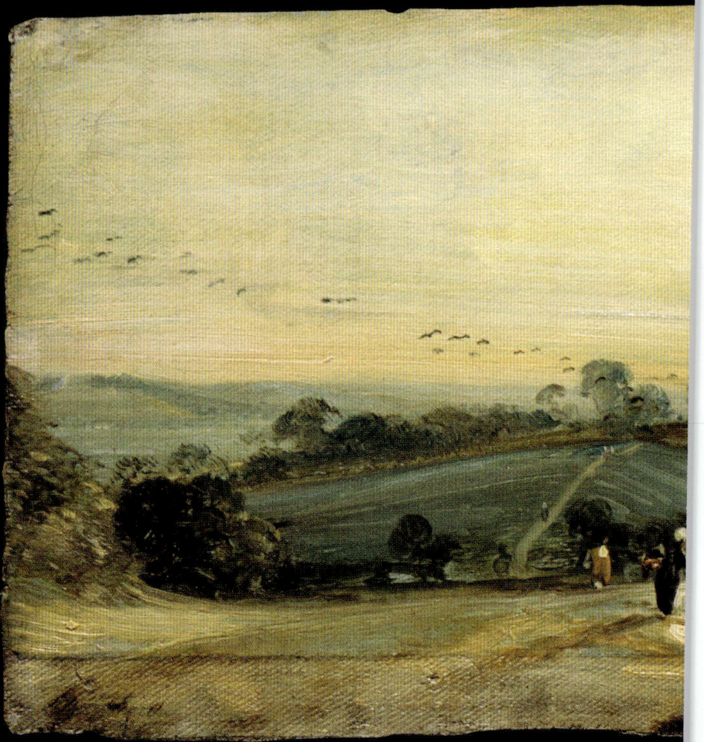

Autumnal Sunset near East Bergholt, c. 1812

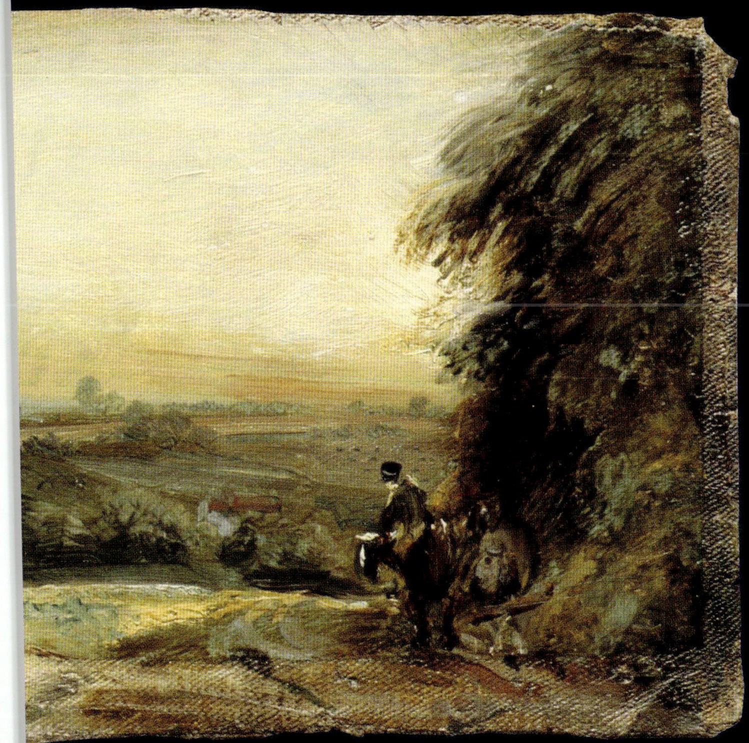

my portraits – but you know I am 'too proud to be vain.' I am however perverse enough to be vain of some studies of landscapes which I have done – 'Landscape which found me poor at first and keeps me so.' I am sure you will laugh when I tell you I have found another very promising subject at *Flatford Mill*. I do not study much abroad in the middle of these very hot bright days. I am become quite *careful of myself*, last year I almost put my eyes out by that pastime. [...]

My mother begs to be remembered to you, and I beg you will present my respectful compliments to Mrs Skey – and believe me, my dearest Maria

for ever most affectionately yours,
John Constable

CONSTABLE TO MARIA BICKNELL
EAST BERGHOLT, 22 JULY 1812

I am sure my dearest Maria you will forgive my great anxiety to hear from you when you reflect in common with me that we are two hundred miles apart and that it is a month since I had the happiness of a letter from you – one line to say that you are well would be some alleviation of this wretched absence.

I was so much disappointed when I found you had deferred your journey that I did not go to London at the time I had fixed (though I believe I have made a great omission), but as I should not have attained my chief object I do not repent of it – especially as we have had this charming season.

I have been living a hermit-like life though always with my pencil in my hand. Perhaps that is not usual with hermits – without we except Swanevelt (the pupil of Claude Lorrain) who was called the 'hermit of Italy', from the romantic solitudes which he loved and which his pictures so admirably describe.

How much real delight I have had with the study of Landscape this summer. Either I am myself improved in 'the art of seeing Nature' (which Sir Joshua Reynolds calls painting) or Nature has unveiled her beauties to me with a less fastidious hand – perhaps there may be something of both, so we will divide these fine compliments between us – but I am writing this nonsense to you with a really sad heart, when I think what would be my happiness could I have this enjoyment with you. Then indeed would my mind be calm to contemplate the endless beauties of this happy country.

In your society I am freed from the natural reserve of my mind – 'tis to you alone that I can impart every sensation of my heart – but I am now too apt to dwell on this melancholy side. Should I not rather think on the thousand blessings which I possess? I am hourly receiving every

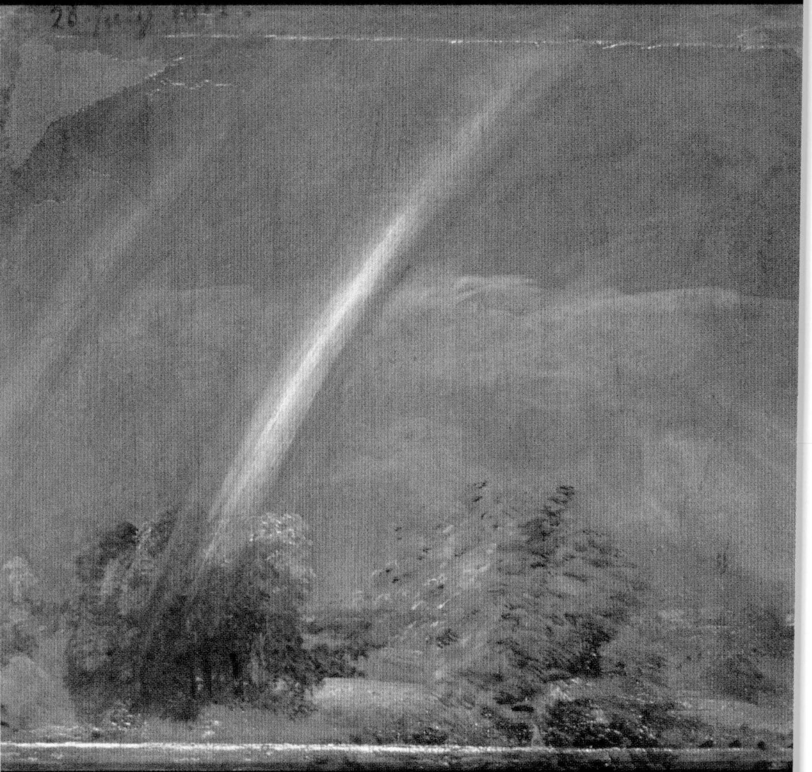

Landscape with a double rainbow, 28 July 1812

kindness from the best of parents – have I not health and time to pursue my darling study? – and above all I have your great love and esteem. I feel that what I desire would be joy too great for me – that I am really unworthy, and my constant prayers are to be deserving of you – and that I may bear this trial, the only one which I have had in the world, with resignation and patience.

I am sure you cannot have left Spring Grove or I should heard from you. Are you still to visit the sea side, with Mrs Skey? I hope Mrs Skey is recovering from the loss of her son. I beg my respectful compliments to her, and remain, my dearest Maria.

Yours most affectionately and truly
John Constable

MARIA BICKNELL TO CONSTABLE, JUNE 1813

I imagine next month you will like to have quitted London for Suffolk as the study of nature will be more agreeable than picture galleries. I will not forget to drink your health in a bumper on the 11th.* Adieu dear friend, why are we thus attached when every thing conspires against us?

Sincerely yours,
M. E. B.

* Constable's birthday

CONSTABLE TO MARIA BICKNELL
63 CHARLOTTE STREET, LONDON, 30 JUNE 1813

When I last had the happiness of seeing you my dearest Maria, I had fixed a day for going into Suffolk – I was however prevented by Mr Lewis's arrival in town from Warwickshire & by a call upon me for portraits – for I assure you my reputation in that way is much upon the increase. They (the pictures) are now gone and I shall leave town this afternoon – one of them, a portrait of the Revd. George Bridgeman (a brother of Lord Bradford's), far excels any of my attempts in that way, and is doing me a great deal of service, as these are people connected with all higher circles – it is to go into Staffordshire to Lord Bradford's seat, where in his library he has portraits of his relations and friends. I have one there already which Mr Bridgeman tells me is preferred to any other in the room.[1]

My price for a head is 15 guineas and I am tolerably expeditious when I can have fair play at my sitter. I have been much engaged by Lady Heathcote, who seems bent on serving me – my pictures of herself and her mother[2] occupy either end of the large drawing room in Grosvenor

1. Portraits of H. G. Lewis and the Rev. George Bridgeman still in the library at Weston Park. 2. These are both copies after Reynolds or Hoppner (see p. 85); private collection.

Square. They have magnificent frames, and make a great dash. She is to bring me a very handsome boy at the Xmas holidays to paint & today afternoon when I took leave of her she presented her hand to me in a very condescending manner. She has 'a little dance' on Friday, when my pictures will be seen for the first time publicly.

I am now leaving London for the only time in my life with pockets full of money. I am entirely free from debt (not that my debts ever exceeded my usual annual bills), and I have required no assistance from my father for some time.

I have arranged matters with Sir Thomas Lennard (who is much occupied with his new house), that I am to pass a month with him very late in the season – which I am delighted to find gives me possession of the three months ensuing to myself – and as I never visit or give time to other people I hope to do a great deal in that time. I do assure you my dearest Maria, I am not trying to give you only a favourable side of myself (that you know would not accord with my disposition which is naturally desponding) but am merely mentioning facts as they have occurred to me within the last 2 or 3 months, during which time we have unfortunately had so little communication with each other – but I am living for you and I trust the time is at hand, when the ground will be rendered smooth for both of us.

You may not probably know that there has been some correspondence between Mr Bicknell and myself. When I thought I was leaving town I wrote to him, to request an interview and that he would consent to some sort of communication between us – he would consent to neither, but I do not repent of what I have done as I was happy at least to have an opportunity of approaching him in a respectful manner.

I am still of opinion that when my situation with you is considered I was justified in what I requested. Could your Father have relented a little towards me, it would have been a great assistance to me in the struggle I am now making – but I thank God daily for a thousand blessings which I enjoy and I can surely lay my hand on my heart and say I have 'a conscience void of offence' – and though I look forward to many happy years with you, I think things might have been rendered more smooth with us, and we might have been spared a world of pain – but we have had experience enough that our sole dependence must be on ourselves and it is in vain to combat the world or its prejudices.

We are now repairing the house here with a thorough painting, and I shall leave orders about the back drawing room. The paper will be a sort of salmon colour and the sofa & chairs crimson (by Lady Heathcote's advice). I think they will suit pictures but I am indifferent about show – though all insist upon it. I ought to have at least one room in tolerable order. Next winter I mean to sleep in a very large bedroom which I think is healthy.

I am quite delighted to find myself so well although I paint so many hours – perhaps too many – but my mind is happy when so engaged – not only by being occupied with what I love, but I feel I am performing a moral duty. My front room where I paint shall be done with a sort of purple brown from the floor to the ceiling – not sparing even the doors or doorposts, for white is disagreable to a painter's eyes, near pictures.

I dined with the Royal Academy last Monday in the Council Room – it was entirely a meeting of artists (none but the members and exhibitors could be admitted) and the day passed off very well. I sat next to Turner, and opposite Mr West and Lawrence – I was a good deal entertained with Turner. I always expected to find him what I did – he is uncouth but has a wonderful range of mind.

John Fisher has [written] in his usual friendly way – he thought 'I did not call enough on the Bishop and his Lady' – and he attributes it to neglect, & not humility. 'Everybody (he adds) does not know as well as myself that there is an Exhibitor and a painter for fame, who is possessed of modesty and merit; and is too honest and high minded to push himself by any other means than

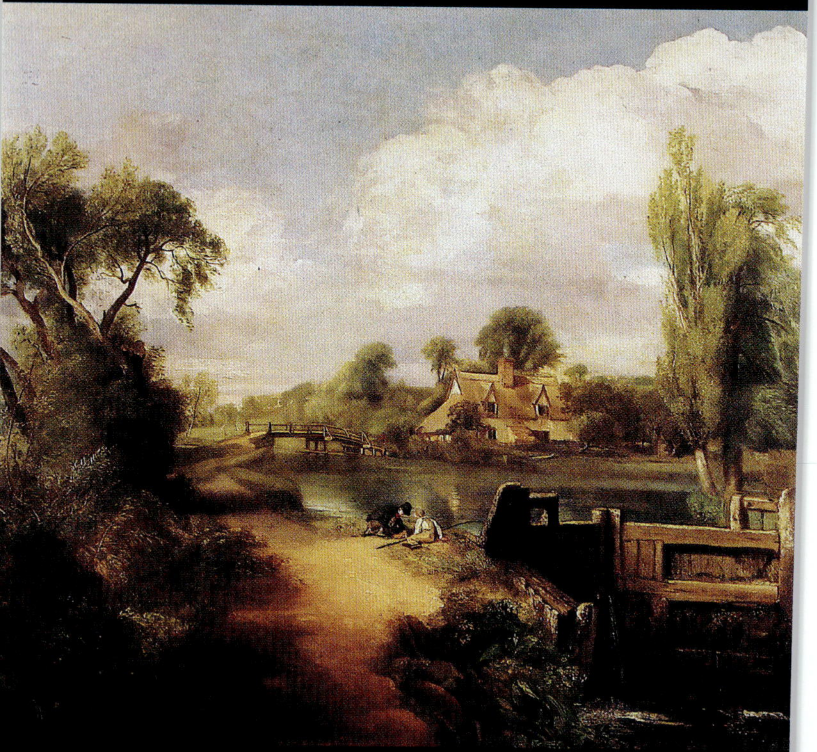

Boys Fishing, 1813

his pencil and his palette.' He says he has met with one good judge who admires my landscape[1] in the Exhibition more than any other there – and it is in his opinion only surpassed by Turner's Frost[2] – but he adds, 'don't repine dear Constable at this decision of mine, you are a great man like Bonaparte & are only to be beaten by a Frost.'

I thank you my beloved Maria for your kind letter, & your affectionate recollection of the eleventh inst. Pray write to me as soon as you can. I hope you are in the country – but am anxious to know. I leave town with a much more comfortable feeling on your account than I had last year. You looked so well and seemed so happy, according to what you said, and to see you comfortable ought to make me happy under any circumstances. Pray remember me to Mrs Skey and believe me my ever beloved Maria

to be most affectionately yours

John Constable

CONSTABLE TO MARIA BICKNELL
EAST BERGHOLT, 28 AUGUST 1814

It was uncommonly kind of you my dearest Maria to write to me again as I requested, and you certainly would have heard of me before now, had I not been called from

1. *Landscape – Boys Fishing*, Fairhaven Collection, Anglesey Abbey, Cambridgeshire. 2 *Frosty Morning*, Tate

home to Tattingstone Hall where I was for several days painting an entire new uniform into the large picture of Admiral Western. This I was obliged to do to my great annoyance, for I grudge the fine weather exceedingly and I sincerely hope this will be the last portrait from my pencil – though I have heard you say you like my portraits.

I am truly sorry to read your sad account of your good mother's health – Brighton may perhaps agree with her better – at any rate the change may be of service to her mind. You do not mention your sister Louisa, perhaps she is at Spring Grove – will you remember me most respectfully to Mrs Skey, she is indeed a charming woman.

I do not know that I can amuse you with any news from this place – you know that I am little interested in any thing that occurs in it out of these walls – but poor Miss Underwood was married a week or two ago and was a widow in four days – this was expected but the young man was a son of her Trustee – as she was not of age it is hoped her property will not suffer so much.

There is a very grand match nearly ready at Old Hall. We have a pleasant family over the way, but I have only seen them at a distance. The clergymen seem to desert this neighbourhood, but that is of little consequence as they are themselves much deserted.

I hope to remain quiet and unmolested here for the remainder of the year. We expect all the Gubbins's to stay a month with us and I hope James will at least join them, which he certainly will do should his regiment remain in England.

Have you been reading any thing very interesting lately, I have always a wish to know. I am delighted with Alison's book on the nature and principles of Taste.* I prefer it to Mr Burke's as I think it more just and its conclusions more sublime – indeed the conclusion of the last essay 'of the Final Cause and of the Constitution of our Nature' is by far the most beautiful thing I ever read. He considers us as endowed with minds capable of comprehending the 'beauty and sublimity of the material world' only as the means of leading us to *religious sentiment* – and of how much consequence is the study of nature in the education of youth – 'as it is at least (amid all trials of society) securing to themselves, one gentle and unreproaching friend, whose voice is ever in alliance with goodness and virtue, who is alone able to sooth misfortune' – have we not my beloved Maria both felt this?

Believe me my dear my thoughts are never a moment from you and I wish for no greater happiness than always to subscribe my self

ever affectionately yours
John Constable

* *Essays on the Nature and Principles of Taste*, 1790, by the Rev. Archibald Alison, a Scottish divine.

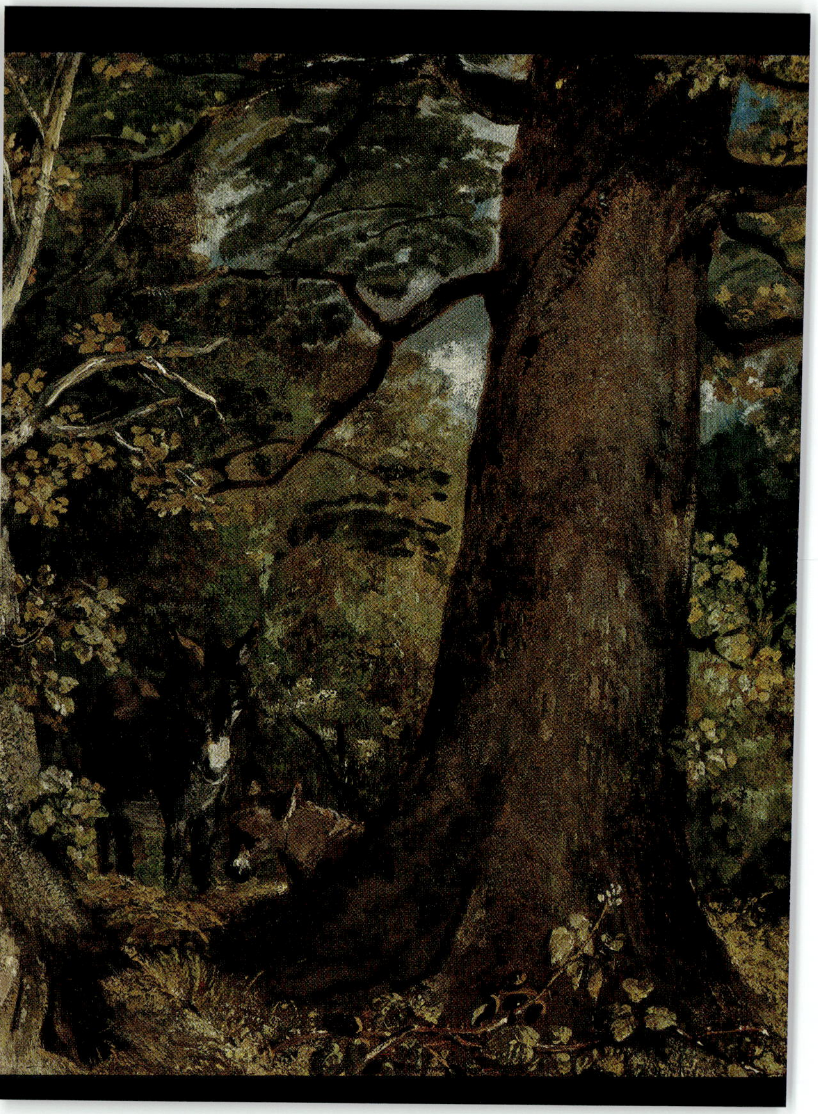

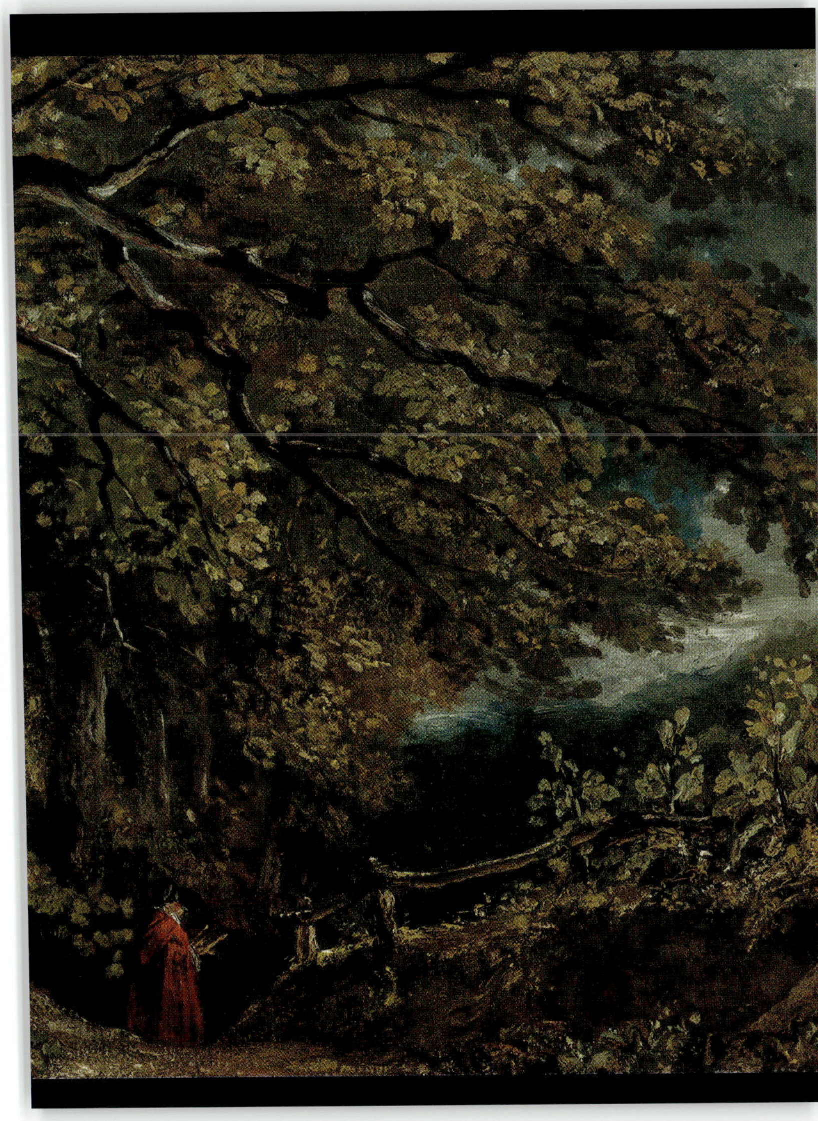

CONSTABLE TO MARIA BICKNELL
EAST BERGHOLT, 18 FEBRUARY 1816

I trust my dearest love that you have allowed yourself to be made as little unhappy as possible by what has been lately passing in your house. I am glad to take the first opportunity of writing to you – you have always been so kind as to believe that my affection for you was never actuated by interested motives – I now more than ever repeat it, and I assure you that nothing that can be done by any part of your family, shall ever make any alteration in me towards you. I shall not concern myself with the justice or injustice of others. That must rest with themselves alone. It is sufficient for us to know that we have at no time done any thing that is blameable, or to deserve the ill opinion of any one.

Our business is now more than ever (if possible) with ourselves. I shall inherit a sixth part of my father's property, which we expect may be at least four thousand pounds apiece, and Mrs Smith of Nayland will leave about two thousand pounds more amongst us* – and I am entirely

* Constable's father did not die until 14 May. Mrs. Smith was Constable's paternal aunt Martha ('Patty') who had commissioned an altarpiece from in Nayland (still in the church). She died in 1820.

Previous pages: Woodland Landscape, 1815

free from debt. I trust, could I be made happy, to make a good deal more than I do now of my profession.

After this my dearest Maria I have nothing more to say – but that the sooner we are married the better and from this time I shall cease ever to hear any arguments of any sort from any quarter. We have been great fools not to have married long ago by which we might perhaps have stopped the mouths of all our enemies.

I shall remain a few weeks longer (perhaps three) in the country – and when I have got my pictures to the Academy, I trust you will not hesitate another moment what conduct to pursue. To part you know as well as me is impossible. What should we be good for, ever after? You know me better than any other person, because I have been less reserved to you than to any one, and in spite of what my enemies please to assert of me I trust my character is wholly unblemished – and that there never will be any want of responsibility in me or in any other part of my family.

Believe me to be, my dearest Maria,
always yours most faithfully
John Constable

I write this for anybody to see – I have no secrets – I wish your father to know what I have written if you likewise think so.

CONSTABLE TO MARIA BICKNELL
EAST BERGHOLT, 17 JULY 1816

My dearest Love

You would certainly have heard from me before, had I left London on the day I mentioned, but I could not get away sooner than Tuesday. I left Aldgate about 2 o'clock – it began to rain about 5, & continued without interruption all the rest of my journey – I drove in at our gate about ten. I did not get at all wet for in addition to my own great coat, Samuel Taylor the coachman lent a large wrapping one, which kept me so warm & comfortable that I was often sound asleep on the coach box.

I found all my friends here quite well, & we make a charming family party, six of us – nine with Mrs Whalley's two children and your portrait[1] (which gives me great pleasure here, as an additional proof of your goodness & kindness to me). We are very happy among ourselves, and when we are all together it is really an interesting sight – I cannot however contemplate it without mixture of old associations inseparable to all sublunary affairs, – so used have I been on entering these doors to be received by the affectionate shake by the hand of my father and the

1. Tate. Illustrated opposite

Opposite: Maria Bicknell, Mrs. John Constable, 1816

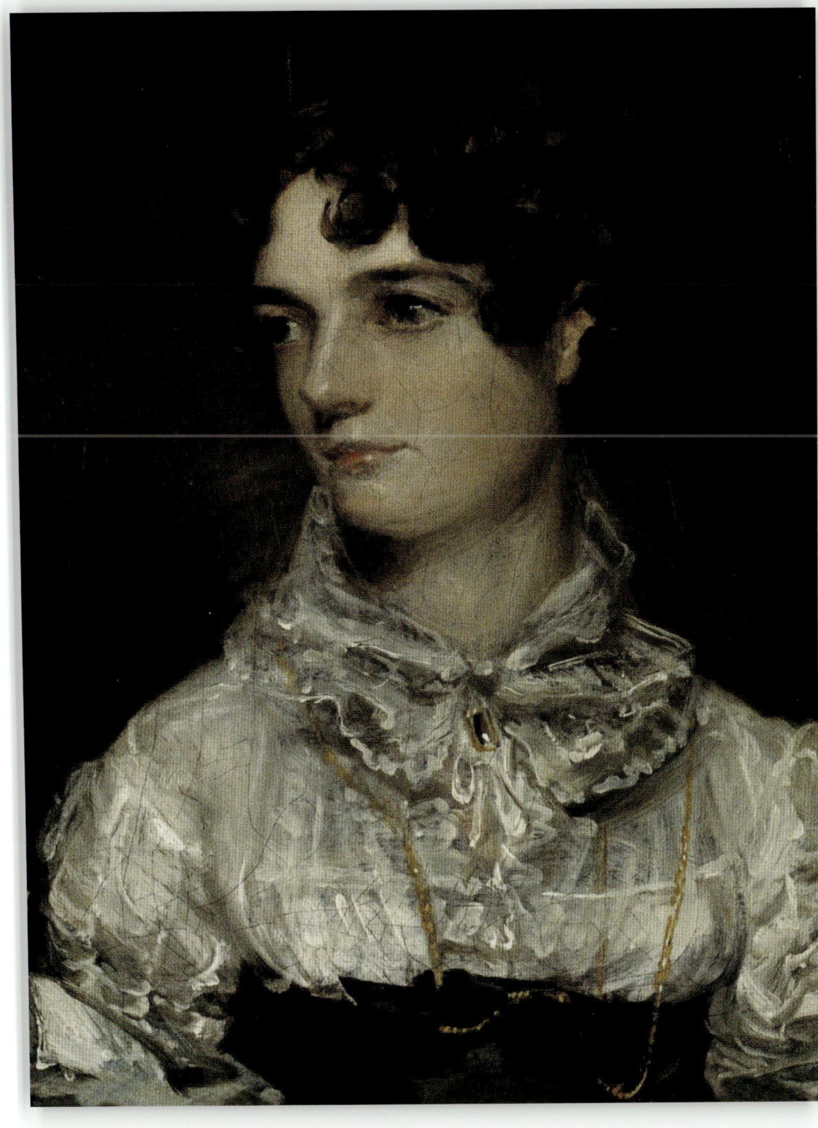

endearing salute of my mother, that imperceptibly I have often found myself overcome by a sadness I could hardly restrain.

Martha Whalley & my sisters desire their kindest love to you. Alicia 'desires her love to the Lady whom we saw by the cannon in the park & hopes she is quite well'.

Nothing can exceed the beauty of the village at this time. The Doctor is here, & I believe quite well, but I have called on no one – and I think I had better not on the Doctor. I hope to hear from you on Sunday morning. How do you like Putney? My kindest love to Louisa & Catharine. I hope sincerely Louisa is going on as you said she was taking long walks & rides.

You cannot imagine what a real beauty the spaniel puppy is – we call him 'Dash' because he is like a charming fellow we once had of that name – but let me know if you have any name you like to have him called better – 'John' you said you did not like, for a *dog*. Believe me, my dearest Love,

for ever more devotedly yours
John Constable

I had sent Johnny away by an early coach & he got home yesterday before the rain. I wished to see Mr Watts before I went & he is but very sad.*

* His uncle was ill and died shortly afterwards, without leaving Constable the money that some family members expected.

CONSTABLE TO MARIA BICKNELL
EAST BERGHOLT, 13 AUGUST 1816

Dearest Maria,

I have been at work all this day and fear that it will not be in my power to write to you so long a letter as I could wish.

I was not able to leave London after I saw you 'till Monday, as I found a picture belonging to a gentleman that was sent to me for some repair – this I stopped to do as it paid my expenses going & coming to London this visit.

I sent as I told you a little book to Spring Gardens – this I hope you have got & that it entertains you as much as it did me the letters will throw a very fair light on the moral feelings and habits of a student of painting, as well as set in a very pleasing view the habits and anxieties of the amiable poet (the father) and his lady – her letters are charming especially her first.* [...]

I hope my dear love does not let the disagreable subject [of Mr. Watts' will] trouble you – I hope your aches and pains of all kinds are at an end. It is kind, it is heavenly of you to remain so faithful & constant to me under all untoward circumstances & I well know I cannot ever make

* Salomon Gessner, *The Letters of Gessner and His Family*, 1804

you amends – but I hope I shall ever have it in my own hands to treat you with never-ceasing kindness and attention. [...]

How is Dash? His food should be bread or a little barley meal well scalded with extreme boiling water, and a bit of fat mixed with it – no more meat than what I speak of. It is the scalding that agrees so well with the stomach of dogs, if not it ferments with them.

Adieu my dearest love – love to Louisa & Catharine – all here desire their kind regards & believe me

always most affectionately yours

J. Constable

Pray write to me very soon. I hope you are quite recovered – ever your most affectionate J. C.

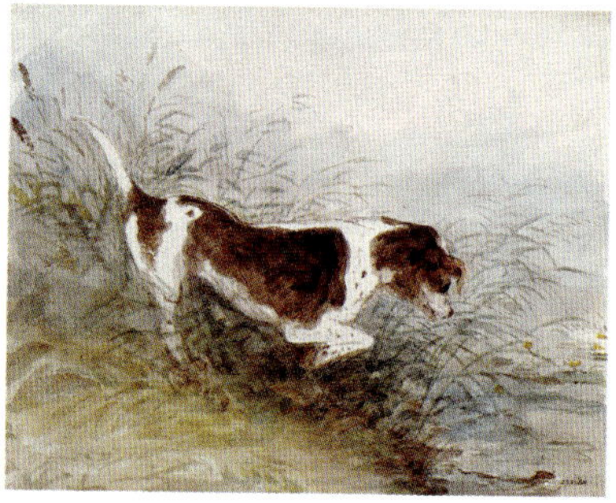

Dog watching a rat, Dedham, 1 August 1831

CONSTABLE TO MARIA BICKNELL
EAST BERGHOLT, 21 AUGUST 1816

My dearest Love

I returned from my very pleasant visit at General Rebow's on Monday [...] This has been a charming day and it will do a great deal of good to the corn which stands much in need of it.

The General and Mrs. Rebow are determined to be of some service to me and at any rate their attentions are agreeable and add much to all that is respectable. I am going there again on Monday and shall stay, a week there in all probability – do be so kind as to let me hear from you before you go to Mr. Lambert's.*

I am going to paint two small landscapes for the General, views, one in the park of the house & a beautiful wood and piece of water,[1] and another scene in a wood with a beautiful little fishing house, where the young Lady (who is the heroine of all these scenes) goes occasionally to angle.[2]

* Family friends of the Bicknells 1. *Wivenhoe Park*, National Gallery of Art, Washington DC. 2. *The Quarters, Alresford Hall, near Wivenhoe*, National Gallery of Victoria, Melbourne

Overleaf: Wivenhoe Park, 1816

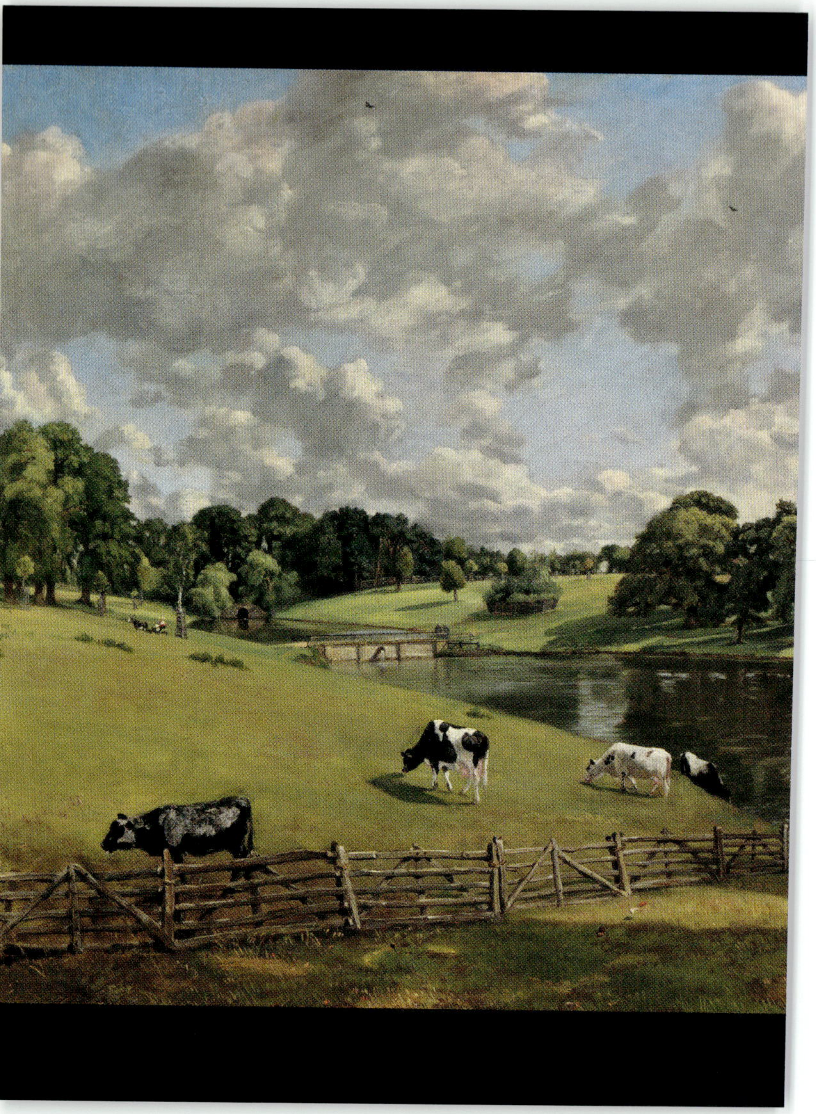

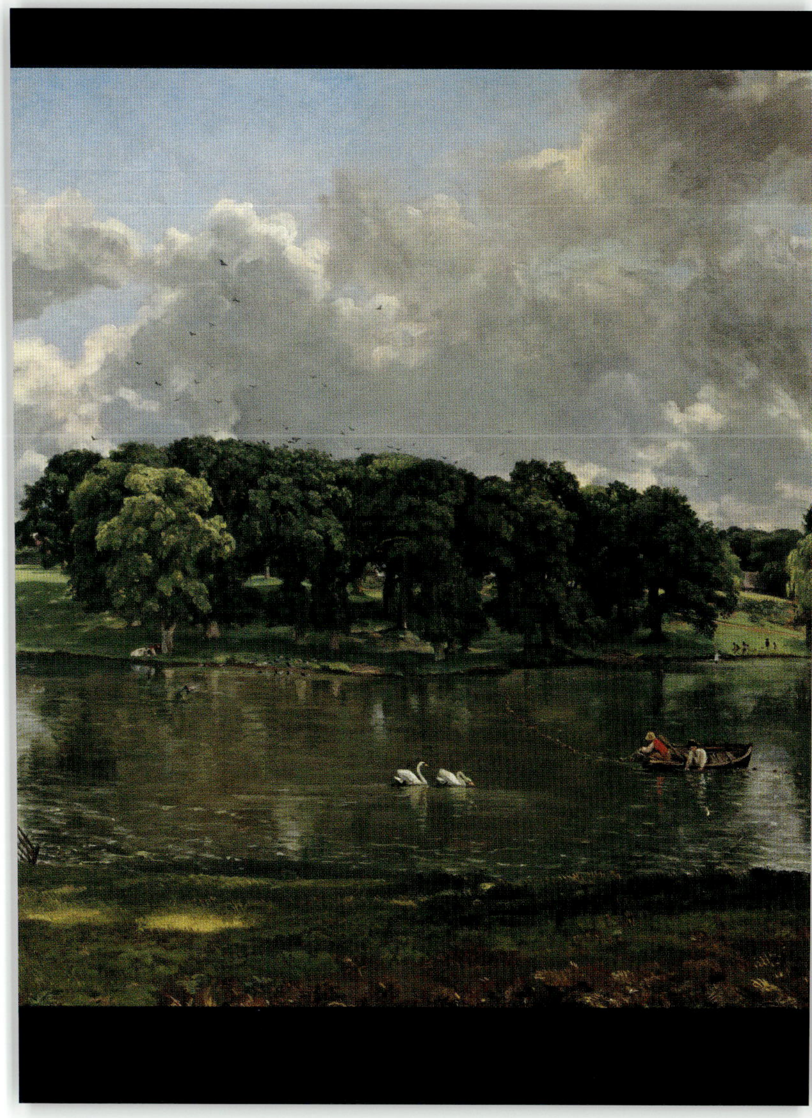

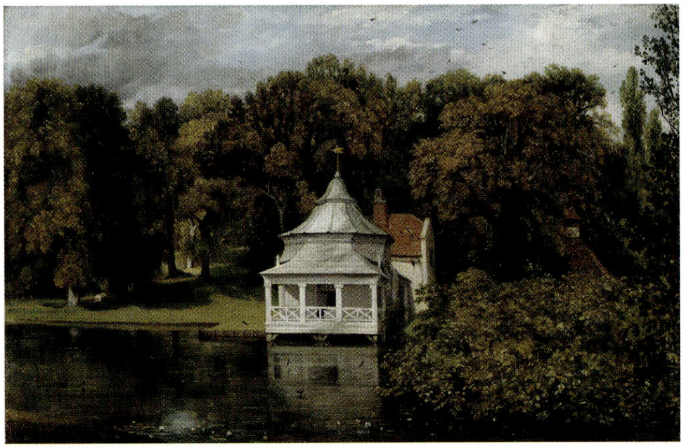

The Fishing Lodge (also known as the Quarters) Wivenhoe, 1816

They wish me to take my own time about them – but he will pay me for them when I please, as he tells me he understands from old Driffield that *we* may soon want a little ready money. Both the General and this good Lady are well acquainted with our history and they both hope to see us there *together*. I am next year to paint another picture of their little girl, with her donkey,[1] for their house

1. This does not seem to have been carried out, but the Rebows' daughter can be seen in a donkey cart at the far left of *Wivenhoe Park*, added when the canvas was extended left and right.

in town (Gloucester Place). This my love is just such a commission as can be of real service to us.

I am getting on as well as I can with my own pictures but these little things of the General's rather interrupt them and I am afraid will detain [me] here a week or two longer than I could have hoped – and it would be a pity not to do as well as I can with what I have got here for a few days longer more or less.

I have been out by the river this morning and am too late for our post, but Mr. Mason is here from Colchester and will put this into the post at Colchester for me – his gig is now at the door.... [...]

Ever yours, most affectionately
John Constable

Constable and Maria were married by John Fisher on 2nd October. There were no members of either family at the service. The honeymoon was spent with the Fishers at Osmington, near Weymouth. The couple would go on to have seven children

Overleaf: The Beach at Weymouth, 1816, painted during the honeymoon

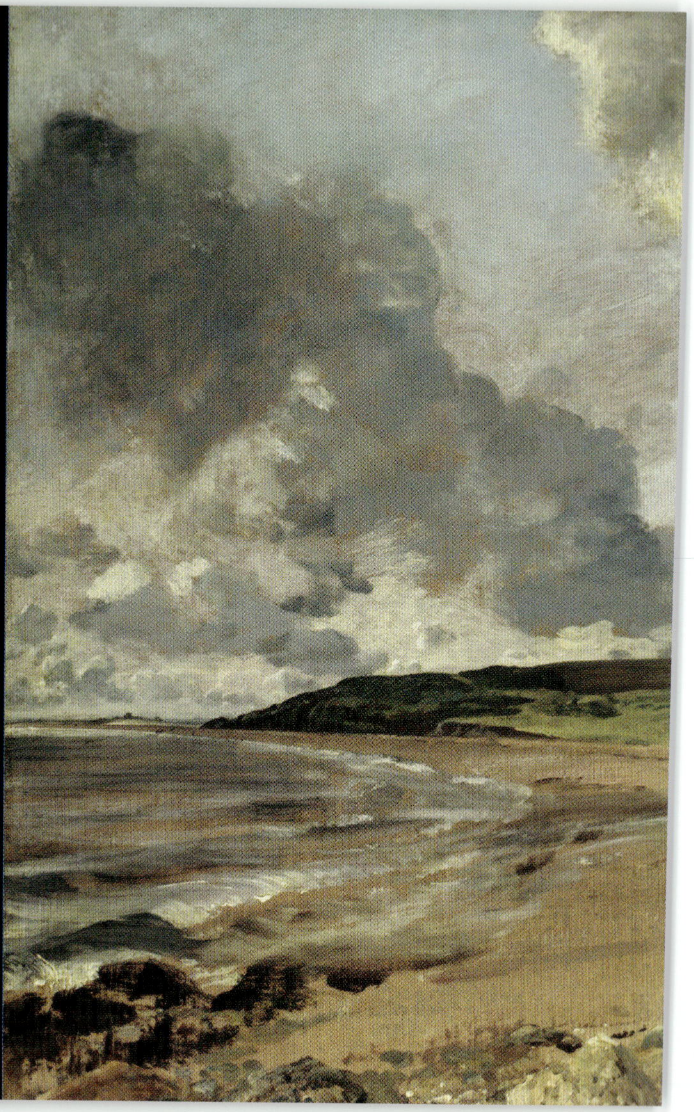

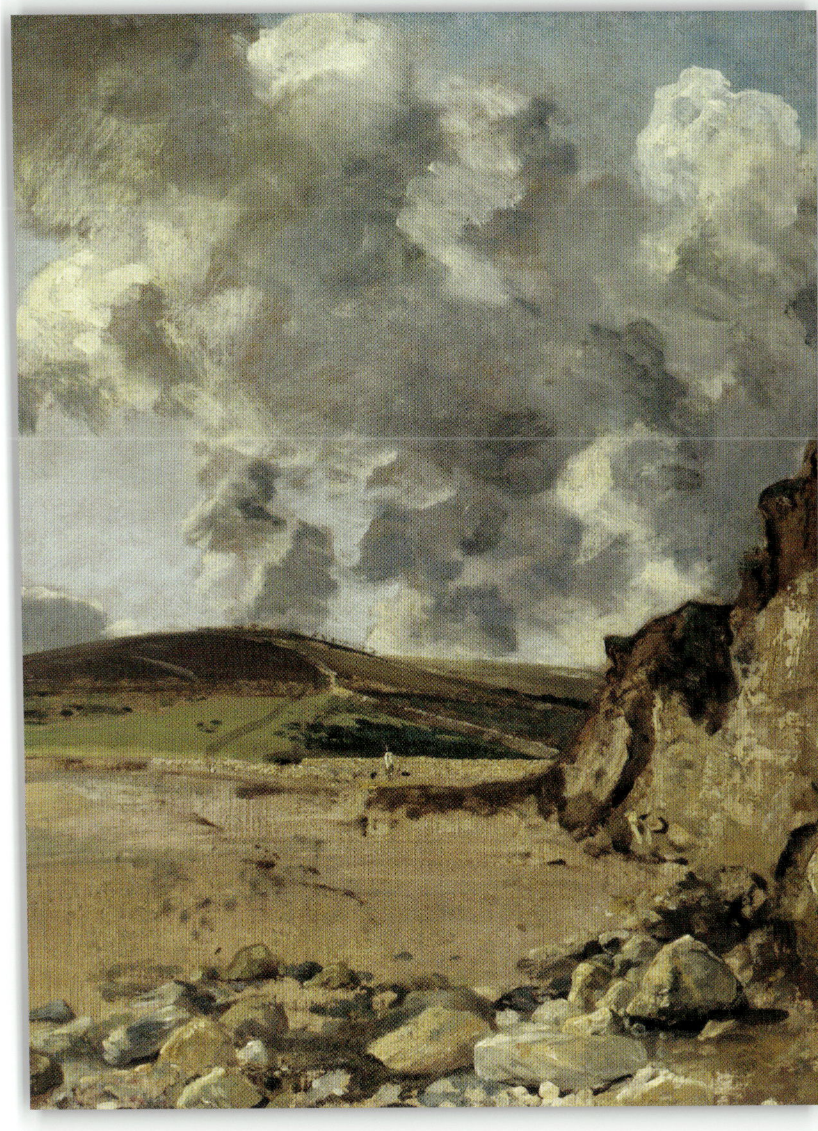

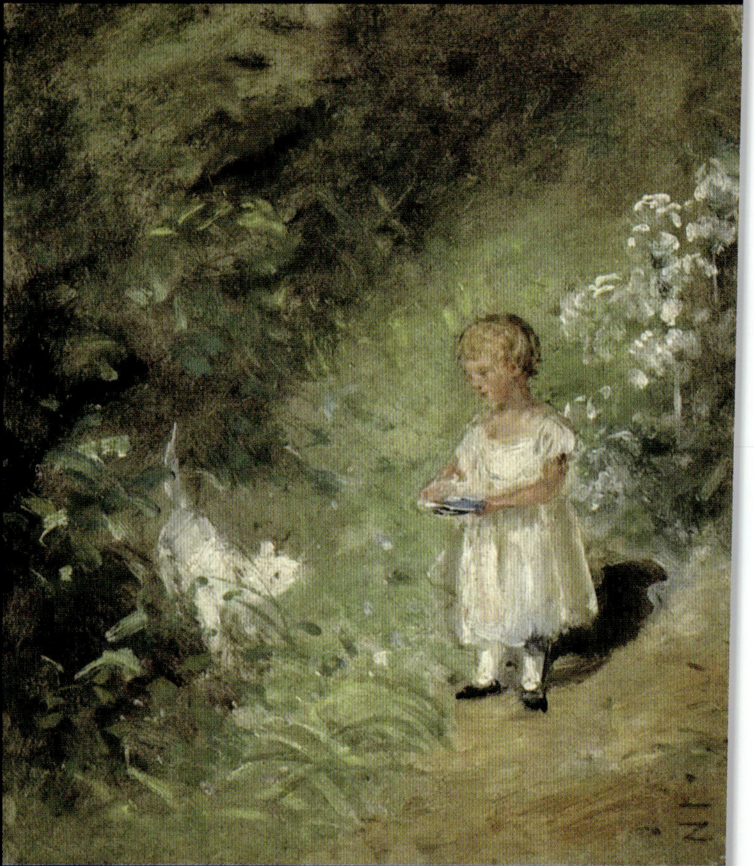

CONSTABLE TO JOHN FISHER
1 KEPPEL STREET, LONDON, 1 APRIL 1821

I trust my dear Fisher you will make every allowance for my occupation and various anxieties in my seeming neglect of you – but I am now relieved of by far the greatest of my anxieties by the safe confinement of my wife who produced a beautiful boy about 2 o'clock on Thursday last. Both are thank God doing well. She was unusually large this time & our children have been ill – and many circumstances have happened to distress her – but God has helped me where I could not have helped myself – and all the rest of my (pictorial) anxieties are giving way to the length of the days and my own exertions –

My picture [ie *The Hay Wain*] goes to the Academy on the tenth. At the same time (as the window on the stairs must be taken out) I shall send Mr Tinney's picture [ie *Stratford Mill*] to Mr Woodburn's – to be packed as the large case is there. The present picture is not so grand as Tinney's owing perhaps to the masses not being so impressive – the power of chiaroscuro is lessened – but it has

Opposite: One of the artist's sons with a dog, c. 1821–3.
Overleaf: Stratford Mill ('The Young Waltonians'), 1821. Bought by John Fisher and given to his friend John Perne Tinney

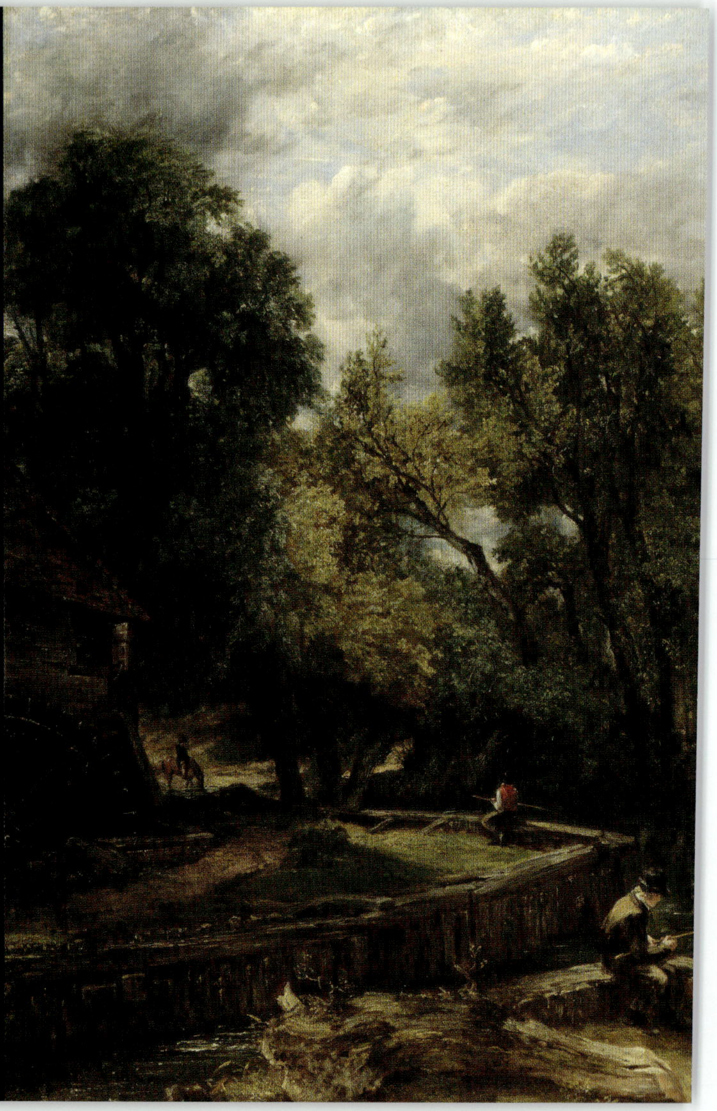

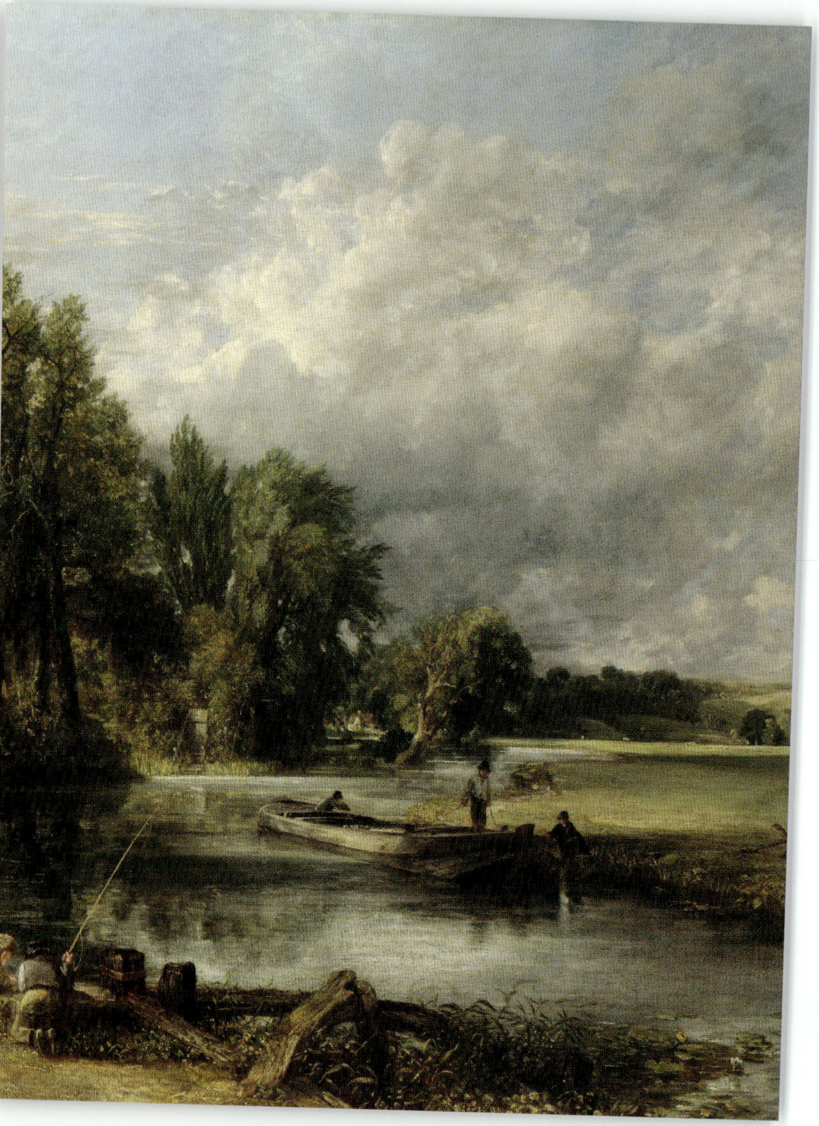

rather a more novel look than I expected. I have yet much to do to it – and I calculate for 3 or 4 days there –

I hear of so many clever pictures for the exhibition especially by Ex members [ie ARAs], that it must be a capital show. They are chiefly in the historical & fancy way – I hear little of landscape – and why? The Londoners with all their ingenuity as artists know nothing of the feeling of a country life (the essence of landscape) – any more than a hackney coach horse knows of pasture. Collins* requested me to return with him to see a landscape by himself for the Exhibition – it was beautifully painted – & I thought the subject might be about the neighbourhood of Bagnigge Wells† – but he named a scene in the most romantic glen in Westmorland as the identical spot he had painted. This I am sure will never do as landscape painting – but I stand on ticklish ground – though that ground is my own – and one might get involved in jarring – & makes ones life uncomfortable. Friendship, and a well regulated mind, are things worth attaining if possible.

How much I am obliged to you for the mention of the books. The Diary is delightful.§ It has given me new information on subjects that I have heard of all my life. There is no doubt but that the Invalid is a clever fellow

* William Collins (1788–1847), landscape and genre painter. † A resort in Pentonville, just outside London. § Henry Matthews, *The Diary of an Invalid*, 1820

– but these Italian tourists think they must talk about pictures & relate anecdotes of painting – I would recommend them always to mention the story of Alexander's visit to the painting room of Apelles. He mentions the landscapes of Gaspard Poussin (whose works contain the highest feeling of landscape painting yet seen – such an union of patient study with a poetical mind). The Invalid (indeed he deserves the name if disease gives it) imagines defects in the landscapes that he may afford an opportunity to '*our own Glover*'* of remedying them – this is too bad and one would throw the book out of the window – but that its grossness is its own cure – and one is led on for the fun of the thing – to be amused with the novelty of shapes which Ignorance appears in –

The mind & feeling which produced the 'Selborne' is such a one as I have always envied.† The single page alone of the life of Mr White leaves a more lasting impression on my mind than that of Charles the Fifth or any other renowned hero – it only shows what a real love for nature will do – surely the serene & blameless life of Mr White, so different from the folly & quackery of the world, must have fitted him for such a clear & intimate view of nature.

* John Glover (1767–1849), highly successful landscape painter, known as the 'English Claude', and also as 'the father of Australian landscape painting'; he had emigrated to Tasmania in old age. † Gilbert White, *The Natural History and Antiquities of Selborne,* first published 1789

It proves the truth of Sir Joshua Reynolds' idea that the virtuous man alone has true taste. This book is an addition to my estate – Carpenter got it for me 2 Vol. Octavo.

Stothard was amused with your mention of his pilgrims – but said he believed many of his prints were to be found amongst the Hottentots.*

I dined last week at Sir G. Beaumont's – met Wilkie, Jackson & Collins. It was quite amusing to hear them talk about Martin's picture. Sir G. said some clever things about it – but he added, even allowing the composition to be something (its only merit), still if the finest composition of Handel's was played entirely *out of tune* what would it be? It was droll to hear Wilkie say '*Gentlemen ye are too severe*' – and then say something ten times worse than had yet been said. Sir G. says he will not go out of town without painting me a picture –

My best regards to all your family – believe me
my dear Fisher
always most sincerely yours
John Constable.

Dr Gooch has just left my door. He says all is going well upstairs –

* Thomas Stothard (1755–1834) had scored a success with *The Canterbury Pilgims,* commissioned by a publisher for engraving. It led to Stothard's rift with Blake who accused him of stealing his composition.

CONSTABLE TO JOHN FISHER
HAMPSTEAD, 23 OCTOBER 1821

My dear Fisher

I trust you will pardon this delay of mine in replying to your last long and very kind letter – I fully expected to have been with you at this time – but I have had many interruptions but what has prevented me has been a good deal of Indisposition in my family. which has made it almost impossible for me to leave home. Our time expires at this place this month – and when I have settled my family in Keppel Street I shall be able to make you a visit for a few days, should it be then convenient to you to receive me.

I have not been idle and have made more particular and general study than I have ever done in one summer, but I am most anxious to get into my London painting room, for I do not consider myself at work without I am before a six foot canvas – I have done a good deal of skying – I am determined to conquer all dificulties and that most arduous one among the rest, and now talking of skies –

It is quite amusing and interesting to us to see how admirably you fight their battles: you certainly take the best possible ground for getting your friend out of a scrape – '(the examples of the great masters)'. That landscape

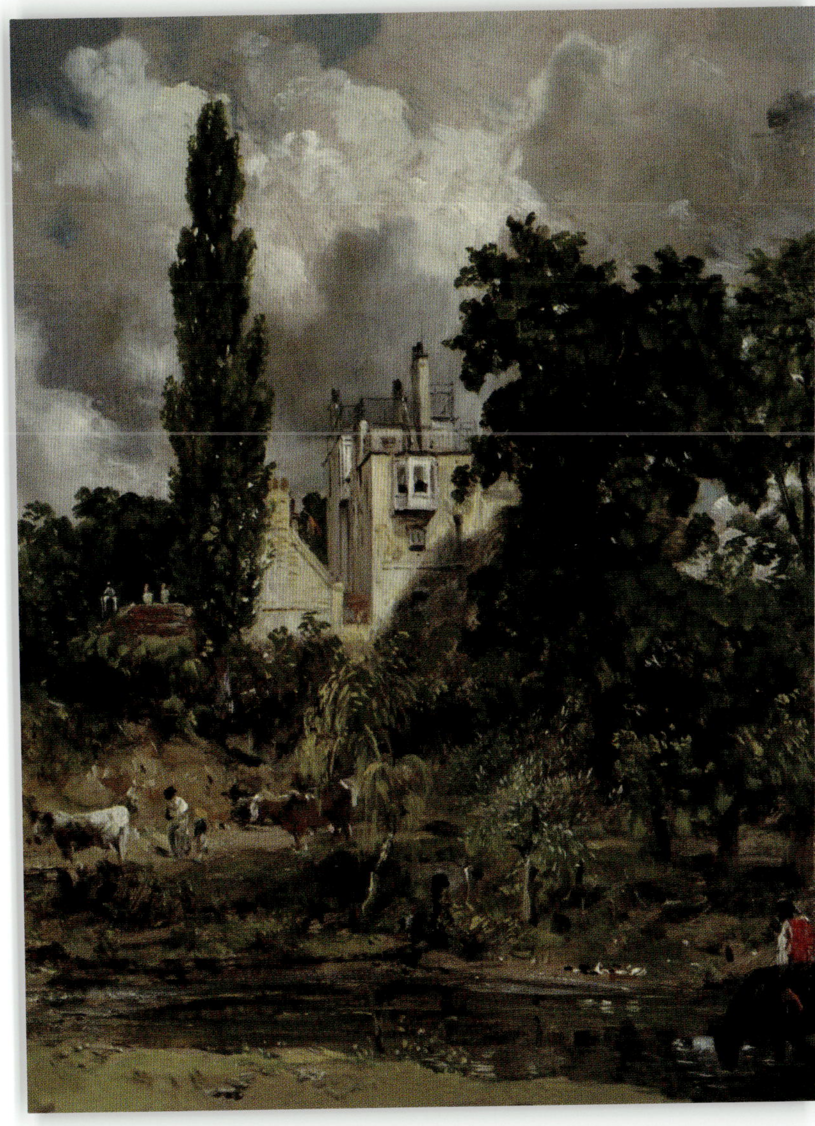

painter who does not make his skies a very material part of his composition – neglects to avail himself of one of his greatest aids. Sir Joshua Reynolds speaking of the 'Landscape' of Titian & Salvator & Claude – says '*Even their skies seem to sympathise with the subject*'. I have often been advised to consider my *sky* – as a '*white sheet drawn behind the objects*'. Certainly if the sky is *obtrusive* – (as mine are) it is bad, but if they are *evaded* (as mine are not) it is worse, they must and always shall with me make an effectual part of the composition. It will be difficult to name a class of landscape, in which the sky is not the '*key note*', the *standard of 'scale'*, and the chief '*organ of sentiment*'. You may conceive then what a '*white sheet*' would do for me, impressed as I am with these notions, and they cannot be erroneous. The sky is the '*source of light*' in nature – and governs every thing. Even our common observations on the weather of every day, are suggested by them but it does not occur to us. Their difficulty in painting both as to composition and execution is very great, because with all their brilliancy and consequence, they ought not to come forward or be hardly thought about in a picture – any more than extreme distances are.

But these remarks do not apply to *phenomenon* – or what the painters call *accidental effects of sky* – because they always attract particularly.

Opposite: The Grove, Hampstead, c. 1821-2

Cloud Study, summer 1821

I hope you will not think I am turned critic instead of painter. I say all this *to you* though you do not want to be told – that I know very well what I am about, & that my skies have not been neglected though they often failed in execution – and often no doubt from over-anxiety about them – which alone will destroy that easy appearance which nature always has – in all her movements. [...]

How strange it is that we should prefer raising up all manner of difficulties in painting – to truth and common sense.

How much I can imagine myself with you on your fishing excursion in the new forest, what river can it be? But the sound of water escaping from mill dams, so do willows, old rotten banks, slimy posts, & brickwork. I love such things – Shakespeare could make anything poetical – he mentions 'poor Tom's' haunts among *sheep cots – & mills* – the water[mist?] & the hedge-pig. As long as I do paint I shall never cease to paint such places. They have always been my delight – & I should indeed have delighted in seeing what you describe in your company 'in the company of a man to whom nature does not spread her volume or utter her voice in vain'.

But I should paint my own places best – Painting is but another word for feeling. I associate my 'careless boyhood'

Overleaf: View on the Stour near Dedham (full size study), c. 1821-2

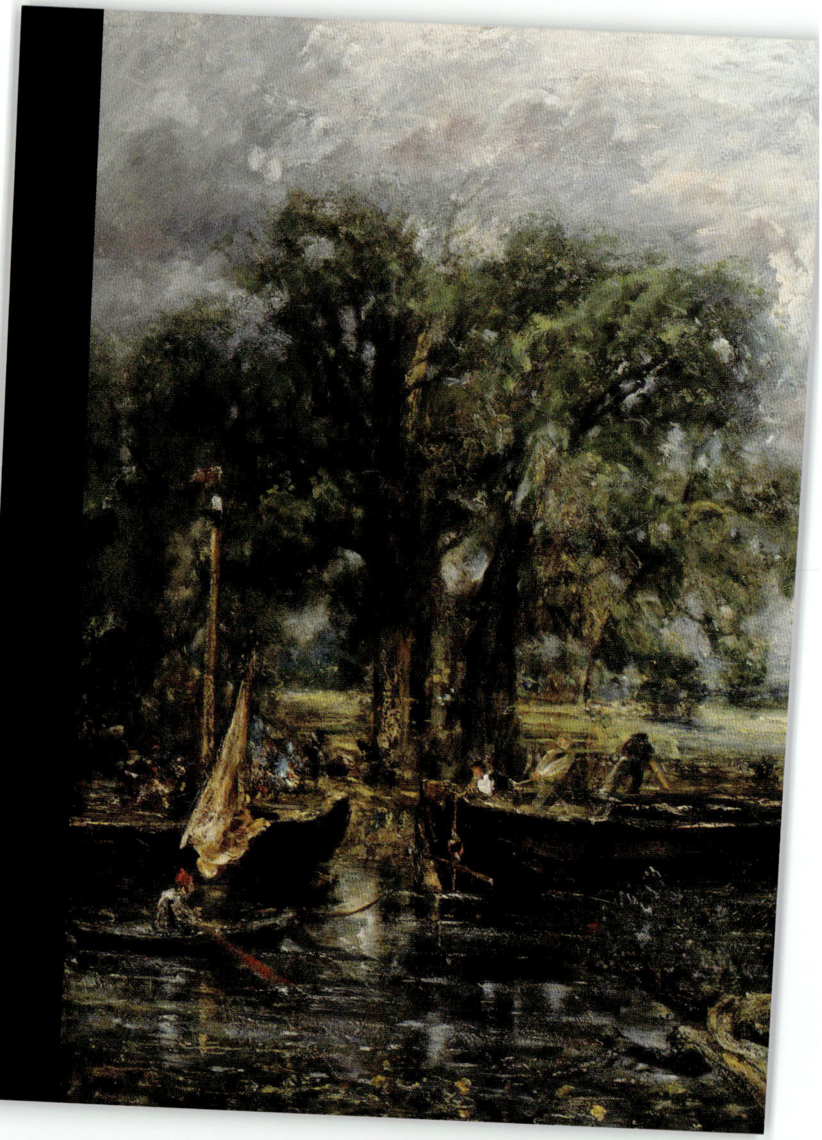

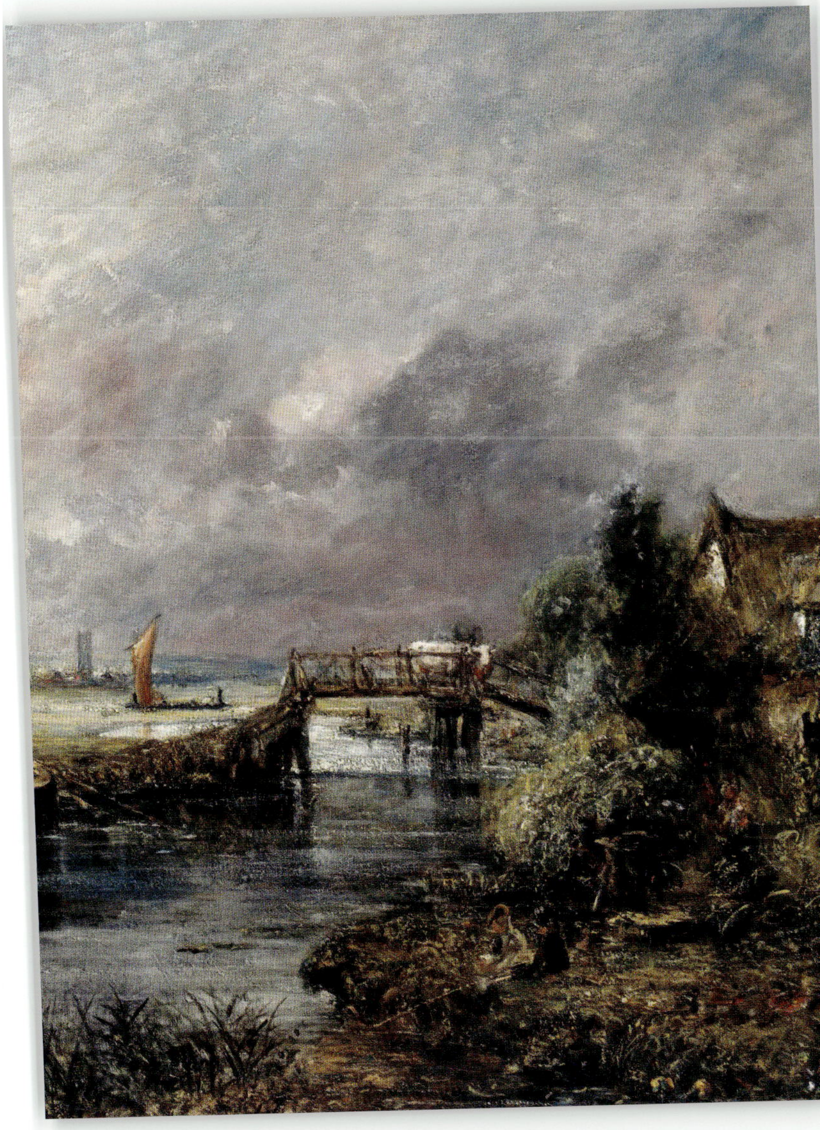

to all that lies on the banks of the *Stour*. They made me a painter (& I am grateful) that is I had often thought of pictures of them before I had ever touched a pencil, and your picture is one of the strongest instances I can recollect of it. But I will say no more – for I am fond of being an egotist, in whatever relates to painting.

Does not the cathedral look very beautiful amongst the golden foliage, its silvery grey must sparkle in it. Poor Read has sent me some copies made at Wilton, the Claude & a Van de Velde – they are very far from bad, and very much better than I expected. I only wished you to call on him, nothing else. Your advice, & notice of him could not fail of being of service to him, in a matter in which the world is led by appearances – I hope he is getting a living. He seems industrious. I have requested the loan of the little Teniers at the Miss Fishers' for him to copy. It is a good tone but rather too hot on the right hand side.

My wife and children are now quite well, the former & my eldest boy having been great invalids. We sincerely hope Mrs Fisher & all your children and relations our good friends at Salisbury are well. Is the *portrait* of which you make such laughable mention, still running the gauntlet at the public house? What can the good Bishop be about? But you fully account for all the scrape – the worst I should fear is that some of the dignity of his high station must go with it – but I will say no more – that *love* *of patronage* which you mention, brought me known to you, and your excellent family, & which has brought with it most of the great blessings of my life. I long to get to work. I shall do another large work of my own, & Savile's picture* – but that is a dead pall. He is not only a fool, but he is as crazy as a fool can be.

My last year's work has got much *together*. This weather has blown & washed the *powder off*. I do not know what I shall do with it – but I love my children to[o] well to expose them to the taunts of the ignorant – though they shall never flinch from honourable competition. I have just paper enough to say adieu – & add my wife's (who is sitting by me) best regards to yourself and all your family. I am yours

John Constable

JOHN FISHER TO CONSTABLE
OSMINGTON, WEYMOUTH, 1 OCTOBER 1822

My dear Constable:

I think you did quite right to lay down your palette for your pen: for if you were painting no better than you wrote your canvas would not be very intelligible. – Over leaf I send you two drafts which you may pay away

* Never painted. Albany Savile MP, foxhunter, was the son of Constable's uncle by marriage, a very rich but dishonest corn merchant.

without the trouble of presenting in person. It is every farthing I can possibly spare. I shall have a deficit this year in my income of not less than £1000. – The sooner you come to Salisbury the better since in November I shall not be alone: and shall have less of your company. I have oil paints & watercolours. My father was at my house in the close a few days ago alone. He said yesterday voluntarily & unexpectedly. 'John that picture of your humming-top friend is a very good one. I did not think the man could paint so well. It is his best. It has less of his meal & white wash.' You must compound the vinegar to get at the oil. He is rather costive in the article of praise you know. – Your house at Hampstead you must for ever give up. I thought it always, & said so, an expense you could not bear. Better your children suffer from hot rooms, than you have your mind torn with the briars [of de]bt. Snuff out one end of your candle. – Captain Forster, a gentleman of property near Windsor, is an admirer of your art. He is to meet you at Salisbury. He was first caught by a sketch book of yours which I had. Your pencil sketches always take people: both learned & unlearned. Surely it would answer to publish a few of them. Get one done in stone as an experiment.* Unless indeed it is derogatory from the

* i.e. as a lithograph – a recently developed method of making prints.

Opposite: Page from one of Constable's surviving sketchbooks, 1813. Reproduced approximately actual size

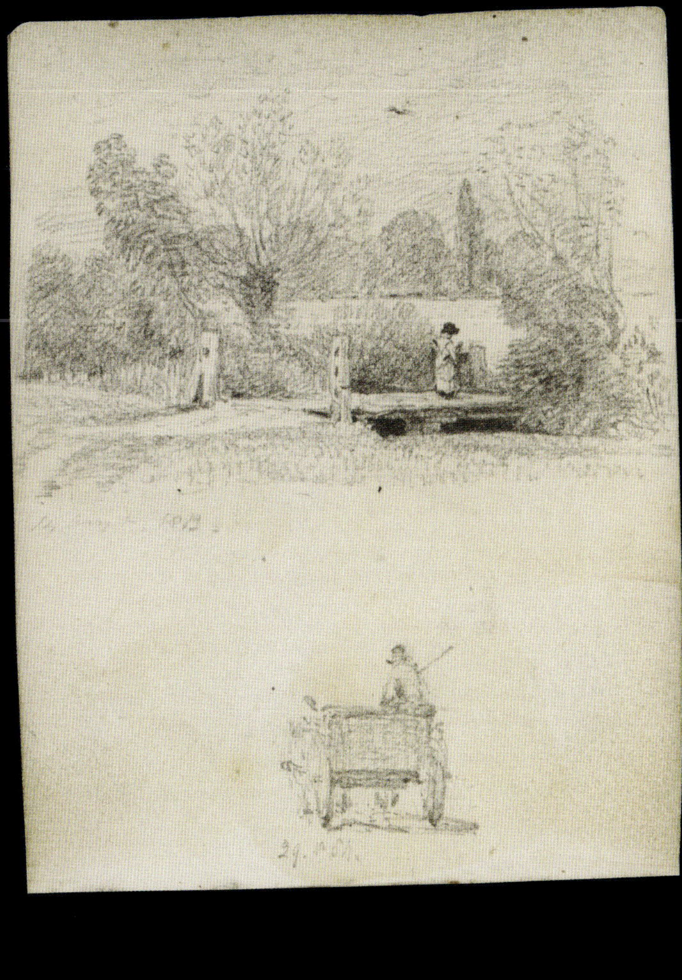

station you hold in the art. In that case I would not advise it – The day before yesterday we had a calm with a clear sky. The NW. wind had blown off all the atmosphere & every thing came sharp close upon the eye. The sea was smooth & a pale white. The hulls of the vessels came off sharp black spots: you might see the men & the small rigging from the shore. Portland was a deep plum colour & close to the eye. — Bring with you my little Novr Salisbury, my wife's coast scene;[1] Dodsworth's Teniers,[2] & the prints you have collected for me. Mrs Fisher hopes Mrs Constable will recover by change of air even that of London. Love to my god-daughter. Believe me

my dear Constable

yours very faithfully

John Fisher.

CONSTABLE TO JOHN FISHER
35 CHARLOTTE STREET, 9 MAY 1823

My dear Fisher

We are bad correspondents – I have made many attempts to write to you during the present interesting season – but without effecting my purpose.

I had many interruptions to my works for the

1. Neither painting has been identified. 2. Private collection. Dodsworth was a verger at Salisbury Cathedral.

Exhibition as you know from various causes so that I have no large canvas there. My Cathedral looks very well. Indeed I got through that job uncommonly well considering how much I dreaded it. It is much approved by the Academy and moreover in Seymour St.* though I was at one time fearful it would not be a favourite there owing to a *dark cloud* – but we got over the difficulty, and I think you will say when you see it that I have fought a better battle with the Church than old Hume, Brougham† and their coadjutors have done. It was the most difficult subject in landscape I ever had upon my easel. I have not flinched at the work, of the windows, buttresses, &c, &c, but I have as usual made my escape in the evanescence of the chiaroscuro. I think you will like it but you could have done me much good.[1]

I have been with the Bishop this morning for this frank.§ I am to *show* the young ladies the Exhibition on Monday. What a treat (it will be to them). I am vexed to see the good Bishop looking ill. It may be a temporary cold – but he breaks, no doubt. This has been a fearful winter for old & young. A gentleman told me last Monday, that he had witnessed at a burial ground in Spitalfields,

1. *Salisbury Cathedral from the Bishop's Grounds*, 1823, V&A, London. Constable painted another version without the dark cloud for the Bishop, now Frick Collection, New York . * London home of Bishop Fisher. † Joseph Hume and Henry Brougham, radical politicians and *bêtes noires* of Constable. § Free postage, a privilege of the clergy.

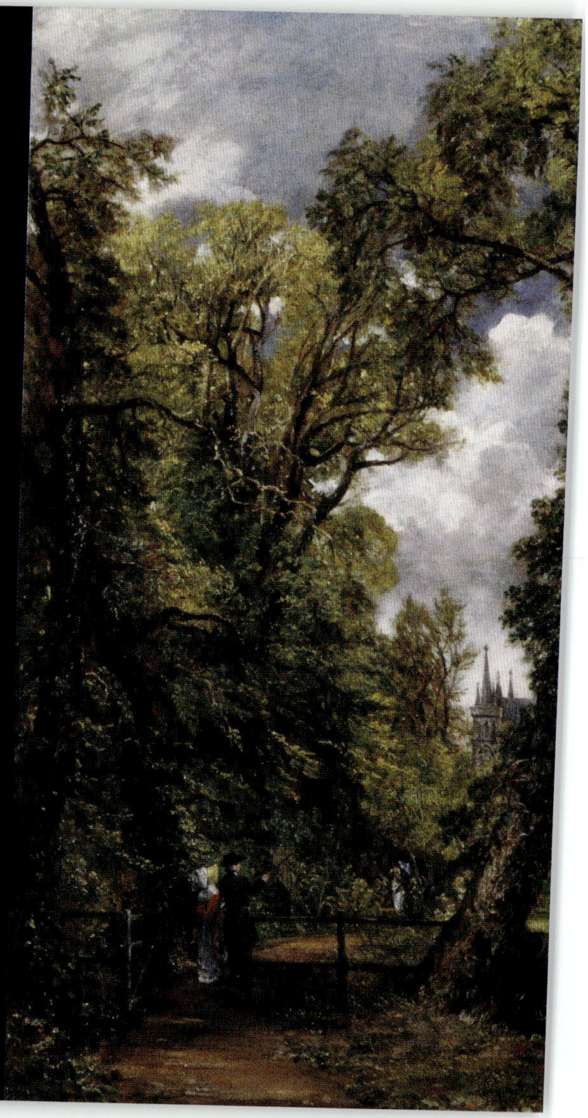

Salisbury Cathedral from the Bishop's Grounds (original version, 1823). Bishop Fisher and his wife can be seen lower left

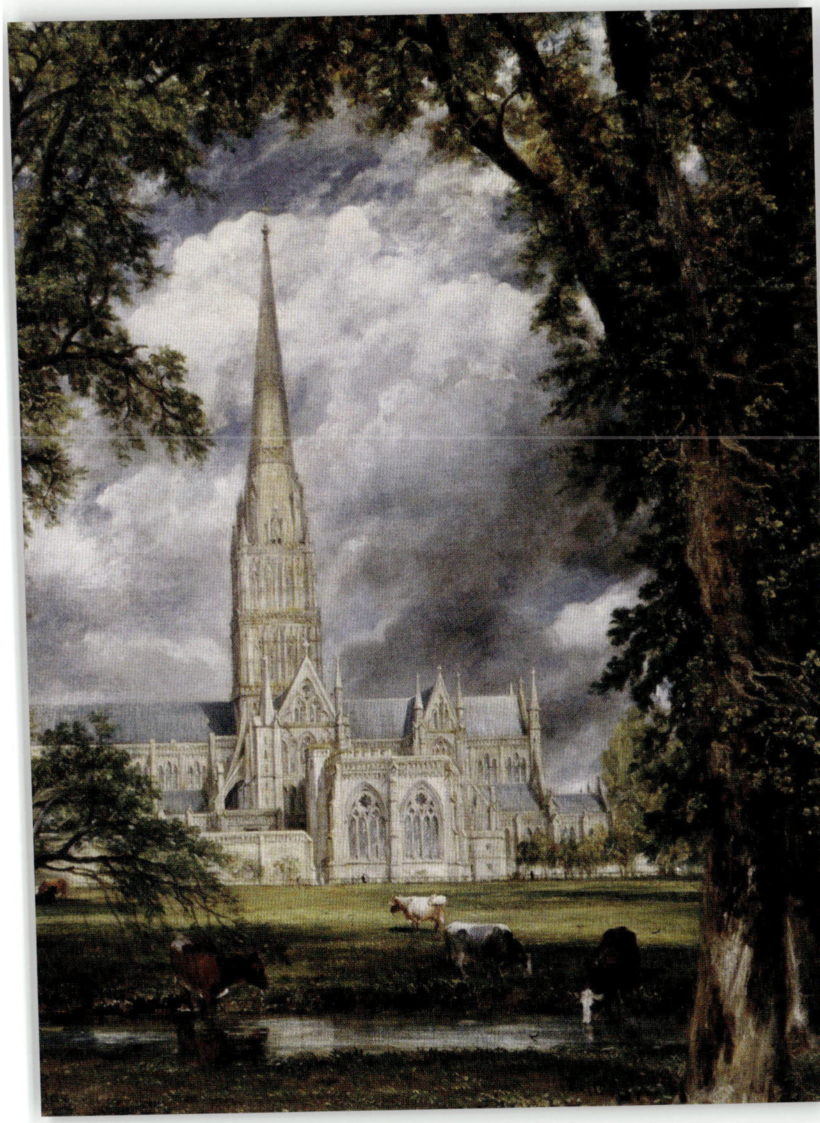

47 funerals one Sunday afternoon, when some others were sent home, as the clergyman was worn out. [...]

It is my wish to come to see you at Gillingham. I want to do something at that famous Mill, a mile or two off. You are in the midst of fine stuff. I am now busy both in portrait & landscape. And when my summer plans are arranged I will tell you of it, & meet you at Salisbury – I should not recognise you in any other place – and besides I have some of my children* there – I have not yet seen Tinney's room.

I was glad to hear this morning that your infant is safe, and that you are all well. I have had a most anxious winter. My boy is getting about, but my wife is extremely delicate – and must be much attended to: my other children are all well, and beautiful.

Calcott admires my Cathedral. He says I have managed it well. He has a poor picture there† – and Turner is stark mad – with ability – the picture seems painted with saffron and indigo.§ Northcote gave him a sad trip up at starting. He was on my arm, when Turner asked him if he (Turner) was in his senses. Northcote said no – certainly you must be mad to do such a thing, but I can tell you

* i.e. paintings. † (Sir) Augustus Callcott, RA (1779–1844). The painting is probably *View of the Grote Kerk, Rotterdam* (with Christies 2006). § Probably *The Bay of Baiæ* (Tate).

Opposite: Gillingham Mill (1823–7)

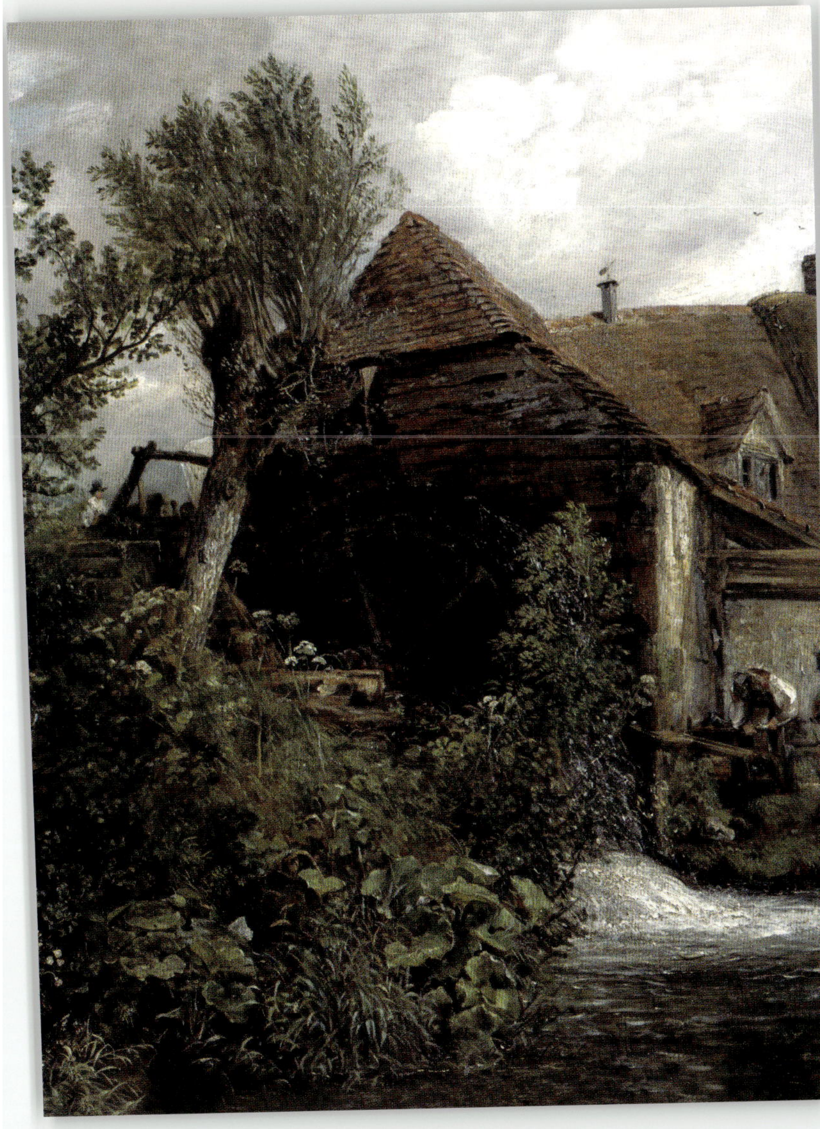

over and over again, if you will persist in imitating '*Martin*' (Paradise Martin of British Gallery fame) you must be ruined.* Turner has often spoke of this as a good *joke* – but as Southey would say, it *sticks*, as [it] is too sure & pungent to be laughed away.

Wilkie's pictures are the finest in the world. Perhaps the outdoor scene is too black.† Fuseli came up to him, and said 'Vell – vhat dis is de new vay – dis is de Guercino. Vel I don't understand it'.§ Speaking of me generally he says – 'I *like* de *landscape* – of Constable – but he makes me call for my great coat', & particularly he says, I am always picturesque – 'of a fine colour – & de lights always in their right places. He makes a good colour' – &c. &c. This nonsense may amuse you when contemplating this busy, but distant scene. However though I am here in the midst of the world I am out of it – and am happy – and endeavour to keep myself unspoiled. I have a kingdom of my own both fertile & populous – my landscape and my children. I am envied by many, and much richer people. –

Let me hear from you – soon. I want to know of your movements, & whether you visit London this season – must you not do so 'ex officio'?

* John Martin (1789–1854) had won several substantial prizes at the British Institution for his megalomaniac paintings. † Possibly *The Parish Beadle* (Tate). § Henry Fuseli, RA (Johann Heinrich Füssli, 1741–1825), was Swiss and never lost his accent.

I have work to do and my finances must be repaired if possible. I have a face now on my easel and may have some more. This is a great chubby boy, who has had an opportunity of running all over Italy, knows nothing of nature or art – being brought up at Oxford – and recollects nothing he saw while abroad – but that in Milan '*the Fantorini puppets* are as *large as life*'.

'Oh dear, Oh dear, I shall never let my longing eyes see that famous country' – are the words of old Richardson.* Am I doomed never to see the living scenes – which inspired the landscape of Wilson & Claude Lorrain? No! but I was born to paint a happier land, my own dear England – and when I forsake that, or cease to love my country – may I as Wordsworth says

> never more, hear
> Her green leaves rustle
> Or her torrents roar –†

I went to the gallery of Sir John Leicester§ to see the English artists. I recollect nothing so much as a

* Approximate quotation of Jonathan Richardson *An essay on the theory of painting*, first published 1715. † Approximate quotation from *The Thanksgiving Ode* (1816) § Sir John Leicester, Bt, MP, later 1st Baron de Tabley, collector and patron of modern British art. He helped to suppress the Blanketeers in Lancashire, and to found the British Institution. He opened his collection to public view in a specially built gallery in Mayfair.

solemn – bright – warm – fresh – landscape by Wilson, which still swims in my brain like a delicious dream.* Poor Wilson. Think of his magnificence, think of his fate! But the mind loses its dignity less in adversity than in prosperity. He is now walking arm in arm with Milton – & Linnæus. He was one of the great appointments to show to the world the hidden stores and beauties of Nature. One of the great men who show to the world what exists in nature but which was not known till his time.

Best regards to all *yours*. Yours most truly
J. Constable.

CONSTABLE TO MARIA CONSTABLE
THE CLOSE, SALISBURY, 29 AUGUST 1823

My dearest love,

I was at Fonthill yesterday.† We have had such sad weather that I have been able to do but little – but I have made one or two attacks on an old mill.

It was very good natured of Fisher to take me to see that extraordinary place – the ticket to admit two persons

* Possibly *Tabley House and Lake* (Whitworth Art Gallery, Manchester, retained at Tabley House, Knutsford). † The grandiose neo-gothic mansion built by William Beckford which he was obliged to sell after losing two of his sugar plantations. At 90m the spire was probably the fourth highest in the country, Salisbury at 123 m being in first place.

is a guinea, beside impositions when you arrive. He says there have been great changes in the articles, since last year – many superb things that are now not there and [divers] others added, especially pictures. One of the latter or I am greatly mistaken (a battle by Wouvermans) I saw at Reinagle's* just before I left town – so that after all it is quite an auctioneer's job.

Yesterday being a fine day a great many people came there. I counted more than 30 carriages, and half the number of gigs, & 2 stage coaches, so that in spite of the guinea tickets there was a great mixture of company – very few genteel people. There was a large room fitted up with boxes like a coffee house, for dinners, &c &c. Mr Phillips's name (the auctioneer) seemed here as great as Buonaparte's – cards of various kinds and boards were put up – Mr P. desires this – Mr P. takes the liberty to recommend the following inns &c &c for beds, &c, &c – but I observed many long faces coming away from the said inns.

I wandered up to the top of the tower – Salisbury at 15 miles off darted up into the sky like a needle – & the magnificence of the woods & lakes, a wild region of the downs to the north, and distant Dorsetshire hills made me long much to be at dear old Osmington, the remembrance of which must always be dear to you & me....

* Ramsay Richard Reinagle RA (1775–1862), painter, restorer, suspected faker and dealer.

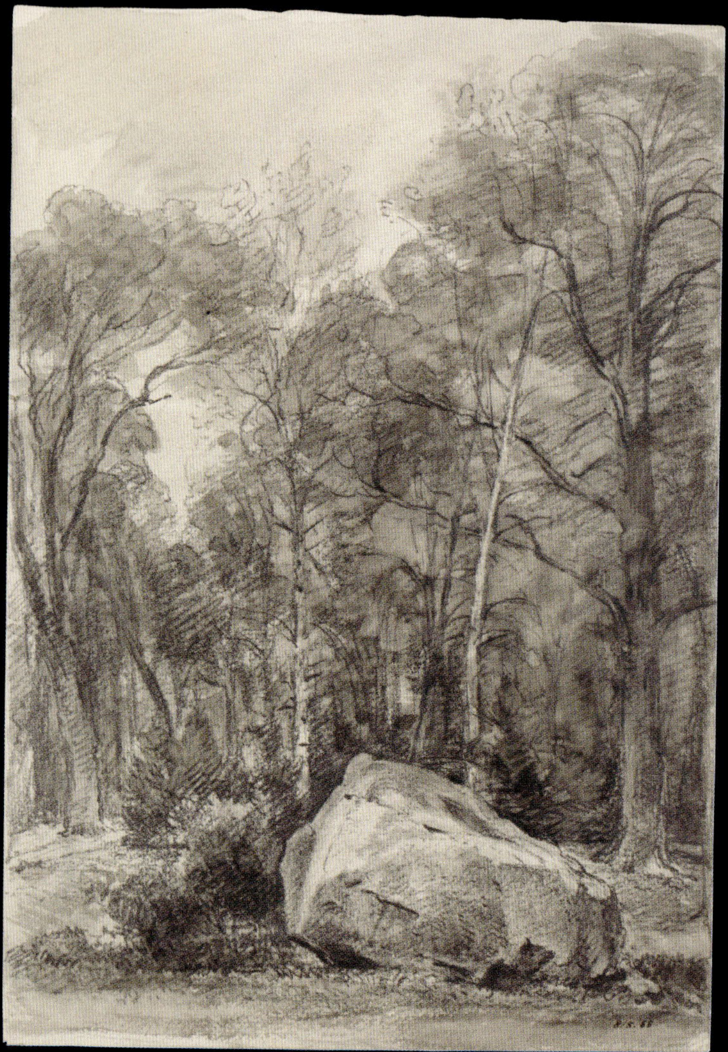

MARIA CONSTABLE TO CONSTABLE
35 CHARLOTTE STREET, 17 NOVEMBER 1823

My dear John,

How came you to disappoint me of a letter to day? You said you would write on Saturday, 'your word once passed should never be broken.' I begin to be heartily sick of your long absence [at Coleorton, staying with Sir George Beaumont]. As to your Claude[1] I would not advise you to show it to me for I shall follow Mr Bigg's advice & throw them all out of the window.

Your friends begin to wonder what is become of you – that great bore Peter Coxe* was here nearly an hour on Saturday reading the paper & talking of himself. I hope you will not admit him so often into your painting room, & Mr Judkin,† another of your loungers, has been here once or twice. Have you heard from Mr Reynolds§ & what is become of his picture? [...]

1. *Landscape with Goatherd and Goats (after Claude).* See p. 36 *Peter Coxe, auctioneer and poet (1752/3–1844). Constable had contributed an illustration to his recent *The Social Day,* probably the first book to use steel engraving. † Thomas John Judkin (1788–1871), clergyman, writer, painter, and friend of Turner. § Samuel William Reynolds (1773–1835), engraver, painter and landscape gardener; trained David Lucas.

Opposite: Stone in the Grove of Coleorton Hall dedicated to Richard Wilson, 28 November 1823

Scene on the Downs, near Brighton, 1824
Reproduced approximately actual size

When summers spent in Hampstead failed to produce any improvement in Maria Constable's fragile health, sea air was recommended. Accordingly, Constable arranged to take lodgings for his family in Brighton at intervals – mainly over the summer – between 1824 and 1828. The good coach service between London and Brighton meant that he could settle his family in the resort for extended periods, then return on his own to his Charlotte Street studio to continue work on his six-foot paintings. Constable claimed to dislike Brighton, with its bustling fashionable crowds, and the sea air failed to provide a cure for Maria's tuberculosis. However, he made some magnificent oil sketches on the beach, and he was inspired to paint a large picture of the Chain Pier which he exhibited at the Academy in 1827 (see p. 52). Furthermore, the journal he wrote for Maria when he was away in London proves a captivating read today, mixing domestic and professional news.

FROM THE JOURNAL
THURSDAY 17 JUNE 1824

Got up at seven and began packing up the box for Brighton – got it done before breakfast. After breakfast walked with Johnny to Oxford Street with it to the stage. Paid 2s. 2d. charges &c. Came home & set to work on Fisher's picture – which I did very well.[1] Willes called. He is in London with his sister from Ireland. Nurse York called. She thought the family she was with would go to Brighton – she seemed in good spirits.

About half past one Fisher called. We had a nice leg of mutton ready at two, and after dinner & a glass or two of sherry we set off for Pall Mall, to the Gallery, & looked in at Christie's. We saw there all Reinagle's collection of pictures & some copies by his son.

We then went to the new Gallery – beautiful rooms, but the most wretched display of pictures that it is possible to conceive – nothing in the world can be worse – too bad too I expect as to look as to gloom, ignorance, [inability], & vanity &c, all that today … Saw the R. I. C. Judkin's picture 'Stolen Moments'* – too bad & vulgar to look at. I called at Lady Dysart's in Pall Mall – she had my letter this afternoon enclosing Golding's.

1. *Gillingham Mill*, Fitzwilliam Museum, Cambridge. * Lost

We returned to tea & coffee – quite tired with our walk. On our way from Pall Mall at the top of the Haymarket we had a full view of the balloon – which looked so near that I could see the divisions of coloured silk. On its rising higher we saw it on a clear blue sky looking like a golden egg. It then went into a white thin cloud – & then emerged from it with great beauty, one side so very bright, & the other so clear & dark. Looked 'till it was hid by other clouds. [...]

FROM THE JOURNAL
SUNDAY 20 JUNE 1824

Fisher took away his little picture of the Mill with a frame. He is quite anxious that I should dine there tomorrow or he says he shall hate the party. I ought to be at the Artists Fund* as it is a particular night.

He spoke very much of the new novel the *Red Gauntlett*,† and was not the least surprised when I told him of Sarah – he said she looked like it, & that her constitution was now impaired & she would never be well again. She is quite poorly to day, & looks sadly. The pigeons make sad work & will not agree when there is an egg. They kicked a beautiful one out to day – this makes four, & poor things

* Artists' General Benevolent Institution, founded in 1814 by members of the Royal Academy. † *Redgauntlet* by Sir Walter Scott

they seem to know how unhappy they are by moping about & sitting with their feathers ruffled.

About 4, Mr Williams our old neighbour in Keppel Street called. Mr Williams is very well & desires his regards to you – & their little boy is quite strong & clever, & forward with his story books. He spoke of their being very comfortable in the country & she liked it.

A note came from Lane in great distress about his pictures & wishing me to come.* I went at nine o'clock, stayed [till] 10, & put all to rights. I am just returned & quite fagged & tired. I found him fast asleep & the room smelling as it always does of paint & dinner & wine & coffee.

A wet night & half past 11 – so good night. I am sorry to say we have not been at church.

FROM THE JOURNAL
MONDAY 21 JUNE 1824

Longest day. Went to Oxford Street after breakfast. Johnny [Dunthorne] to Sir G. B. Returned and got to work on the little picture of Cum Pauls, for Mr Arrowsmith.[1] Got

* Samuel Lane (1780–1859), portraitist. A pupil of Thomas Lawrence, he was deaf and dumb as a result of a childhood accident. 1. Untraced, but probably related to *Sir Richard Steele's Cottage, Hampstead* . 'Cum Pauls' was a family nickname for St Paul's Cathedral. John Arrowsmith was an Anglo-French dealer and collector.

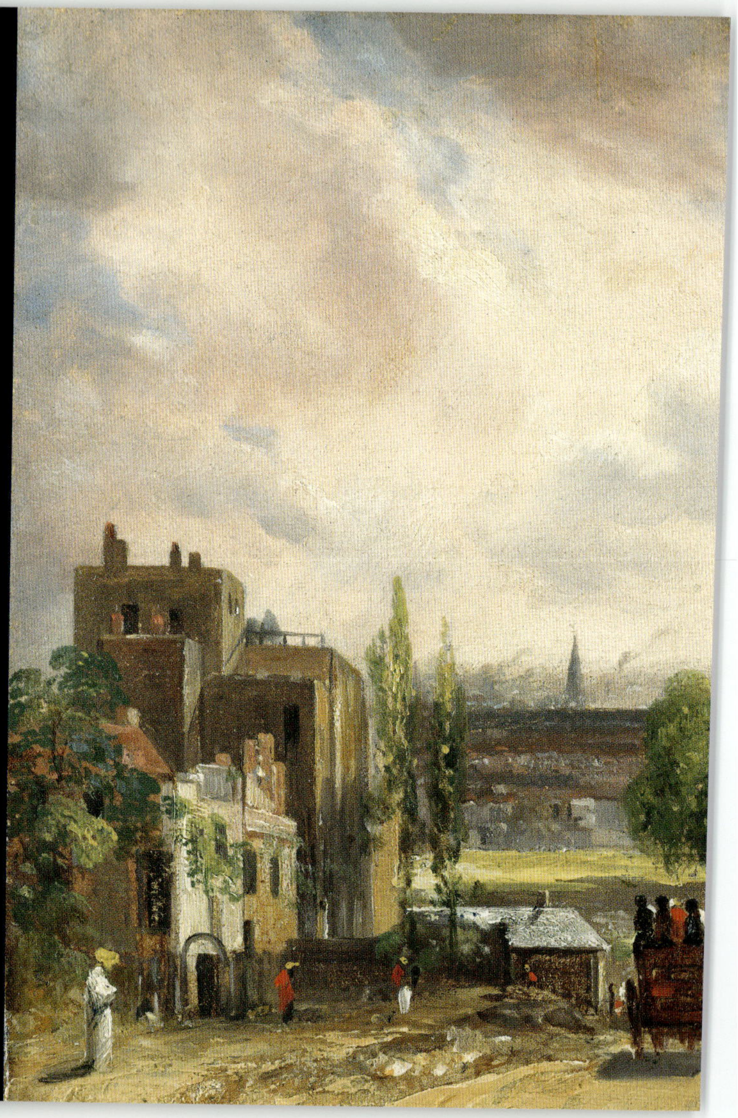

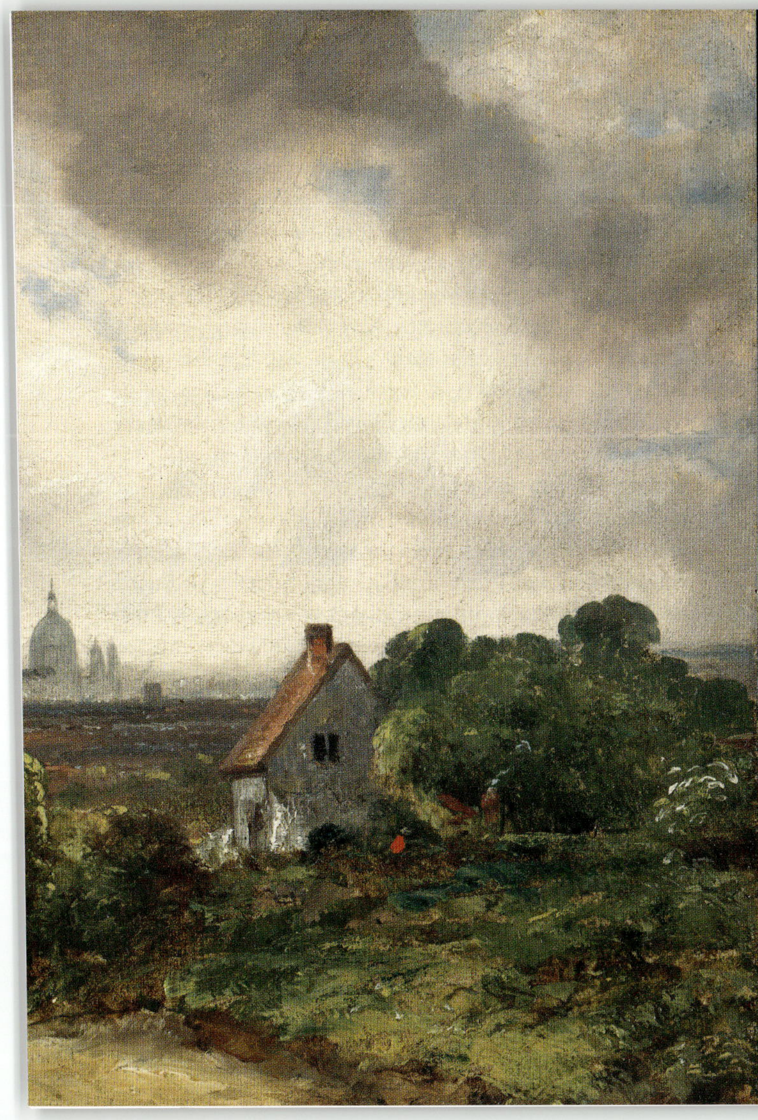

to her. It was dark green & lined with dark blue, quite fashionable & genteel. Wrote to her to come & see me & judge for herself. Called on Manning. He did not think Sarah would be ever strong again, seems almost worn out. Ellen says she is never fit.

Just as I had done my letter & was going to start painting, Judkin called. He talked in quite a friendly [way], & all was very well 'till he asked me how I liked his picture of 'Stolen Moments'. I told him that I could not help saying that it was not a thing for a clergyman to paint, that the very title was a 'double entendre' – and that the picture was very far indeed from what it ought to be. He seemed quite hurt – & I do hope I have scared him away.*

Fisher came on his way to Piccadilly to the coach, so Judkin took his leave. I went with Fisher to the coach & we had dinner in the Coffee House. I drank ale – & 2 glasses of brandy & water. He did the same. We parted quite delighted with having seen so much of each other – he longs like me to get to his darling wife & children.

Got back at 4 o'clock – went to work as (...)† – and to-morrow by the middle of the day shall complete 2 out 3 of Mr Arrowsmith's pictures. Mean to send you my journal tomorrow by coach. Mr Paul the Norwich lad called to

* Judkins later wrote a sonnet comparing Constable to Wordsworth.
† Words deleted by a later hand, perhaps because they referred to the effects of brandy (RB).

show me a picture. He stopped [to] tea. Tonight Kennedy is very busy brewing about 2 bushels of malt & I have just lashed the wort.

Mr Edmonds is going to send me another pair of pigeons. Ours are most beautiful birds, but when one egg is laid or near it they scold each other about sadly. In their bustle the other day, they followed each other into the back drawing room where we found on going up hearing the noise, an egg broken & feathers &c. Johnny saw the Mouse – and he is getting very fat. I take him rinds of cheese.

To day beef steak pudding. We are both … ed up and going to bed. Met Dr. Anderson in Bond Street. He will send you the ginger beer receipt. Mrs Everard has passed through town again and sent us their card. Mr Weight has got an artist in his floor – the cap business ended in cap pulling, not cap making.

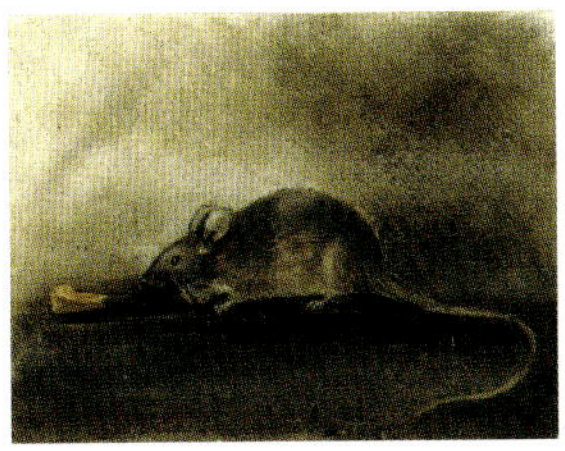

Mouse with a piece of cheese, 1824

FROM THE JOURNAL
WEDNESDAY, 7 JULY 1824

Got up at 7. Packed the fruit for my darling and took it to the stage[coach]. Went with John to Sir G[eorge] B[eaumont]'s to overlook such of his pictures as he wished [to] lend me. Brought away another specimen or two and a nice rich upright one like Rembrandt, and he lent me his lovely little Rubens, & the Teniers and another German landscape to take care of. We brought them all home in the coach, & it rained hard.

After dinner got to work and did up a picture for Sir G. Mr B[igg]* called – & in the evening went to tea & met the Chalons, Newton,† &c &c at Mr Rochard's in Bond Street.§ A pleasant evening enough. He has got on the new Waterloo. Saw a newspaper on his table, the Traveller of this evening. In it was a paragraph, 'the Column of *Original and Select News*.' [It] was this.

* William Redmore Bigg RA (1755–1828) painter of rustic genre scenes and restorer. † Alfred Edward Chalon RA (1780–1860), Geneva born portraitist, and his brother John James RA (1778–1854), well known for their party-giving. Gilbert Stuart Newton RA (1794–1835), Nova Scotia-born painter. § Either Simon-Jacques ('Mahogany') Rochard (1788–1872) or his brother François-Théodore (?1798–1858), French-born miniaturists. The reference to Waterloo is unexplained.

> Two landscapes from the pencil of Mr Constable, the eminent English artist, have arrived at Paris, and are to occupy a place in the approaching exhibition of the works of living artists in the Louvre. These landscapes have attracted great attention in Paris, and are justly admired by the French artists.*

The pictures have caused great stir. The French critics by profession are very angry at the French artists for admiring them. All this is funny enough – and very amusing, but they can't get at me on this side of the water, and [I] will never forsake old England, the land of my happiness. I have some recollection of a verse of Wordsworth's.

> O, England – if I – forget thee
> May I never more
> Hear thy green leaves rustle
> Or thy torrents roar –

I can't recollect them particularly. [...]

*Three paintings were shown at the Paris Salon: *The Hay Wain* (1821), now National Gallery, London; *View on the Stour near Dedham* (1822), now Huntington Library and Art Museum, San Marino, CA; and an unidentified Hampstead subject. A fourth painting, a view of Yarmouth Jetty, was also sent to Arrowsmith in Paris at the same time.

Overleaf: The Hay Wain, 1821

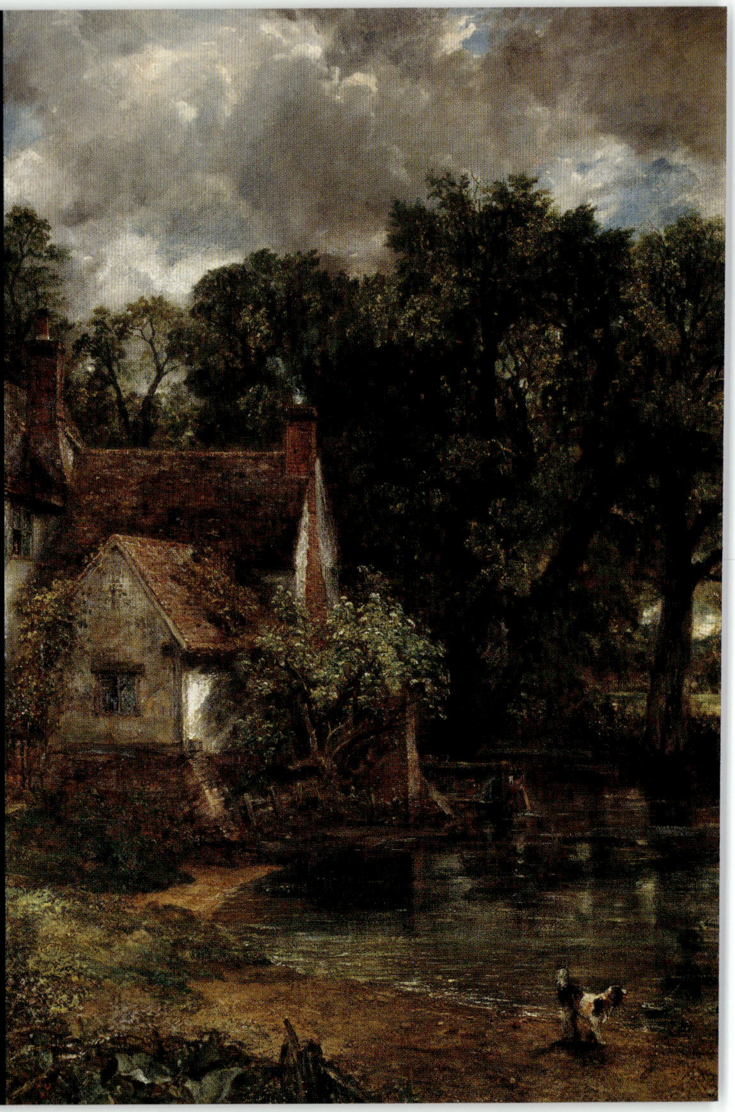

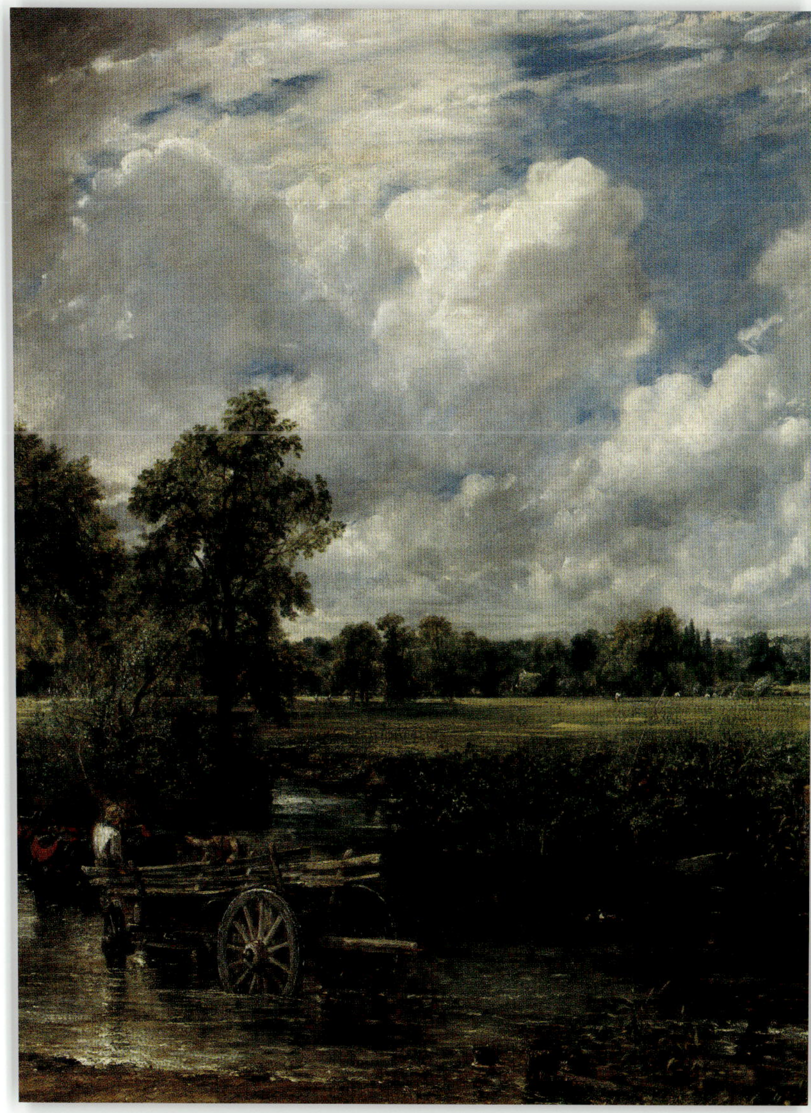

JOHN FISHER TO CONSTABLE
THE CLOSE, SALISBURY, 6 AUGUST 1824

My dear Constable;

Tinney readily consents to your exhibiting your picture when the Gallery opens. But he begs that he may have it *till* then. He particularly wishes for it at the Music meeting, the 16th August. You will do well to send it directly or you will really disoblige him.

I am on my road to Southampton [...]. I have discovered a beautiful old Mill in a secluded part of our valley on the spot where Fielding wrote his Tom Jones.

Believe me ever yours
John Fisher.

CONSTABLE TO JOHN FISHER
9 SOBER'S GARDENS, BRIGHTON, 29 AUGUST 1824

My dear Fisher

I am disappointed at not having heard either from yourself or Tinney of the safe arrival of my pictures at Salisbury. No doubt the pick-pockets and fiddlers who have of late made your cathedral the scene of their depredations must have put all other thoughts aside.

I was piquing myself how promptly I had obeyed your

demands – did you like the picture I sent you to *show*? Had I recollected your objection to that picture (The 'Nass'*) I should have sent you Hampstead.

I am living here but I dislike the place – & miss (in this my solitude) any letter from you especially when I may expect to receive one. I am however getting on with my French jobs.[1] One of the largest is quite complete, and is my best, in freshness and sparkle – *with repose* – which is my struggle just now. A friend here wished Ld Egremont to see it. It was shown him. He recollected all my pictures of any note, but he recollected them only for their defects – so that my friend's good intentions failed. But I will do his Lordship & myself justice. The truth is that landscape affords him no interest whatever.

Brighton is the receptacle of the fashion and offscouring of London. The magnificence of the sea, and its (to use your own beautiful expression) everlasting voice, is drowned in the din & lost in the tumult of stage coaches – gigs – 'flys' &c. – and the beach is only Piccadilly (that part of it where we dined) by the sea-side. Ladies dressed & *undressed* – gentlemen in morning gowns & slippers on, or without them altogether about *knee deep* in the breakers – footmen – children – nursery maids, dogs,

* Probably the name of a lane in Suffolk; see below, p. 170. 1. Most likely the pair of pictures of Hampstead, painted for the dealer Schroth, replicas of which Constable later sold to Francis Darby (see pp. 178ff).

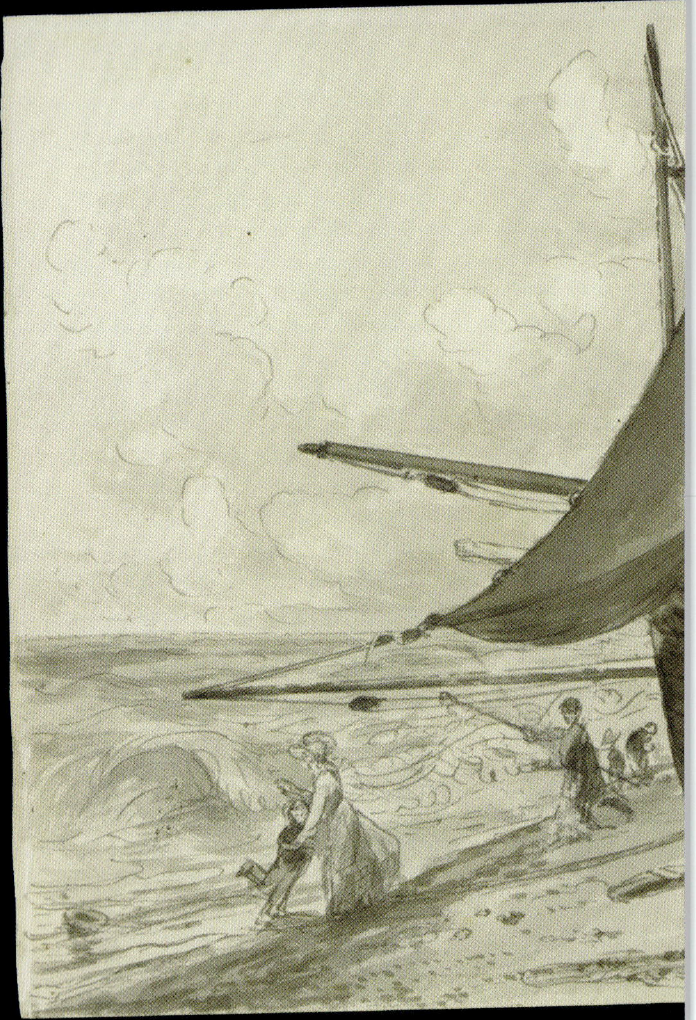

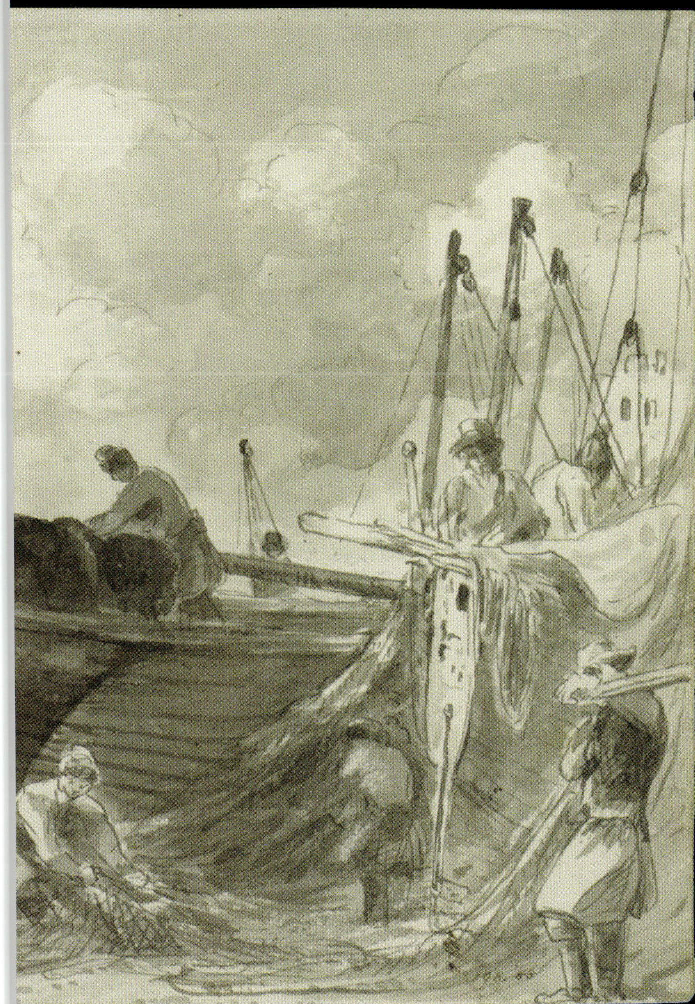

boys, fishermen – *preventive service men* (with hangers & pistols), rotten fish & those hideous amphibious animals the old bathing women, whose language both in oaths & voice resembles men – all are mixed up together in endless & indecent confusion. The genteeler part, the marine parade, is still more unnatural – with its trimmed and neat appearance & the dandy jetty or chain pier, with its long & elegant strides into the sea a full 1/4 of a mile. In short there is nothing here for a painter but the breakers – & sky – which have been lovely indeed and always varying. The fishing boats are picturesque, but not so much so as the Hastings boats, which are luggers. [...] But these subjects are so hackneyed in the Exhibition, and are in fact so little capable of that beautiful sentiment that landscape is capable of or which rather belongs to landscape, that they have done a great deal of harm to the art – they form a class of art much easier than landscape & have in consequence almost supplanted it, and have drawn off many who would have encouraged the growth of a pastoral feel in their own minds – & paid others for pursuing it. But I am not complaining – I only meant to call to your recollection that we have Calcott & Collins – but not Wilson or Gainsborough.

While in the fields (for I am at the west of this city – and

Previous pages: Scene on the beach at Brighton, c. 1824

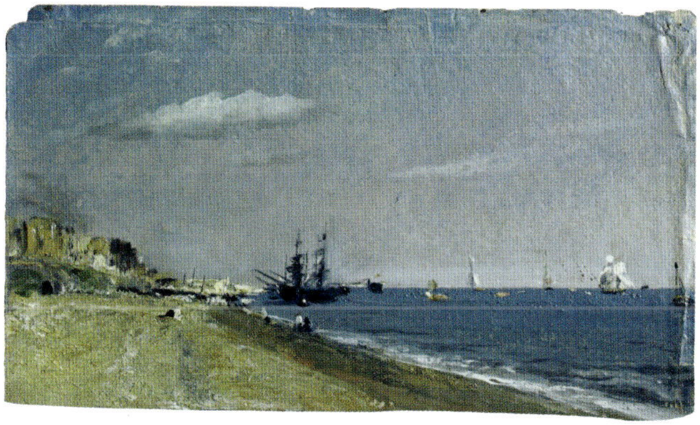

Brighton Beach with Colliers, 19 July 1824. The Parade is to the left, and the Chain Pier in the distance. It was painted on Constable's daughter Maria's birthday, and a few months later sent to John Fisher, her godfather

quite out of it), I met with a most intelligent and elegant man Mr Phillips* – we are become intimate & he contributes much to our pleasure here. He is a botanist – & all his works on natural history are instructive and entertaining – calculated for children of all ages – his history of trees is delightful – I shall buy them – & I think you would if you saw them –

* Henry Phillips (*c.* 1779–1840), botanist, horticulturalist and landscape gardener, then working on grandiose development schemes across Brighton and Hove.

Our next door neighbour is Mr & Mrs Masquerier, a portrait painter* – retired from business with a fortune – she a Scotch woman, a niece of Ld Buchan's – vulgar – & clever – with the assurance of the devil. Masquerier & I have no one feeling in common on the Art. On the score of the Academy the grapes are sour, & although he has made a fortune in the Art, he enjoys it only as a thief enjoys the fruits of his robbery – while he is not found out. He would (I see) give half his fortune for half my reputation.

No. 9, Mrs Sober's Gardens – so called from Mrs Sober the Lady of the Manor – & rich in estates here – which are more so now by their new buildings. She is of the *good*, and has built a Chapel in which she preaches herself. I have heard this story – a man was taken before the Magistrates quite drunk – when asked what he was, he said he was one of Mrs Sober's congregation.

Last Tuesday, the finest day that ever was, we went to the Dyke – which is in fact a Roman remains of an embankment, overlooking – perhaps the most grand & affecting natural landscape in the world – and consequently a scene the most unfit for a picture. It is the business of a painter not to contend with nature & put this scene

* John James Masquerier (1778-1855), portraitist and his wife Rachel Forbes, niece by marriage to the 11th Earl of Buchan.

(a valley filled with imagery 50 miles long) on a canvas of a few inches, but to make something out of nothing, in attempting which he must almost of necessity become poetical. But you understand this better than me.

My wife & children are delightfully well. Ever yrs. most truly

John Constable.

JOHN FISHER TO CONSTABLE
THE CLOSE, SALISBURY, 13 NOVEMBER 1824

My dear Constable;

This moist muggy weather, seems to have deranged everybody: and among others your humble servant. I have been as the old women say 'quite poorly' this last week & not up to the energy of a letter.

The obstacle to your getting a fresh loan of your picture, is not mine but Tinney's. His assertion that I should not like to have 'the White Horse' again removed, was gratuitous. He did not ask me. However on the receipt of your second letter, I went & made the offer; stating what I guessed to be your reason for wishing to have it viz to 'whip up' your present pictures by. But I met with no success. He will not part with it, until the time promised. The application is hopeless, though the refusal is politely worded. I assure you I did not need any bribe to induce me to comply with your wishes. I am indeed already in your debt for the loan of the 'shady lane'. But the offer of the virgin sketches is too tempting to be resisted. – Perhaps it will be as well if I return you 'the Lane'. I will send for the Carpenter & order it off; unless you write to forbid me. Would the following request interfere with your occupations? To make me a sketch of a gothic chair to correspond with our choir. Or would you get it done for me. We have at last ordered our altar on *Sundays* to be temporarily brought down between the two pillars at the end of the choir. We want the chair as an accompaniment. Is my sketch comprehensible? – The Cathedral brings poor Dodsworth to my mind. He has had two paralytic seizures. The second has drawn one eye up into his head, & has left him a woeful figure. But he still toddles about with his silver stick on his shoulder. *After thoughts*. If the request about the chair occupies any thing but an idle minute, or gives you the least trouble forego it. It is of no consequence. It is generally reputed that there will be a grand explosion in Ireland next spring. Some popular prophecies (Pastorini's) predict the year 1825 as the first year of Irish *liberty*. Every thing seems tending to a rebellion. And then it is the opinion I hear of the D[uke] of W[ellington] that the country must be *conquered*. So much for the result of Opposition politics, ministerial conciliation, & Catholic Emancipation.

I hope that you will a little diversify your subject this year as to *time of day*. Thomson you know wrote, not four Summers but *four Seasons*.* People are tired of mutton on top mutton at bottom mutton at the side dishes, though of the best flavour & smallest size.

When you write again, give us a little history of your wife and children. Believe me

yours always
John. Fisher.

CONSTABLE TO JOHN FISHER
35 CHARLOTTE STREET, 17 NOVEMBER 1824

My dear Fisher

Thank you for your letter of yesterday. I wrote rather a long letter to Tinney a few days ago – which will I hope set all right about the picture. You are both mistaken as to my motives for desiring it so soon as I at first requested to have [it] – I wished for it not to '*whip up any other pictures by*' – my Lock which now hangs in my room, being far beyond it in that respect – but my anxiety was to have it in readiness and by me as an inducement for the Wise Men from the Institution, to receive it – should it fail after all I must trouble you for your White Horse.

* Constable was fond of quoting from James Thomson's *The Seasons* (1726–30) to amplify the titles of his pictures.

See my letter to Tinney if you can? I have endeavoured to awaken him to some perception of the feeling which must govern artists and poets in their productions – but though he '*respects*' the thing, his constitution and all the *habits* of his life, make it quite impossible for him to enter into any work of '*imagination*'. It is different with you and was so from the first. You saw at once the right things in spite of the milk & water of the Bishop, & the Colonel, and the dirt & varnish which begrimed the walls of poor Douglas's drawing rooms.

I am at work again & I have my friend John Dunthorne with me – he cheers & helps me so much that I could wish him always to be with me. He forwards me a great deal in subordinate parts such as tracing, squaring &c &c. This morning a gentleman called on me who has '*nine telescopes*'. You may judge how thick they soon got. It is John's forte. He is to see them tomorrow.

I am planning a large picture – I regard all you say but I do not enter into that notion of varying one's plans to keep the public in good humour – subject and change of weather & effect will afford variety in landscape. What if Van de Velde had quitted his sea pieces – or Ruisdael his waterfalls – or Hobbema his native woods – would not the world have lost so many features in art? I know that you wish for no material alterations – but I have to combat from high quarters, even Lawrence, the seeming plausible arguments that subject makes the picture. Perhaps you think an evening-effect – or a warm picture – might do. Perhaps it might start me some new admirers – but I should lose many old ones –

Reynolds the engraver tells me my 'freshness' exceeds the freshness of any painter that ever lived – for to my zest of 'colour' I have added 'light': Ruisdael (the freshest of all) and Hobbema, were *black* – should any of this be true, I must go on. I imagine myself driving a nail. I have driven it some way – by persevering with this nail I may drive it home – by quitting it to attack others, though I amuse myself, I do not advance them beyond the first – but that particular nail stands still the while. I can't mention one strong living instance of what greediness of trying every thing has brought his very original mind to.* No man who can do any one thing well, will ever be able to do another different as well – I believe that from our physical construction no man can be born with more than one high & original feel – this in my opinion was the case with the greatest master of *variety*, Shakespeare.

I will leave this stiff work – and speak of what has happened to me – and about me. [...] Williams [...] is an instance of what a dissenter can do – he was paid for a

* The reference may be to Turner.

Following pages: The Leaping Horse, 1825

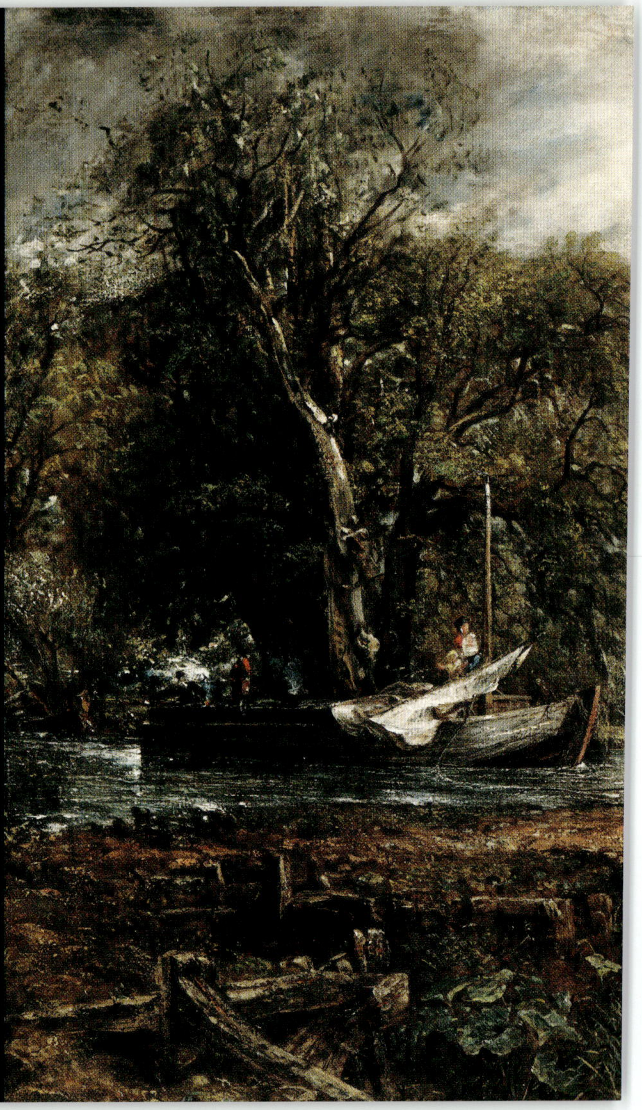

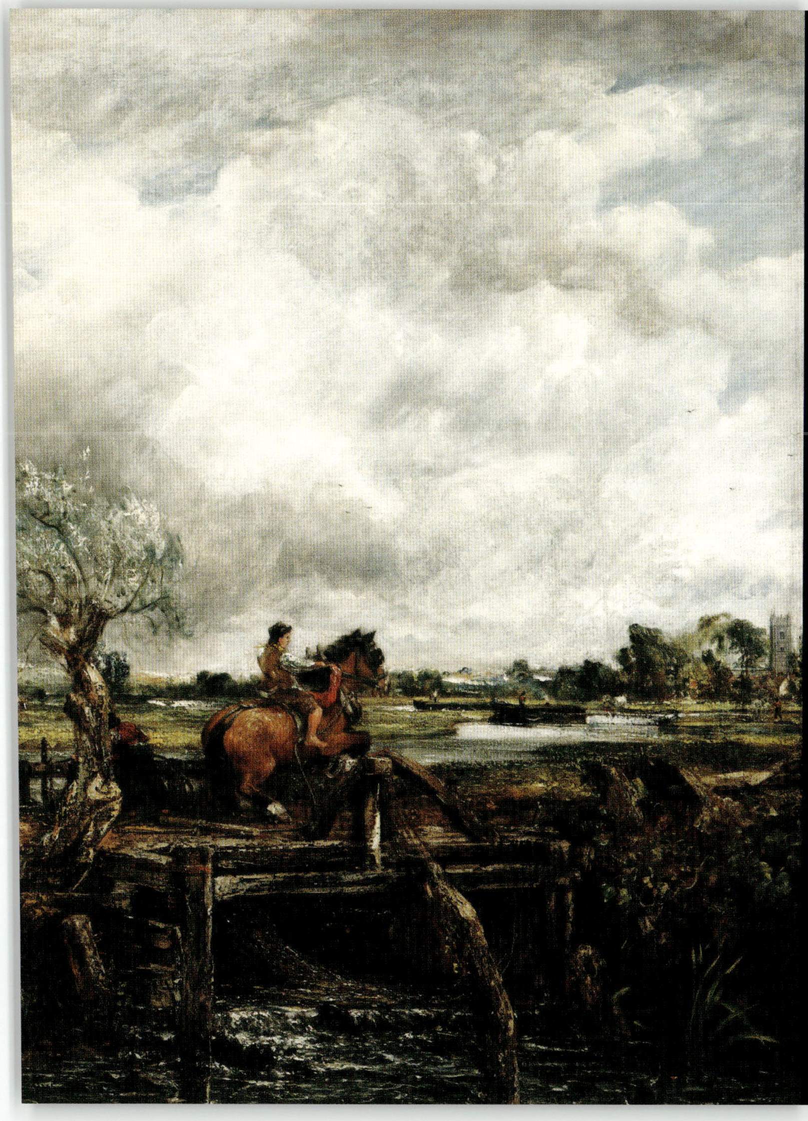

sermon on the Thursday at this church, had no more to do with the parish than you – and was hated by the Rector for his principles – when he called himself the faithful servant of the parish for 16 years. He is owner of a dissenting chapel at Homerton in which he does all the duty.

A Calvinist is capable of any thing – the *Revd* Dr. Richardson of Dunmow, late of Dedham, was caught by Mrs Richardson – in bed with *their favourite* servant, Bridget Hursell. Nobody however is *surprised* at the circumstances but Mrs R. herself, to whom he has been of late so very *affectionate*. [...]

JOHN FISHER TO CONSTABLE
4 BELLE VUE, BATH, 8 APRIL 1825

My dear Constable;

I rode yesterday out of the white atmosphere of Bath into the green village of Bath-Easton; & found myself by instinct at the *mill*, surrounded by weirs, backwaters nets & willows, with a smell of weeds, flowing water, & flour in my nostrils. I need not say that the scene brought you to my mind, & produced this letter.

My poor dear wife has been lamentably ill again with inflammation of the lungs. She is now apparently recovering. But I have yet my fears for the final result. I have now been so long habituated to contemplate her as in danger, that I should submit to the blow with fortitude. But life would be a blank for the future; saving only the green spot of your friendship. Children are a dubious good.

I have not expected to hear *from* you, knowing how you were employed. But I have heard *of* you; by the repetition of one of those speeches which you have a talent at making. I mean, which a man cannot forget it he would. Mary White reports you as saying 'that your wife and you are going to *exhibit* at the same time'. Which is to me as complete a history of your goings-on, as if you had written a volume.

I will send you in a week or so, your sketches back & Pullan's Collection. In the same box I shall enclose as a sort of remunerating fee, 2 vols of Paley's posthumous sermons, which you may read to your family of a Sunday evening. They are fit companions for your sketches, being exactly like them: full of vigour, & nature, fresh, original, warm from observation of nature, hasty, unpolished, untouched afterwards. There is prefixed to a new edition of his works a life of Paley by his son in which the inner man is laid open. If you can get it, there are parts that will delight you. He appears to have been a strong-minded, guileless simple hearted man who told the truth & declared his honest opinion to every man he met with, friend or foe. Hence he was *sometimes* in scrapes.

I hope to be able to get a peep at the Metropolis and

your picture about the 20th of June. If I find I can leave my wife. We are going to set up our staff at Osmington immediately. I expect to be fixed there by the 20th of May. – In a letter I had from the Charterhouse some months ago it was mentioned that you were out of spirits seemingly & had lost your glee in conversation. What cog of the wheel wanted grease? – [...] My kind regards to Mrs Constable and wishing her well through her approaching 'exhibition' believe me yours very sincerely

John Fisher

CONSTABLE TO FRANCIS DARBY OF COALBROOKDALE
35 CHARLOTTE STREET, 24 AUGUST 1825

Sir,

I had the honour of receiving your very kind letter this morning. I waited Monday and yesterday 'till after the general post hours, when fearing that I had already given you too much cause to think me dilatory and that I had already troubled you with too many of my letters, I was determined to look about for a conveyance myself – having your direction.

The pictures left London yesterday evening by *Brown & Co's* waggon from the Green Man and Stile, Oxford Street – they speak of the journeys being three days. The case is directed to you at the Jerningham Arms,

Shiffnall – perhaps it would have been better had there been a case for each picture, but I have no doubt of their safety.

I am obliged to you for your kind enquiries of my health. I always find business a cure for all *my* ills. I am not the worse but much the better for my endeavours to attend to your wishes, and besides your letter afforded me the best excuse in the world for coming away from the apothecary.

I ought not to trouble you, Sir, with myself, but the truth is, could I divest myself of anxiety of mind I should never ail any thing. My life is a struggle between my 'social affections' and my 'love of art'. I daily feel the remark of Lord Bacon's that 'single men are the best servants of the public'. I have a wife (daughter of Mr Charles Bicknell of the Admiralty) in delicate health, and five infant children. I am not happy apart from them even for a few days, or hours, and the summer months separate us too much, and disturb my quiet habits at my easel.

This disposition is no doubt to my disadvantage, as I have pressing invitations to push my success on the Continent by visiting Paris, &c, &c, but I cannot speak a word of the language, and above all I love England & my own home. I would rather be a poor man here than a rich man

Following pages: Branch Hill Pond, Hampstead, 1824–5; one of the paintings sold to Francis Darby

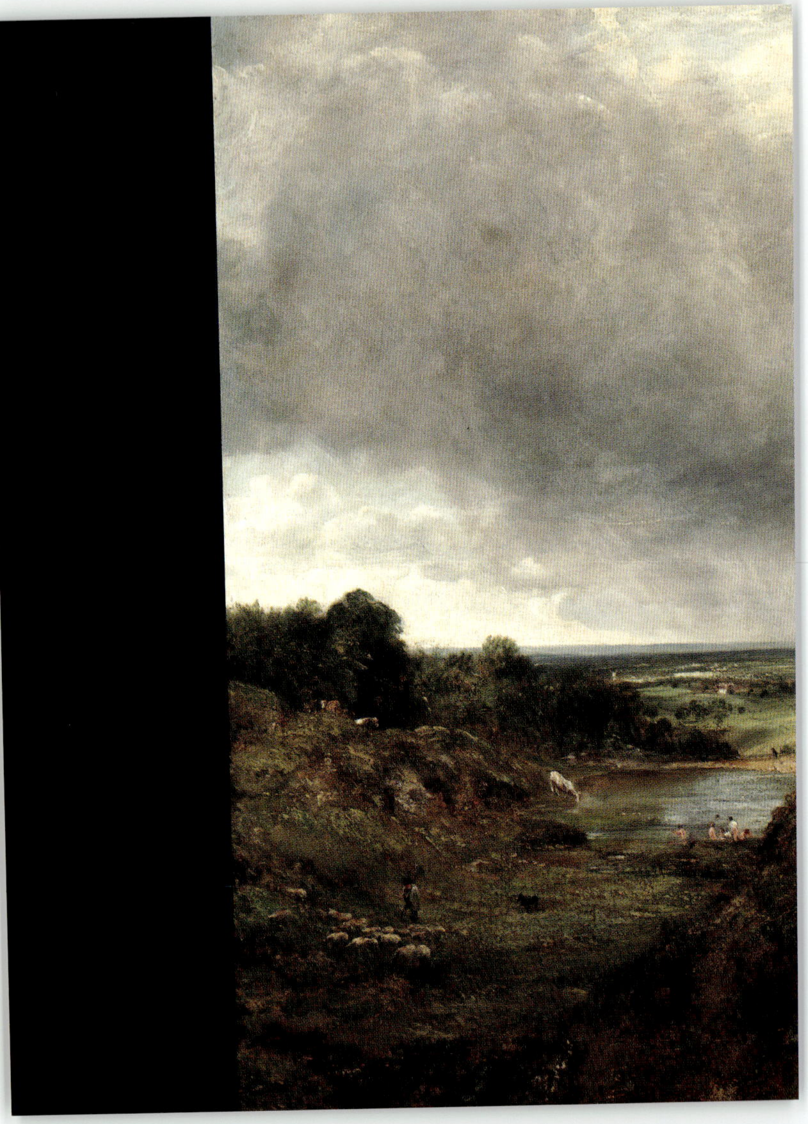

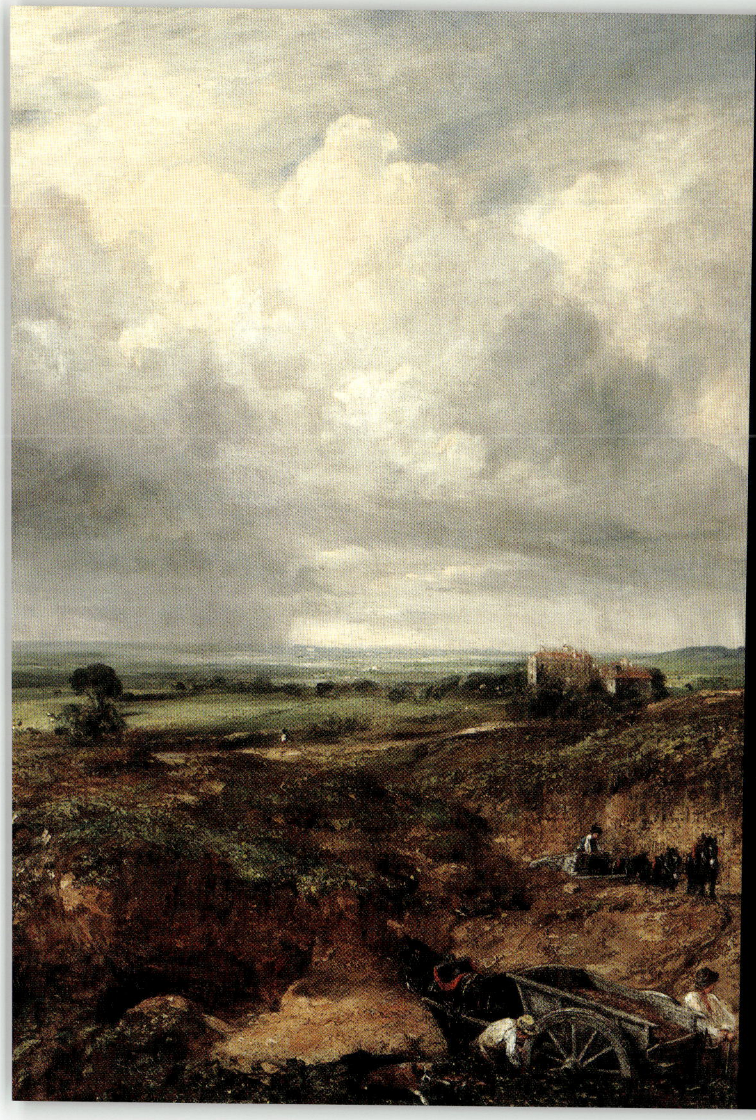

abroad. I am neither an ambitious man, nor a man of the world, but am sincerely grateful to providence and my own exertions for being enabled to do that for myself which no human being could have done for me.

I am certainly proud of my degree of reputation, for it has been honourably gained by my pencil alone – the height of my ambition has ever been to attain excellence, and to gain the public for my patron. And I now repeat that the circumstance of your having purchased my pictures has been most highly gratifying on that account. One of my large pictures in Paris is purchased by a nobleman[1] (a great collector, I know not whom) for twice or three times what I sold it for.

Your pictures were purchased by Mr Hebbert of the Strand – corner of Arundel Street. A few weeks ago he wrote me a kind and polite letter, to say that should any other purchaser be found, he should in prudence resign them though most unwillingly, owing to some serious losses in India. Accordingly I did not send him the pictures from the Exhibition. He is now entirely chagrined at having lost them, and almost angry with me for not making him acquainted with your offer. On no account did I choose to do so. I left the pictures to speak for themselves or not as I have always done and would neither make use of your name to Mr Hebbert or Mr Hebbert's name to you.

1. This was not in fact the case.

I ought indeed, Sir, to beg pardon for this most unconscionable letter which I have now written to you.

I am, Sir, always your much obliged servant
John Constable

Maria's health remained precarious. A daughter, Emily, was born prematurely in 1825 and further weakened her. Again the family was separated during the summer months and Constable renewed his journal.

FROM THE JOURNAL

CHARLOTTE STREET, MONDAY, 15 MAY 1826

Had a note to say Mrs Treslove does not come till Tuesday. Went to Reynolds to see how he is doing the copy of the Bishop. It is so bad I could not talk to him about it – it was hopeless & beyond my advice. What a pity they did not come to me. It is money worse than thrown away – because they buy a lasting disgrace – but he has promised to make it better.

No letter from Suffolk and I sadly vex myself about poor Abram – but I shall hear nothing to day as it is past post hours.

FROM THE JOURNAL
TUESDAY, 16 MAY 1826

Mrs Treslove has been sitting and we have got on pretty well – but she left me at two. Her little girl got well of the measles – the other little girl fell out of the book case just as Mrs Treslove was coming here, but though she pulled it down & it fell on her head it did not hurt her materially. Our sitting was much interrupted by callers.

Mr Ward called with a finished print of Mr Walker, looking very nice.* Mrs Masquerier called and wanted to see what John is about. I introduced her to Mrs Treslove – and she amused her a good deal. She talked wholly of themselves as usual – and though they desired to live in style with a good establishment, yet John did not like to be put out of his way – for 'any of them'.

The Strutts called† – and Mrs De Wint,§ and just as Mrs Treslove was gone in came Fisher just got out of a post chaise from Blackwater this evening – with his children

* William Ward (1766–1826), engraver. The print is a mezzotint after Constable's portrait of William Walker, chaplain to Lincoln's Inn. † Jacob George Strutt (1784–1867), landscape and portrait painter, engraver and poet. His wife Elizabeth wrote novels, travelogues and devotional works. § Harriet de Wint, wife of the watercolourist Peter de Wint and sister of the portraitist and history painter William Hilton.

and one of them with the croup. These are in lodgings in the Regent's park – and he was in his way to the Charter House. I walked to the gates with him – and on my return I called to ask if Mrs Treslove's little girl was hurt & she was not, but out in the carriage with her nurse. They are going out of town for a week – so this will stop my picture.

Fisher's stay in town, and every thing else belonging to him, is uncertain – but he will call tomorrow – & we shall then settle if he has my bed. He is going to Cambridge to canvas for the Solicitor General – Copley – chairman of a committee.

You will see the pleasing letter of Mrs Phillips giving such a good account of our dear boy, and it is plain our letters gave no offence.

Leslie called last evening with the pleasing news of Mrs Leslie's safe confinement & a lovely little boy had at last made his appearance. He was much worn with anxiety and glad it was over – as she had suffered a good deal – but was doing well. This happened on Sunday – I gave joy in your name.

Sir G. Beaumont called. He was delighted with the large picture of Mr Allnutt by Gainsborough* – & today sent Lady Beaumont to see it. [...]

* Mr. Allnutt had bought *Ploughing Scene in Suffolk (A Summerland)*, 1814; but Constable is probably referring to a lost portrait of the corrupt politician and lawyer Thomas Nuthall (exhibited 1771).

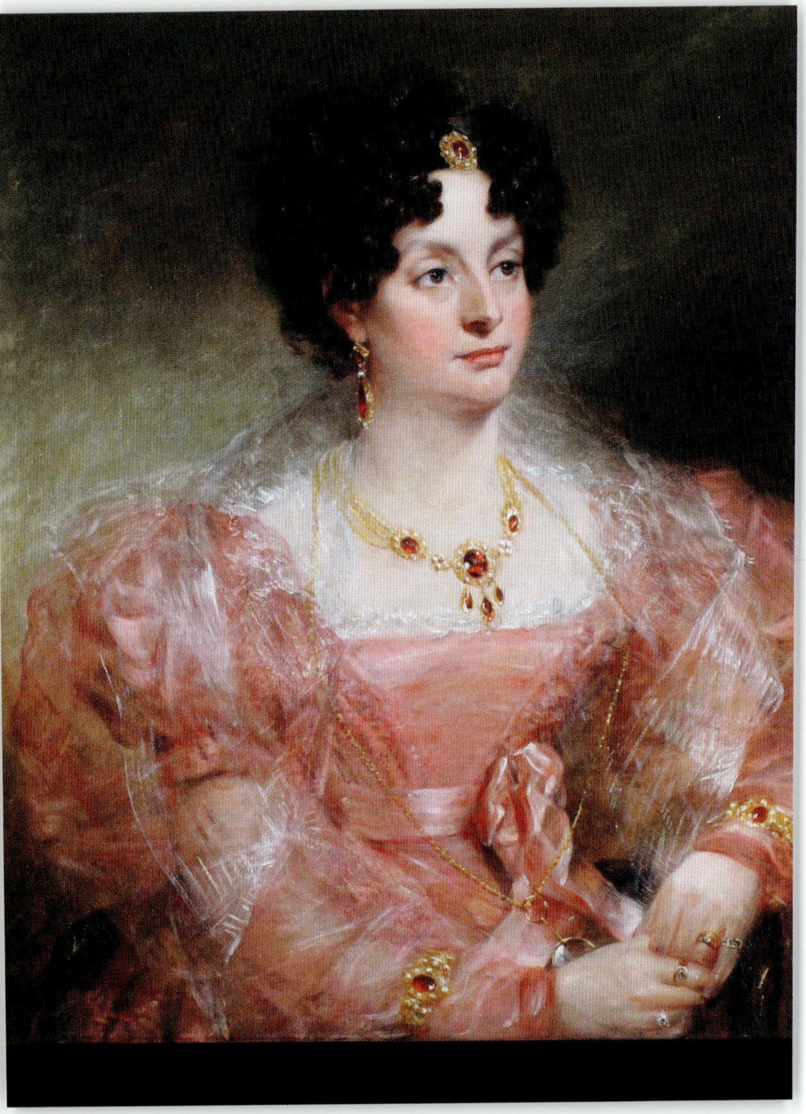

FROM THE JOURNAL
TUESDAY, 23 MAY 1826

I find it difficult to recollect what I meant to write to you on Monday – though only one day has passed between. I am now writing at 7 o'clock (Wednesday morning) so I will pass on to Tuesday – when soon after breakfast called Mrs Treslove, & I painted till two, & got the head on so well that I shall now finish the picture in [dress] &c, &c, before I do any more to the face. Both her girls had the measles so nicely, that it is delightful – if they could have brought so good a sort here – but we are too young at present in our nursery.

Fisher called just as she was gone – and stopped the rest of the day & was very agreeable. I did not go out but worked all the time. Young Carpenter called & said his wife had been into the country & returned better.

I will attend to all you say – had not Mrs Treslove come I should have gone on with my journal to you & it would have passed your letter on the road – but I found it almost impossible to avoid interruptions. Ambrose has taken down the window curtains, hangings, &c in our bedroom. I shall pay Sheppard's bills, &c. Captain Tudor has paid me the money £30 advanced to Mr Ward.

Opposite: Mrs. Treslove (1826, retouched 1829)

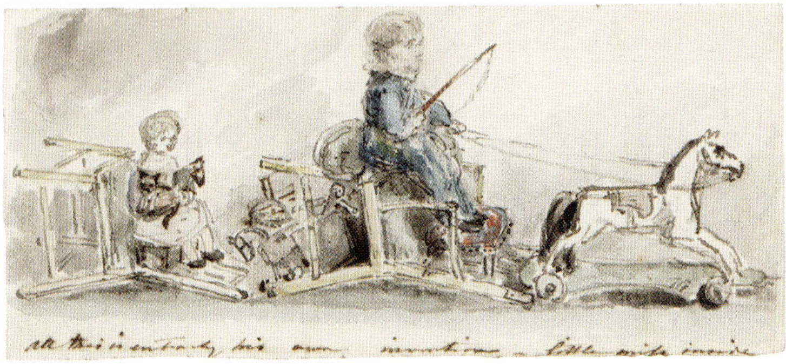

Charles Golding and Minna playing coach and horses (c. 1822)

FROM THE JOURNAL
WEDNESDAY, 24 MAY 1826

Got up quite early to write to you before 8 – Saw the children at 7 – Emily's eyes were open & she was smiling – Isabel sitting up in her crib & saying, come here papa – & Charley was kneeling up in his bed which was full of things – chiefly boats – M[inna] & Roberts not awake.

Fisher did not advise much to be done for Charley's teeth – took my stuff as he thought it would be better to let it have a rein & he gave him a little stuff that gave a quiet night, so he is quite well & nice this morning.

I am sorry to say that I yielded to the importunities of the Saviles – & must go with them to the Exhibition this morning. They will call for me at 11 (then we shall be sure of *time*) – but their stay is short. But they did enquire kindly after you, & the children – the wretches who have just left here & these unhappy beings are well met.

Love to all. Yours truly

J. C.

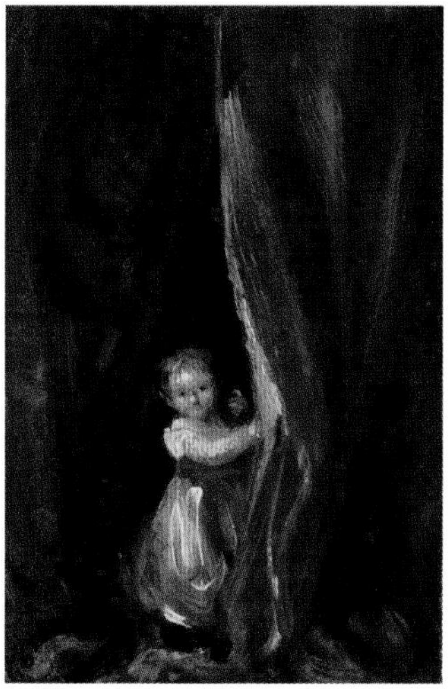

Minna playing Bo-Peep (c. 1822)

Maria's health did not improve. She had two more children: Alfred in November 1826, and Lionel in January 1828. The pregnancies left her 'in a sad and weak condition'. The visits to Brighton in 1825–6 and in the early summer of 1828 had brought no relief, and in November 1828 Maria died.

CONSTABLE TO GOLDING CONSTABLE
35 CHARLOTTE STREET, 19 DECEMBER 1828

Dear Golding.
Your goods went off this day all nicely packed – in all – *20* parcels – *cheap* – *sound* – *seasoned* and *good* and free from the '*buggery*' – for what I know it is a noble bed – and Ambrose was determined you should have it reasonable enough for after he had put it at almost nothing he has given you the easy chair in – (for I would not have parted with it) it has a capital cover – & the shit pot will be found carefuly packed in it – in spite of your orders to the contrary – Abbot may want if you don't – but it is no bad thing for either in a cold showery night on Bargell [i.e. ?Bergholt] heath when taken short – – I forgot the spring for the door – so John Dunthorne has kindly take charge

of it (no charge) – I wish you had looked at my hard ware – a great assemblage if not variety of pokers – tongs & fire shovers – but short of fenders – so 'tis all very well – only they were there –

Pray remember that while I am joking in this way – that I am very glad to be rid of so much of my stock in trade – & that Ambrose assures me that you pay me a very fair price – & full as much or more than he himself would give.

Shall I pay his bill for you & you add it to mine when you pay Abram for I know you are a ready many [i.e. ?money] man – '*a qualified man Sir*' – at all times. The ship sails to day at 11 o'clock – I have no doubt – & the Cap^{n} came to me here yesterday & told me he should – our cart was with him at 9, or ¼ past – a full well topped up van load – pray take quite your leisure in paying for them = shall Ambrose send you the whole account – or perhaps he may – he had your orders to do so.

Lady Dysart has sent me some venison as she said, very good the haunch on Sunday.*

My poor boy gets on sadly – Your namesake is a noble boy – my dear little girls will be here tomorrow – I shall fetch them home to dine & then I shall have my seven children under my roof – hourly do I feel the loss of my

* Golding Constable was employed by Lady Dysart as her gamekeeper at Helmingham.

departed angel – God only know how my children will be brought up – nothing can supply the loss of such a devoted – sensible – industrious – religious mother – who was all affection – but I cannot trust myself on the subject – I shall never feel again as I have felt – the face of the world is totally changed to me – though with God's help I shal endeavour to do my next duties –

God bless You my dear Golding.
Your ever afft. Brother
John Constable

God grant You health and many many happy years in your new home – I hope to see it soon – I should like to come to see you all for a day or two – but poor dear Bergholt will fill me full of – sad – sad – associations – especially the sight of the Rectory – & its dark trees – but a few year will set all these sorrows at rest – but I cannot recover my lost happiness – the loss grows upon me – but I must turn to my dear Infants. J. C.

A carpet for M[rs] Whalley – makes one of the twenty parcels – A[bram] C[onstable] – will forward it to her – by barge or van.

Shortly after Maria's death Constable was finally elected to the Royal Academy

JOHN FISHER TO CONSTABLE
LODGE, CHARTERHOUSE, 11 FEBRUARY 1829

My dear Constable;

Although I fully expected the event, your note gave me the greatest pleasure in confirming the fact, that you are a Royal Academician. It is a double triumph. It is in the first place the triumph of real Art, over spurious Art; and in the second place, of patient moral integrity over bare chicanery, & misrepresented worth. Your rewards are beginning now to flow in upon you with full tide; although, as everything is ordained in a state of trial, the painful is mixed with the sweet. My mother sends her congratulations which are worth the having. Tomorrow I go with you & call upon your friends.

The event is important to me, since my judgement was embarked in the same boat with your success. Most faithfully yours

John Fisher

Turner's presence was a high compliment. The great landscape painter by it claimed you as a brother labourer.

Overleaf: A Boat passing a Lock (1826). This is the painting that Constable chose to present to the Royal Academy as his Diploma work, required upon election

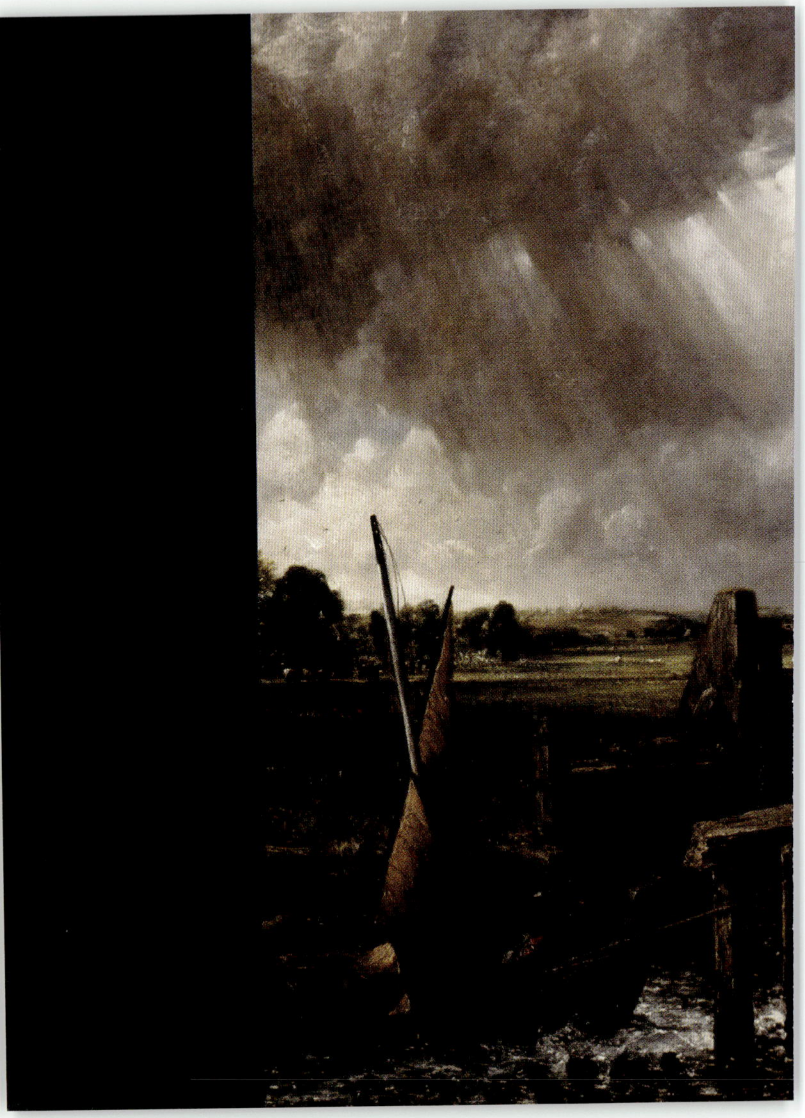

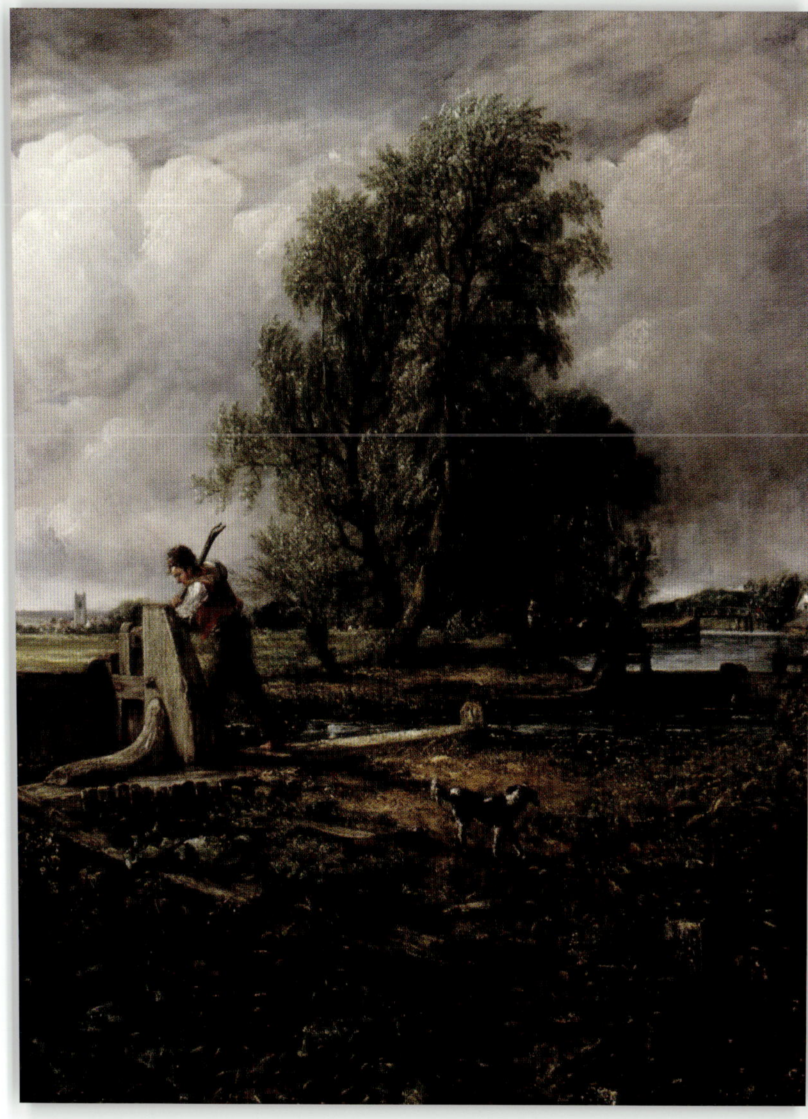

In the years following his election to the Academy, Constable became increasingly preoccupied with, and anxious about, the portfolio of mezzotints that he commissioned from the engraver David Lucas

CONSTABLE TO DAVID LUCAS,
LONDON, 12 MARCH 1831

Dear Lucas

My indisposition sadly worries me and makes me think (perhaps too darkly) on almost every subject – nevertheless, my 'seven infants', my *time of life*, and state of health, and other serious matters, make me desirous of lightening my mind as much as possible of unnecessary oppression – as I fear it is already overweighted.

I have thought much on my book [i.e. *English Landscape*], and all my reflections on the subject go to oppress me – *its duration, its expense, its hopelessness of remuneration*, all are unfavourable – added to which I now discover that the printsellers 'are watching it as their lawful prey', and they alone could help me: for 'I cannot dig, & to beg I am ashamed'. I can only dispose of it by giving it away. My plan is to make the whole number of plates now in hand only to form the book, for which I see we have about twenty. The three present numbers make 12 – others begun are about eight or ten more, some of which may not be resumed – & we must begin the frontispiece.

I am led to conclude of this definition of our book – finding that it grievously harrasses my days, and disturbs my rest of nights. The expense is too enormous for a work that has nothing but your beautiful feeling and execution to recommend it – the painter himself is totally unpopular and ever will be, on this side of the grave certainly – the subjects nothing, but '*The Arts*,' and 'buyers' are totally ignorant of that. I am harrassed by the lengthened prospect of its duration – which seems quite undefined. Therefore I am come to my first plan, of *twenty*, including frontispiece & vignette – & we can now see our way out of the wood. I can bear this perhaps – because I then know the worst. I can bear the irritation of delay (from which I have suffered so much that I attribute my present illness to it in part) no longer. Consider, not a real fortnight's work has been done towards the whole in the last four months – years upon years must roll to produce the 26 prints – & all this time I shall not sell a copy, but must stand ready to part with every *fifty* or *hundred* pounds of my ready money – till it comes to £1000.

Remember dear Lucas that I mean not to think one reflection on you – every *thing* with the *plan* is my

Overleaf: Progress proof of David Lucas's mezzotint of Spring, *with Constable's comments and corrections in white*

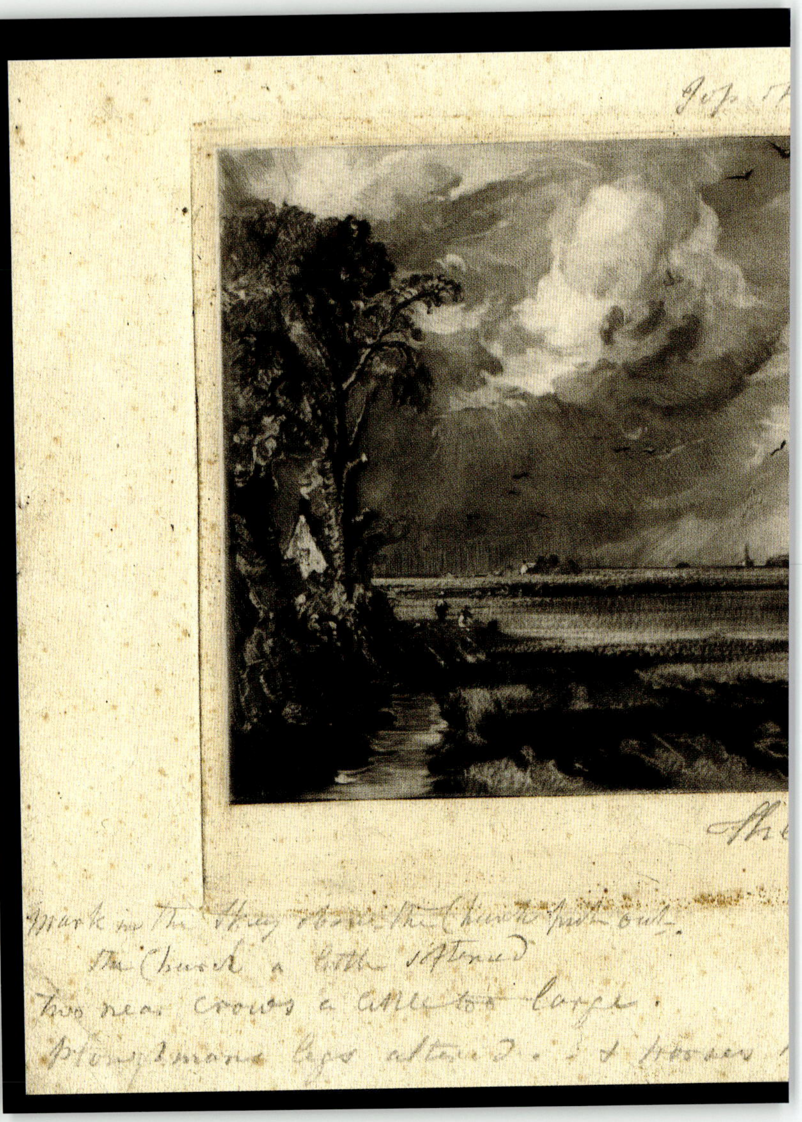
Mark in the Sky above the Church put out.
the Church a little softened
Two near crows a little too large.
Ploughmans legs altered . . & horses

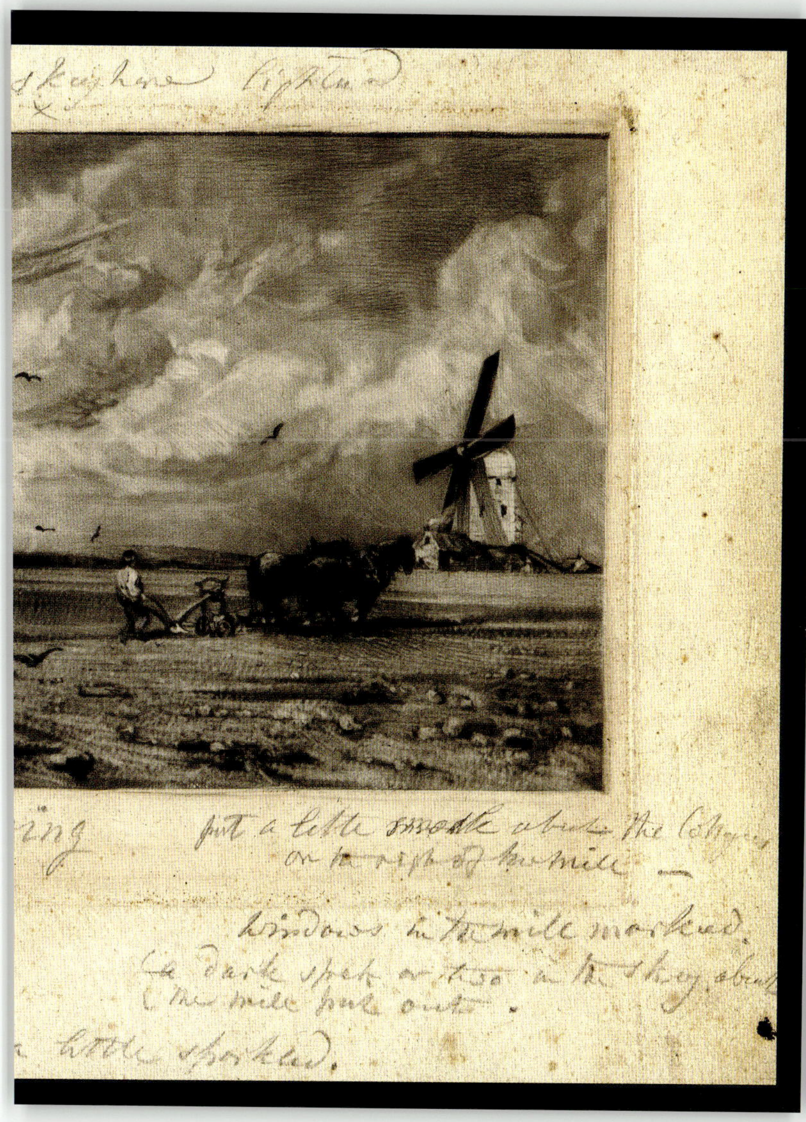
windows in the mill marked.
a little sparkled.

own – and I want to relieve my mind of that which now harrasses it like a disease – & looking forward as I now do I think of it with delight as an occupation, though utterly hopeless in its result. Do not for a moment think I blame you – or that I do not sympathize with you in those lamentable causes of hindrance which have afflicted your house. Nobody will do me any good – even that man who thinks he is sure of going to heaven by dipping his arse under water – I mean Mr White of Brownlow Street – offers to propagate & guarantee the money for Turner and his liber stupidorum for *15 per cent*, & will not do the same for me under *35 per cent*. Therefore let us protect ourselves, by drawing the circle a little closer – & complete & that as rapidly as possible whatever is began, be these what they are. We have no really bad subjects amongst them, at least one is as good as another of them, & let us get them out of hand – the sooner the better.

Pray let me see you soon. I am not wholly unable to work, thank God. I hope poor Mrs Lucas is better. Dr. Davis has been to see me & my poor boy John, who is very ill, Mr Drew giving me medicine & pills – so that both of their medicines (which I take together) may get me well at double quick time.

Yours truly
John Constable

CONSTABLE TO C. R. LESLIE
LONDON, 9 SEPTEMBER 1831

My dear Leslie

My servant told you of my being at the Coronation. I was at the Abbey eleven hours, and saw with my own eyes the Crown of England put on the head of that good man, William IV – and that too in the chair of a saint. I saw also the gentle Adelaide crowned, and I trust, what may now be called the *better half* of England's crown has sought its own wearer in this instance. I saw also Brougham with his crown on, a sight than which nothing could be more ridiculous – for as his coronet was perched on top of an enormous wig, he bore the external shape of a Jack in the Green, as he stood with his back towards me a full hour.

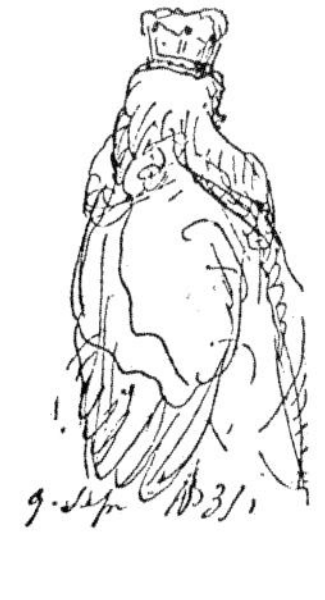

I sat so that I commanded a view of all the peers placed in raised ranks in the south transept. The moment the King's crown was on, they all crowned themselves. At the same instant the shouts of 'God save the King,' the trumpets, the band, the drums of the soldiers in the nave, and last – though not least – the artillery, which could be distinguished amid all this din, and the jar even felt, made it eminently imposing. The white ermine of the peers looked lovely in the sun – I shall sketch some of the effects I saw at the Coronation – the tone of the walls was sublime – they were heightened, no doubt, by the trappings like an old picture with a newly gilt frame.

In a day or two I shall have a third number [of *English Landscape*] to offer you, it is at the binders. I am afraid Lucas has not always attended to my wishes in taking you an occasional proof which may come good for something *by accident*.

Affectionate wishes of all – yours truly
John Constable.

Will you tell Lucas by letting your servant take him this bit of paper, that I shall be at Charlotte Street Saturday afternoon for the evening – I wish to see what he is about.

J. C.

CONSTABLE TO C. R. LESLIE
LONDON, SEPTEMBER 1831

My dear Leslie

Accept my 3rd number with my best regards. I hope Mrs Leslie was not the worse for her visitors yesterday. The dear infant has not been a moment from my *sight* since I left you – they were happy days with me when I had infants… .

Will you come any day, when we can look at the old masters in Pall Mall?* I sleep in town tonight!!

How are you now with the portrait picture?

Ever truly yours
J. Constable

CONSTABLE TO C. R. LESLIE,
LONDON, 12 SEPTEMBER 1831

I am glad I saw the show in the Abbey. It was very delightful & I can now say I *have seen* a Coronation.

Everybody seemed amused at Brougham – the annoyance to him must have been great.

J. C.

* The National Gallery was still at John Julius Angerstein's house in Pall Mall.

CONSTABLE TO C. R. LESLIE, LONDON, OCTOBER/NOVEMBER 1831

Dear Leslie

Greatly do I lament going to the Academy. I am much worse than when you and Mrs Leslie were here. The truth is I have long been getting ill and it will surprise you to hear that I have always had the *worst tongue* possible. The mischief that has been so long hatching has at length come to a head. Evans tells me I must take great care of my health for my children's sake – I much doubt if my life is of any use to them, but I love them and they love me, so the parting, at least, will be sad [...]

What makes me dread this tremendous attack on the constitution of the country is, that the wisest and best of the Lords are seriously and firmly objecting to it – and it goes to give the government into the hands of the rabble and dregs of the people, and the devil's agents on earth – the agitators.[...] and the slimy marshes of Chelsea and Paddington & St. Pancras. When the 'equitable adjustment' took place my children's £20,000 would be balanced out to me at less than 10,000 – then what use [is] it to me. I look for all gone – buy, by the great Lords, I must buy cursed bricks at last – at four times their present value.

Do you think that the *Duke of Wellington* & the

Archbishop of Canterbury & *Copley* & *Eldon* & *Abbott* – and the best & wisest men we have – would all have opposed it, if it was to have [done] good to the country? I do not.

No Whig government ever did or can do good to *this* peculiar country – they are always the blocks as well as the Whigs – and always when in power, are our worst stumbling blocks. They never made a grander push than this because it is so long since they have had so very great a fool on the throne. [...]

CONSTABLE TO C. R. LESLIE
35 CHARLOTTE STREET, 4 NOVEMBER 1831

My dear Leslie

I know not how enough to thank you and dear Mrs Leslie for the kind interest you both take for me. I am now perhaps quite well – and I can give you no greater proof of it than to inform you that the 'Reform bill,' now gives me not the least concern – I care nothing about it – & have no curiosity to know if it be *dead* or *alive* – or whether it will rise from its ashes.

Lucas will take you this note – I came here this afternoon. Old Stothard called on me just now – he mentioned your telling him I was kept at home. [...] I shall come here on Monday afternoon – will you call on your way, & ride down with me to the Academy. I took hurt last time – but I was not fit – and that restless groom Baily who was fidgeting for his 'pint & pipe' would have the *window open*.

I have escaped a great deal by being out of the way. The two *great* Bones have each called – they would have been *bones* in my throat – & I am glad I missed them.

I think a sculptor ought to be the one but who I know not. If an architect, I think I will always vote as an Academician, for *Gandy*. I think he is a man that has been hunted down – & that too, most cruelly and unfairly – but that is time enough.*

I hope to pass a quiet and domestic winter. All my illness has been fretting – pining for my children – of whom I saw little or nothing, only night and morning. I shall now call Hampstead my *home* – Charlotte Street my *office*. Arnald has been here often. Only think I had the children here only 3 or 4 months all the last year – & then took them to Hampstead like parboiled rabbits fairly hunted down, by doctors – 'death – & pain.'

* Constable was voting for a new member to be admitted to the Academy, which was open to sculptors and architects as well as painters. Edward Hodges Baily (1788–1867) was a prolific sculptor, later responsible for the statue on Nelson's Column. The Bones were a family of miniaturists, and the Gandys a family of architects, though Constable is probably referring to the visionary Joseph Michael Gandy ARA (1771–1843). George Arnald (1763–1841) was a rival landscape painter.

I shall nevertheless be much here. I have begun on Mr Wells's picture.*

Make my best regards to Mrs Leslie. I hope herself & children are well. Ever my dear Leslie yours affectionately

John Constable

CONSTABLE TO C. R. LESLIE
6 WELL WALK, EARLY JANUARY 1832

Dear Leslie

We intend reaching Charlotte Street pack & package with my *seven* children about Thursday – the day the little girls disperse. I am not certain however of myself – for Evans says I *may* not be *fit* for removal by that time.

He (Evans) is a skilful, & honest doctor – a very sensible man – with great acquirements and a most sincere friend – so that I have *many* blessings – yet.

I am not sorry to have missed the Visitorship† in the Life this year – & next year I am ineligible. [...] My youth being gone, I cannot hardly stand the fags I lay on myself – in whatever relates to duty to others.

Now – my kindest regards to dear Mrs Leslie & your dear small children, I hope all is well with you – yours ever affectionately

John Constable

* A copy of a painting by Greuze (private collection). † Responsible for setting the model and pose for life studies at the Royal Academy.

CONSTABLE TO C. R. LESLIE

FROM MY BED, 35 CHARLOTTE STREET, 14 JANUARY 1832

My dear Leslie,

Accept my thanks for your kind letter; a proof of your anxiety. I rejoice to hear that you and Mrs Leslie and the dear children got through your journey [to Petworth] so comfortably, and I trust their colds will not be of long continuance. For myself, I regret to tell you that I have had rather a severe relapse, but I passed last night almost wholly free from pain, the first I believe for these three weeks, so that I hope the worst is now over, and I have before me the pleasurable prospect of recovery. The very great pleasure of seeing my brother (by whom I was much spoiled), with regard to family matters, he entering with so much cordiality into all my wishes regarding my children, in whom he seems to take a lively interest; the exertion was no doubt too great for me, but Evans assured me last night he had not yet seen me looking so well.

Your delightful little picture is always before [me], beaming a ray of friendship upon my bed, and that ray (though it could receive no heightening) is tinged with all the delicious hues by which the pencil of Rubens has so long fascinated the world. I am much interested with the account of the pictures. I remember most of Turner's early pictures, as they came occasionally to be *rubbed out* at Mr Bigg's; I must say however, some of them came to him in a most miserable state of filth, shined on in haste for the exhibition. Amongst them was one of singular intricacy and beauty, it was a canal with numerous boats, making thousands of beautiful shapes, and I think the most complete work of genius I ever saw.*

The Claude I well know, grand and solemn, but cold, dull and heavy, a picture of his old age.† Claude's exhilaration and light, in which he was the first to delight the world, he departed from at the age of between 50 and 60, and he then became a professor of the *higher walks of art*, and he [fell], in a great degree, into the manner of the painters round him, so difficult it is to be natural, and so easy to be superior in our own opinion.

When we have the pleasure of being together in the National Gallery, I think I shall not find it difficult to illustrate these remarks, as Carr has sent a large picture of the latter description.§ Hobbema if he misses colour is very disagreeable as he has neither shapes nor composition.

Your mention of 'a solemn twilight' by Gainsborough, has awakened all my sympathy. Do pray make me a sketch

*Possibly *Sun Rising through Vapour* (also known as *Dutch Boats*), *c.* 1807, cleaned by Bigg in 1819, National Gallery, London † Possibly *Landscape with Jacob with Laban and his daughters,* 1654, Petworth. § *Landscape with David at the Cave of Adullam,* 1658, National Gallery, London

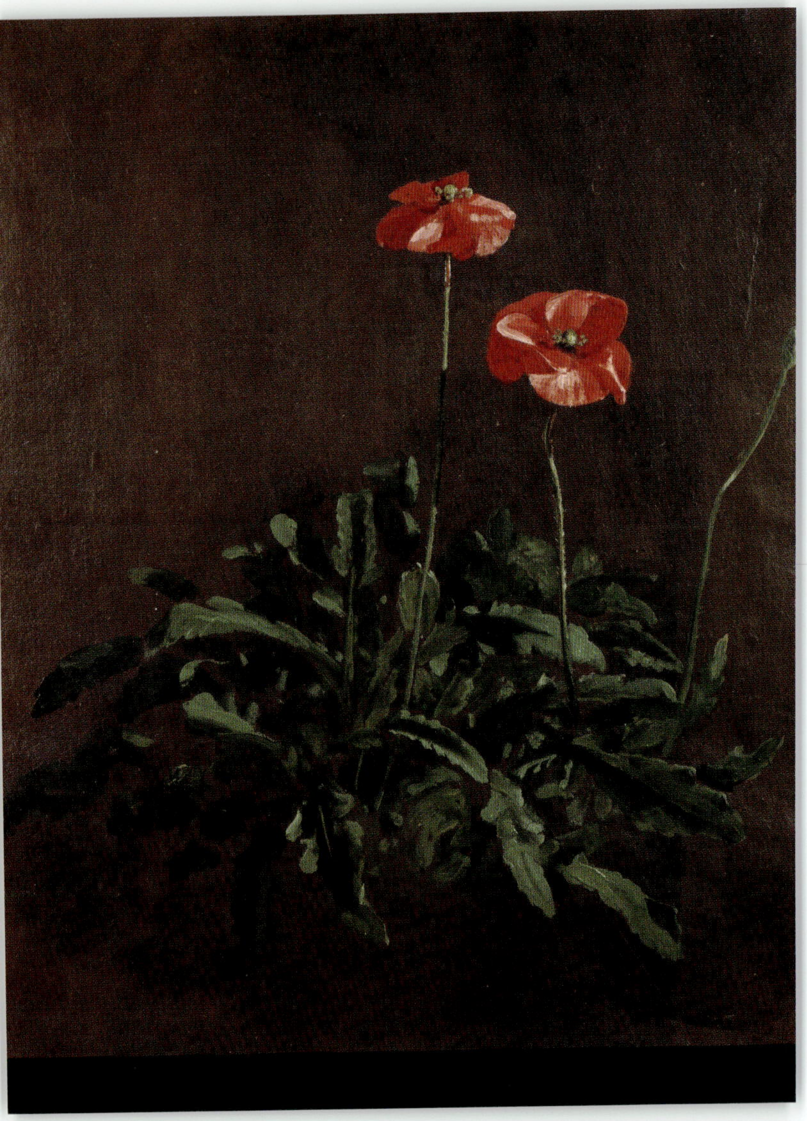

of it, of some kind or other, if it is ever so slight a splash. As to meeting you in these grand scenes, dear Leslie, remember the great were not made for me, nor I for the great, yet, perhaps, things are better as they are. My limited and abstracted art is to be found under every hedge, and in every lane, and therefore nobody thinks it worth picking up, but I have my admirers, each of whom I consider a host. My kindest regards to Mrs Leslie –

Yours affectionately, John Constable

CONSTABLE TO C. R. LESLIE

FROM MY BED, 35 CHARLOTTE STREET, 17 JANUARY 1832

My dear Leslie

It is a pleasing sentiment that after 3 weeks inability to hold my pen, I resume it for the first time again to *write to you*!! – so far I had written when your letter [...] arrived. Thus [duly] is the sentiment answered by the proof of how much do our minds really mingle.

I am [much] better, recovering as I may say fast. I am beyond the fear of relapses – but certainly as you say excitement under illness is a much worse thing than is generally believed.

I sat up yesterday – dressed, by the fire – and ate a small fish for my dinner – to the great delight of Alfred who

Opposite: Study of poppies, c. 1814-32

would dine with [me] – as 'he it was who nursed me well' as he said – and truly.

How heavenly it is to wake up as I do now after a good night – and see all these dear infants about my bed all *up early* to know how papa passed the night – even little Lionel puts out his little face to be kissed and smacking his lips like a fish, says, 'Are you well-better to day.' Your jewel of a little picture I now more & more discover to [be] an exquisitely finished thing. I shall treasure for my life as an 'epoch,' and among things I love. I am often enquired for by kind friends – & the sympathy of my real own & dear friends is great indeed. I have got my *Church* from Hampstead to hang at the foot of my bed to amuse me. Thus do I cheer my sick bed – and it is wise always to look for the bright side of things, for however sad they may be – still there is always a bright side. It is beautifully shown by Burton in his Anatomy of Melancholy – & followed by Milton –

> These delights do Melancholy give
> And I with her will chuse to live.

Thus I may truly say how *delightful* has this grievous illness been to me. [...]

Kindest regards to dear Mrs. Leslie & all your little flock. Yours affectionately, John Constable

Opposite: John Charles and Maria Louisa ('Minna') fishing from a barge at Flatford Mill, 5 October 1827

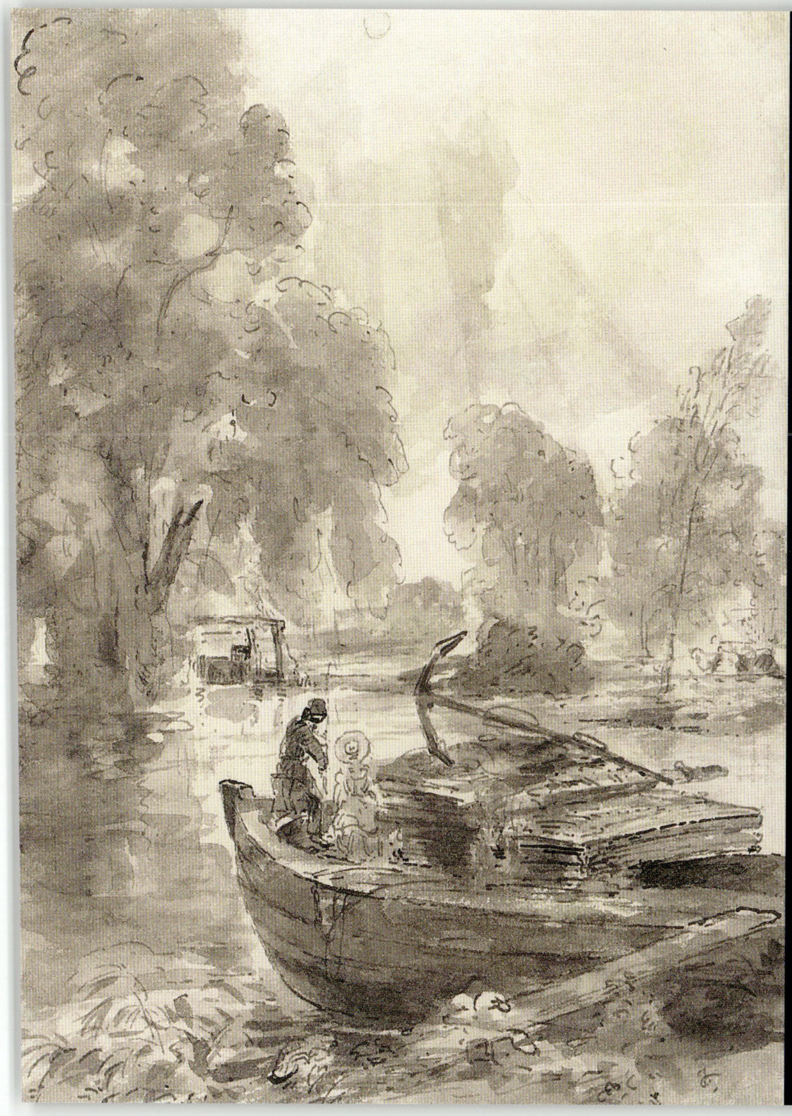

CONSTABLE TO C. R. LESLIE
LONDON, 4 SEPTEMBER 1832

My dear Leslie

You will be grieved to hear that I have lost my dear friend Archdeacon Fisher. He went with Mrs Fisher to Boulogne, hoping there to find some relief from a state of long and severe suffering both mental and bodily. He was benefited at first, began to take an interest in what was about him, & poor dear Mrs Fisher was cheered with the prospect of his being speedily restored to health and spirits – when on Friday August 24, he was seized with violent spasms and dead in the afternoon of Saturday the 25.

I cannot say but this very sudden and awful event has strongly affected me. The closest intimacy had subsisted for many years between us – we loved each other and confided in each other entirely – and this makes a sad gap in my life & wordly prospects. He would have helped my children, for he was a good adviser though impetuous – and a truly religious man.

God bless him till we meet again – I cannot tell how singularly his death has affected me.

I shall pass this week at Hampstead, to copy the winter piece – for which indeed my mind seems in a fit state.

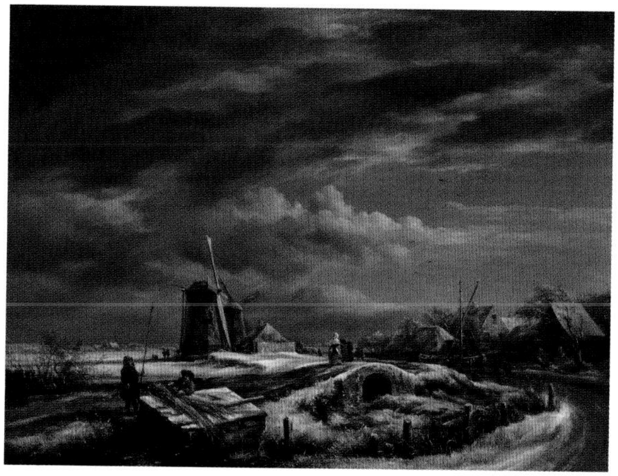

A Winter Landscape with figures after Ruisdael, 1832
This was the 'winter piece' that Constable worked on to console himself after the death of John Fisher. It was the last picture he showed to John Dunthorne before the latter's premature death in November 1832

Evans has returned with his nice bride. My best regards.

Yours most truly
John Constable

I send a frame and glass of yours which conveyed to me your kind present of the drawings from Gainsborough at Egremont's.

CONSTABLE TO DAVID LUCAS
6 WELL WALK, HAMPSTEAD, 14 NOVEMBER 1832

Dear Lucas –

I send a copy of the part of a letter which I received from Mr Lane, relating to the print – it may be useful & serves to confirm what we thought about the letter, hand &c, &c.

I returned last night here, after seeing the last of poor John – no one can supply his place – either with me, his friends, or the public. 'God's will be done'.

I shall be in Charlotte Street tomorrow at five or six. Can you meet me – & can you bring anything. We stand still here – waiting for you.

I do not change my opinions on all the subjects discussed at our meeting – on the contrary I agree more & more with my conclusions. But of the 'Stonehenge' I am pretty fully determined – and that it be as a companion to 'Old Sarum'. In the last chapter of Hebrews is the line in question!!

Can the plate of 'Old Sarum' (the engraved part) be a little extended so as to allow the 'Stone Henge' to be elongated?

Today is dear Alfred's birthday, and the house kept me a willing guest. – An angry neighbour has killed my fine black cat, which used to call me up in the morning – but she had been very naughty and killed his ducks. I should like to meet you, tomorrow afternoon – not later than six. We stand still in the *tacking* and *packing* way, which Bonner* does very nicely. We must first pack & tack before we can crack, with the work.

Yours truly
John Constable

In the coach yesterday coming from Suffolk, were two gentlemen and myself all strangers to each other. In passing through the valley about Dedham, one of them remarked to me – on my saying it was beautiful – 'Yes Sir – this is *Constable's* country!' I then told him who I was lest he should spoil it.

J. C.

* *Charles Bonner, of German extraction, was a tutor to Constable's sons*

Overleaf: The Glebe Farm, 1827. Constable had written 'My last landscape is a cottage scene – with the church of Langham – the poor bishop's first living [...] It is one of my best – very rich in colour – & fresh and bright – and I have "pacified it" – so that it gains much by that in tone and solemnity.' Later he wrote that 'this is one of the pictures on which I rest my little pretensions to futurity.' He was so anxious about it that Lucas's first attempt at engraving seemed a disaster: 'I could cry for my poor wretched wreck of the Glebe Farm – a name that once cheered me in progress –now become painful to the last degree.'

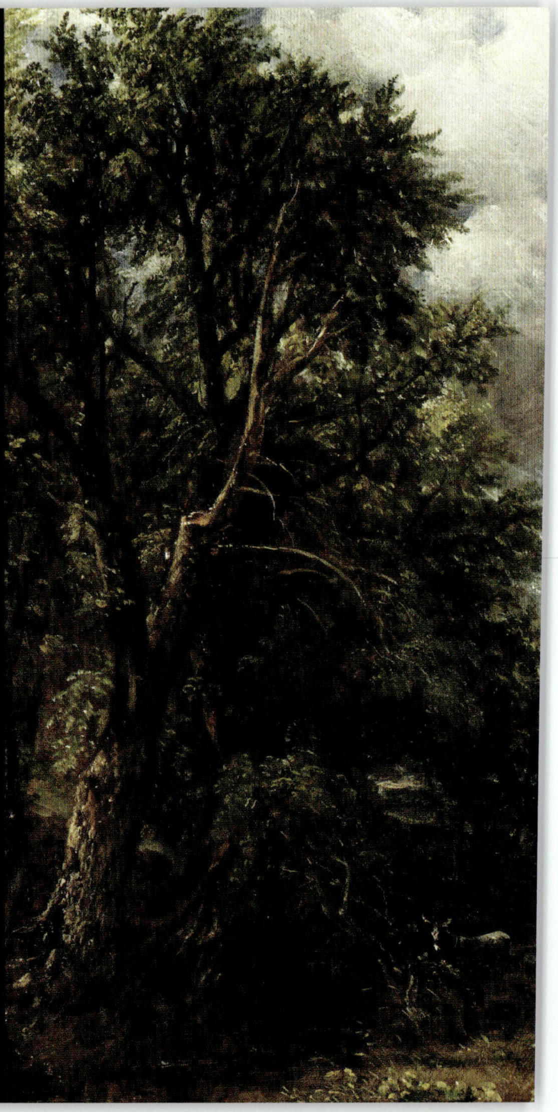

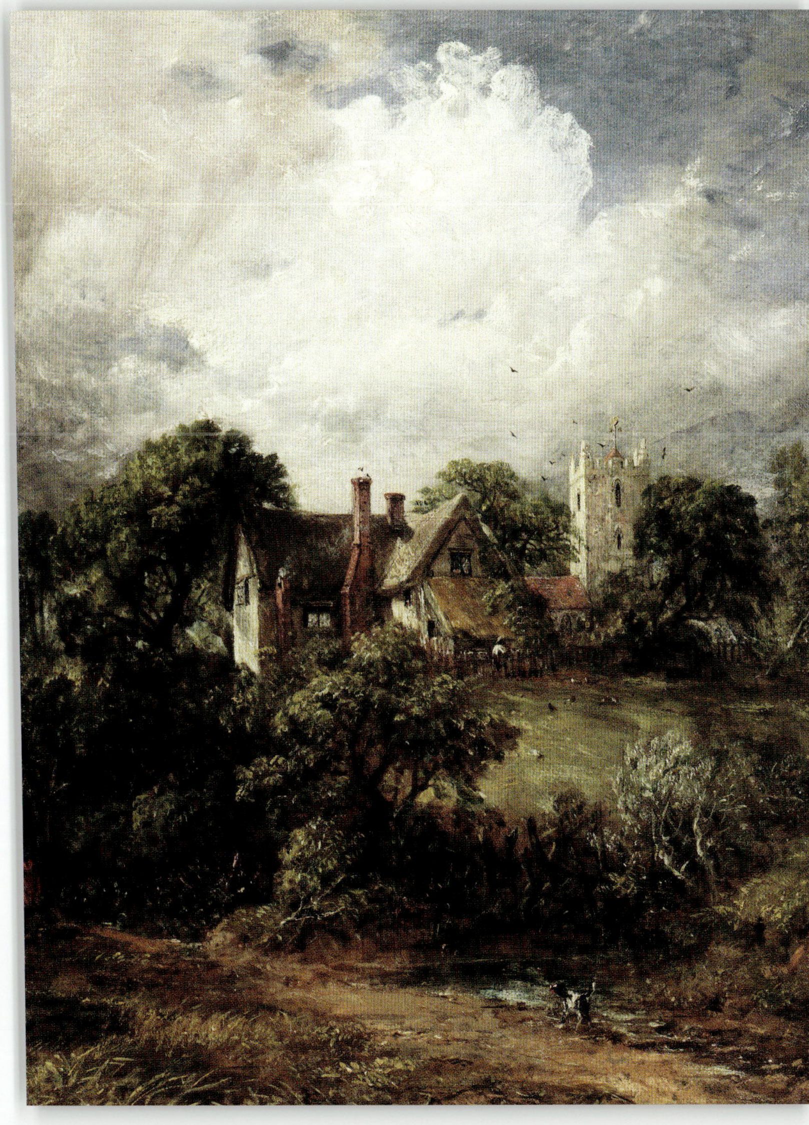

JOHN CONSTABLE TO C. R. LESLIE
35 CHARLOTTE STREET, LATE MARCH 1833

My dear Leslie

I haven't wholly shaken off my cold – but I will have the great pleasure of dining with you to day at *three*.

I have laid by the Cenotaph *for the present*.[1] I am determined not to harass *my mind* and HEALTH by scrambling over my canvas – as I hitherto have too often done. Why should I – I have little to lose and *nothing* to gain. I ought to respect myself – for my friends' sake, who love me – and my children. It is time at '*56*' to begin at least to *know* '*one's self*' – and I do know what *I am not*, and your regard for me has at least awakened me to believe in the possibility that I may yet make some impression with my 'light' – my 'dews' – my 'breezes' – my *bloom* and my *freshness* – no one of which qualities has yet been perfected on the canvas of any painter in this world.

What a galaxy have you had in your house – and as you say who is to supply their places. The sentiment is a melancholy one.

I should have been delighted in seeing you yesterday – and how is poor Dunlop? Can you and Mrs Leslie and all your community hold 'Easter Sunday' in remembrance

1. *Cenotaph to the Memory of Sir Joshua Reynolds*, 1836, see p. 240.

– and make my little girls happy in dining with them here on that day!!

Evans was here yesterday from Hampstead. Mrs E. is in a 'fair way' &c &c. I told Bonner that Evans had *poisoned his wife*. He looked quite frightened and said 'Indeed! has he given her any thing by *mistake*?' I wish I could help writing nonsense. Best regards.

Yours truly
John Constable

MARY CONSTABLE TO CONSTABLE
FLATFORD, 7 NOVEMBER 1833

My dear Brother John,

Abram and myself have the pleasure of sending off a Flatford Goose which we hope will fly in the direction of your house & there alight. Will you then have his wings and his head taken off & a spit run through his Body – *& roast him well* – and eat him up as a token of kind *thoughts* of you and your's?

We sincerely hope ere this you have received better accounts from Kent. I am sorry to say Abram has a troublesome cough – it is a session of trial to the tender. Poor Mr Quilter is no more. Abram thinks Mr Whalley declines – he had lately suffered great pain in one hip.

Alicia frequently passed through 'Morvern Park' where

you have formerly passed some time with the late Mr Lewis – the present family did not directly succeed to the estate – I do not recollect the name, but the *young squire* is the *only son*, not thirty years old – he has three sisters – the father and mother living – all together at 'Morvern Hall.'* Alicia saw a little of the young squire who thought everything Alicia did *was right*. I only wish he may meet her again in the same mood. I recollect you made a picture of 'Malvern Hall'. I should very much like to have something done from it that she might show it to him the next visit she makes in that neighbourhood – it might possibly prove a charm to win *ten thousand* a year *for her*. I expect she may make a second visit next summer. [...]

I was glad to find you had seen Lady Dysart again, renew your visit when you can – it is one of the pleasures of your life to have had such a friend as her – who will never come any more. We had need make much of present good which is granted to us in this world.

My lovely swans come smiling up and seem to say 'We

* Malvern Hall was the seat of Constable's patron Henry Greswolde Lewis, and the childhood home of Lewis's sister Magdalena, Lady Dysart (d. 1823, not to be confused with Lady Louisa Manners, *née* Tollemache, later 7th Countess of Dysart, Constable's life-long friend). Constable visited Malvern Hall in 1809 and 1821, and painted the house a number of times, but Mary may be referring to the painting of 1809 which he had kept for himself (see pp. 34–5).

wish Mr John Constable could see us –he would appreciate our beauty.' It will afford you a glad heart to know that your warm blanket gives comfort to the poor Widow Abbott – she thanks you humbly – she said 'What a good thing it is that the family notice me' – Howard & John begged me to add their duty & thanks to you when I wrote. Poor dear Widow Hart – how kind you were to her – she is gone before us, I trust to a better inheritance.

Our beautiful London cat has brought up her three lovely kittens & they 'turn out quite to her liking' & the favourites of everybody – 'Marquis' & 'Jessey' & 'Gipsy' are their names. If I write the word 'Horse' it renews great vexation, so I pass over loss upon loss.

Next Monday would be the anniversary of our coming to live at Flatford, *14 years ago* – to retrace the blessings which have been showered down upon us time must prove too short – but I trust we may seek the path which conducts mankind to happiness – temporal trials are our lot only for moments – all must meet them.

No time to spare so excuse this from your's ever affectionately to all of you.

M. C.

[...] Abram but sadly – lungs oppressed – spirits down – business troubles here – Golding we see but once a week – pray eat a *medlar*.

Dame Hope's quite brisk.

CONSTABLE TO C. R. LESLIE
ARUNDEL, 16 JULY 1834

My dear Leslie

In all my walks about this most beautiful spot I am continually thinking of you. How much your company would enhance the beautiful things which are continually crossing my path. John is enjoying himself exceedingly. The chalk cliffs afford him many fragments of oyster shells and other matters that fell from the table of Adam in all probability – but our friend here Mr George Constable* is a most sensible man in all matters of science and he has won John's heart by a present (the arrival of which in Charlotte Street I shall much dread) of an electrifying machine. In the drawing room in which I am now writing, are many enormous pieces of stained paper by Copley Fielding, as well as of poor Robson, and Havell, and some 'oils' by Wm. Daniel – therefore I hope you excuse whatever this letter may contain.

The Castle is the chief ornament of this place – but all here sinks to insignificance in comparison with the

*George Constable of Arundel, brewer, amateur scientist and painter, was no relation of John's, but had become a close friend after meeting in 1832. He had invited John to convalesce in Sussex; and had given young John a collection of fossils.

woods, and hills. The woods hang from excessive steeps, and precipices, and the trees are beyond everything beautiful: I never saw such beauty in *natural landscape* before. I wish it may influence what I may do in future, for I have too much preferred the picturesque to the beautiful – which will I hope account for the *broken ruggedness of my style*. Some parts of the castle, such as the keep and some old walls, are as grand as possible – but the more modern part is not unlike a London show place, or tea garden. The Baron's Hall, is a grand room though strangely vulgarized by some hideous figures *larger* than life in *painted glass*, by Oliver, A.R.A., in all the windows. These ruffian looking fellows look like drunk bargemen dressed up as crusaders, and are meant to be the 'barons bold,' the former lords of the estate, who spread the English name over Palestine with holy wars – but so are the mighty fallen, you would take them to be the very men who are engaged this hot weather in watering the streets in London. It makes true what Lord Orford (Horace Walpole) says of the painters and architects of the middle (or dark) ages as we call them. He says, it would not be easy now 'to know where to go to order a painted window' like one he was describing.

The meadows are lovely, so is the delightful river, and the old houses are rich beyond all things of the sort – but

Overleaf: Arundel Mill and Castle, 1837

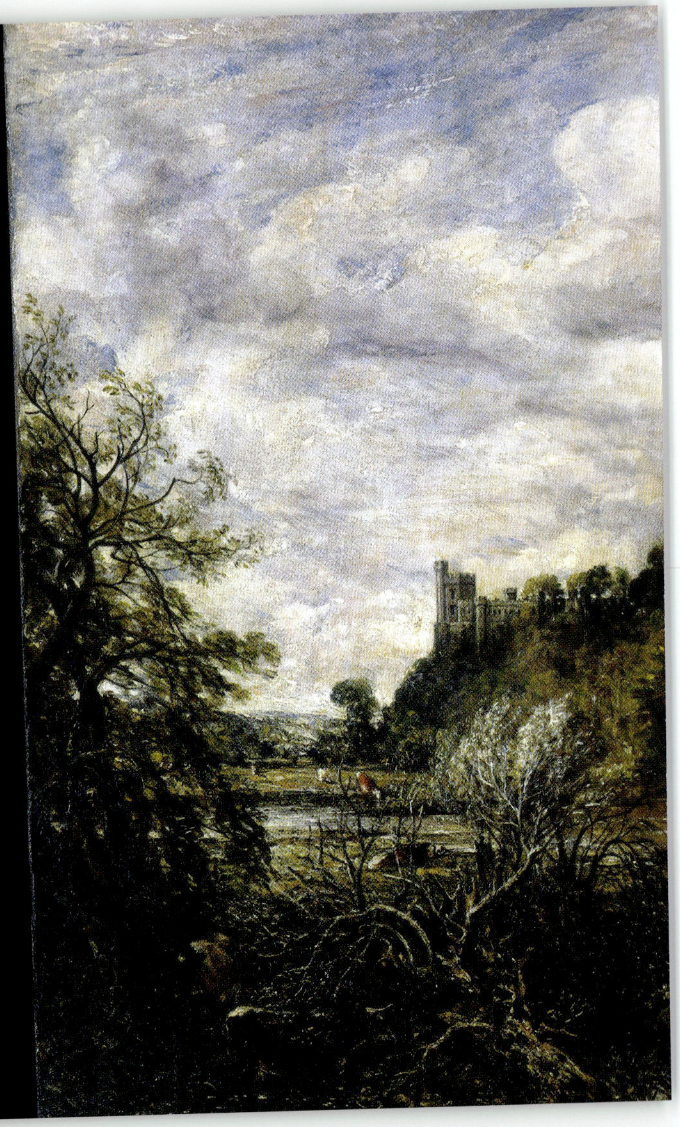

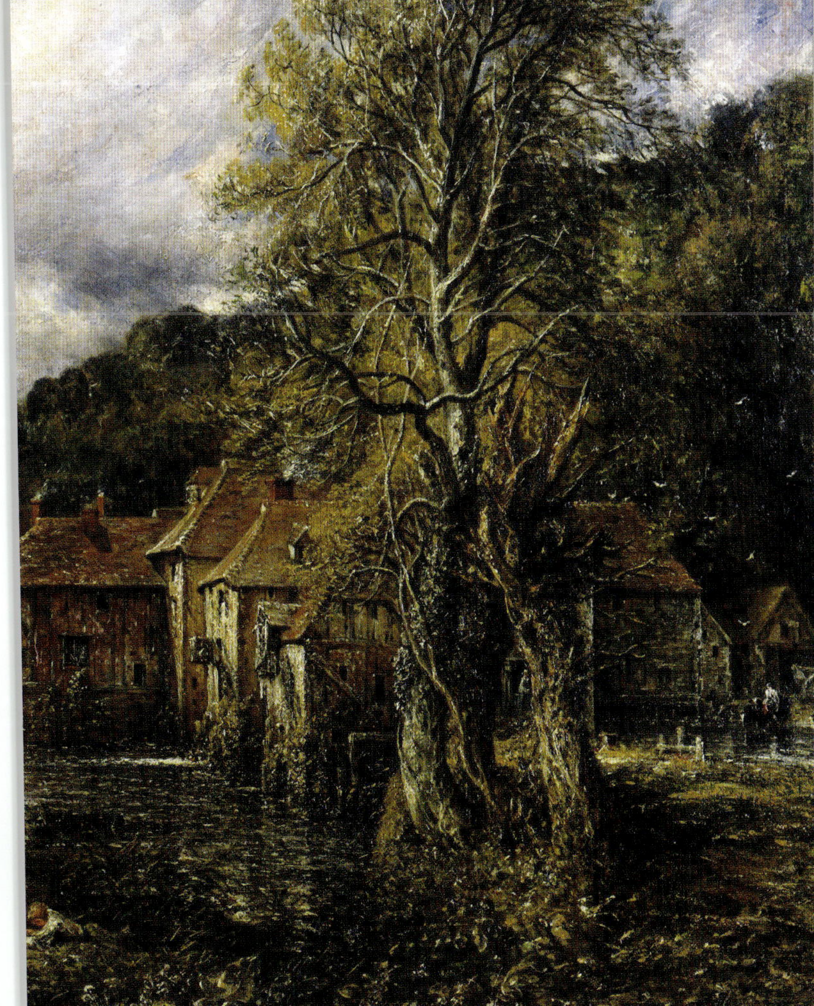

the trees above all, but anything is beautiful. Only last night by chance I stumbled on an old barn situated amid trees of immense size, which is … as old as of King John, and tended by a lady.

But we have been to Petworth. [The collection of] pictures forms a chief attraction. I have thought of nothing else but this vast house & its contents – [and] the Earl the master of all was there. He was [pleased] to come out to me, and to Mr and Mrs Constable and their daughter. He wanted me to stay all day – nay more he wished me to pass a few days in the house. This I was much pleased at, but I excused myself for the present, saying I would so much like to make that visit while you was there – which he took very agreeably, saying let it be so then, if you cannot leave your friends now. He came out to us 3 times, & once to the riding house from which I was sketching the [view], all of which pleased him. I had a very kind letter of Phillips's to him for me.

Have you seen Bonner? My best and kindest regards to you & Mrs Leslie [and] all the dear children. Lord Egremont asked me if you had a nice home. I told him it was delightfully [placed], only a little further on than the last. You, my dear Leslie, what matters to me, are there.

Affectionately
John Constable

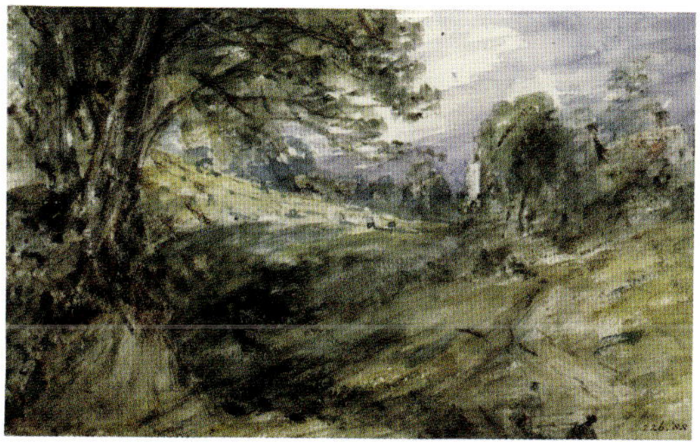

Study of cottages on high ground, Sussex, 1834 or 1835

ABRAM CONSTABLE TO CONSTABLE
EAST BERGHOLT, 23 APRIL 1835

Dear John,

I should certainly have written before had not Mary kept her pen going, who I knew would inform you of all things upon the anvil just now – I was delighted with your letter giving an account of your picture[1] just then sent to the Academy, as well as the pleasing intelligence of its sale, there are but few people can make a piece of canvas worth *£300*. I already long to see it, & hope when the Exhibition is open I shall pay an early visit to it.

1. *The Valley Farm* (Tate), sold to the collector Robert Vernon for £300, the highest price Constable achieved for a picture in his lifetime.

The prints you were so kind as to send us are a constant delight, I certainly derive more pleasure from them than from any other prints I ever saw, there seems more effect combined with beautiful minutiæ than is usually seen as far as I am a judge. Most likely the picture this year will furnish the subject for another print, of a very delightful kind.

[...] I have not yet seen Mr Gosnall upon the business we talk about, the price he asks is terribly high, and unless he will take less, it seems like madness to me to purchase, as there is every possibility that the rents of land must come down considerably, generally, still we can try what we can do, & some sacrifice you seem willing to make, it would be very comfortable to have such a house with a little land attached, to retreat into when you grow tired of the smoke & dirt of London. – I will see Mr G. very shortly & sound the ground – I want to come to London & shall then see you of course.

Your plan & prospect for your Hampstead incumbrance is very cheering, & I hope it is now off your hands even though at a yearly loss of a few pounds. [...].

The weather is beautifully fine, & dry, but showers would be delightful for *Sir John Barleycorn*.

We are selling flour at eighteen pence a stone, the lowest price I ever remember it to have been at the milling trade in the country, & in London for country millers, is sad indeed, I am very uneasy about it, as I see no prospect of amendment, or of paying my interest. I should not care about accumulating money could I but clear my way from year to year, as I have no family or heavy expenses.

You did not tell me which set of your books of prints I was to give to James Revans, perhaps it had better remain till you come to us again. [...]

Kind love from all here to you all,
& believe me Dear John
as ever yours affectionately
Abram Constable

ABRAM CONSTABLE TO CONSTABLE
EAST BERGHOLT, 20 MAY 1836

My dear John,

Although I have not written to you lately I have thought more about you than usual but M. C. having more leisure she has communicated most to you. Indeed I should have written last week had she not told me of her letter to you, and though I have nothing very particular to write about, I am anxious to prevent you supposing for a moment that you can be long absent from my mind, & I ought in this first to thank you much for your kindness in sending me the syllabus of your Lectures the first of which is next Thursday, & I feel no doubt of your success in arresting & keeping possession of the attention of your hearers – & it is no small thing to appear before an assembly like that in the first city of the world.

There will be many first rate people there, & some that will be able to appreciate the research & ability of the lecturer: the card is drawn up in a way to open the subject to the reader of it, & not only prepare him for the lecture but afford him much insight into the subject matter.

I am very desirous of being present if possible next Thursday, but I very much fear I shall not be able to accomplish it, should I be able to leave home I shall come up on Tuesday, be in the City & Mark Lane [ie the Corn Exchange] on Wednesday, & drink tea with you on Wednesday evening – this is in my mind, but I may be prevented, having many things to attend to, this much is certain if I can start from here you will be sure to see me on Wednesday evening.

Sidey is at home & has brought G. C. two beautiful prints which he has hung up I hear in his house but I have not seen them. Golding is much delighted with his acquisition of land, indeed it is *now* complete, Old Cuthbert's cottage is not necessary to him, although I should advise him to buy it if possible but the old man asks such a foolish price, considering his determination to keep possession without paying rent or interest, & he may live these 10 years – I know no man at his age, more likely so to do.

M. C. & you have got the farm and old house – & I

have paid £200, deposit – M. C. anticipates much pleasure, & I trust will experience it, & without loss, – she had engaged old Crosbie & his wife, one to see to the farm & the other to dairy – &ccc.

How very dry the weather has been now for three weeks, it seems to promise to be such another season as the last two were, the wind has been at east for the last month, I have been quite distressed for coals, the ships not being able to stir. I am glad to say my flour has pleased …, I think it has improved. … Mr Scourfield is at the Rectory, & has given me this frank which I am glad of, for I am sure this laboured epistle is not worth postage.*

I am anxious to thank you for sending me a catalogue of the Exhibition. I hear that your picture[1] is mentioned in many of the papers, & very favourably. I think *Stonehenge* is a drawing – where did you get the quotation for it?[2]

The eclipse on Sunday was very interesting though the darkness was not so great as was expected by many – but the correctness of the calculations excited my admiration. We went into Church at 5 in the afternoon instead of 3.

I hope all your family are well. […] Yours Dear John affectionately

A. Constable

* Clergymen were entitled to post letters for free with a 'frank'. 1. *The Cenotaph* (see p. 240). 2. *Stonehenge* (1835) for which Constable wrote a long caption himself (see overleaf).

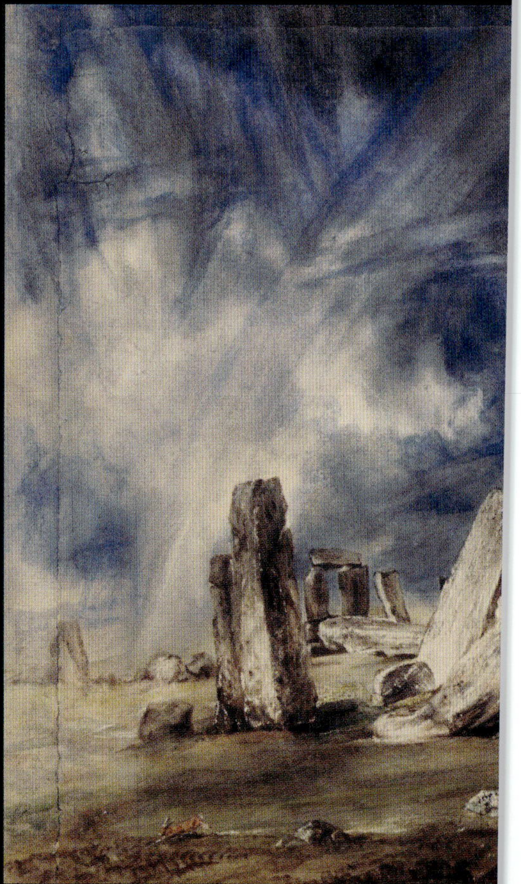

Stonehenge, 1835

Constable wrote this caption: 'The mysterious monument of Stonehenge, standing remote on a bare and boundless heath, as much unconnected with the events of past ages as it is with the uses of the present, carries you back beyond all historical records into the obscurity of a totally unknown period'

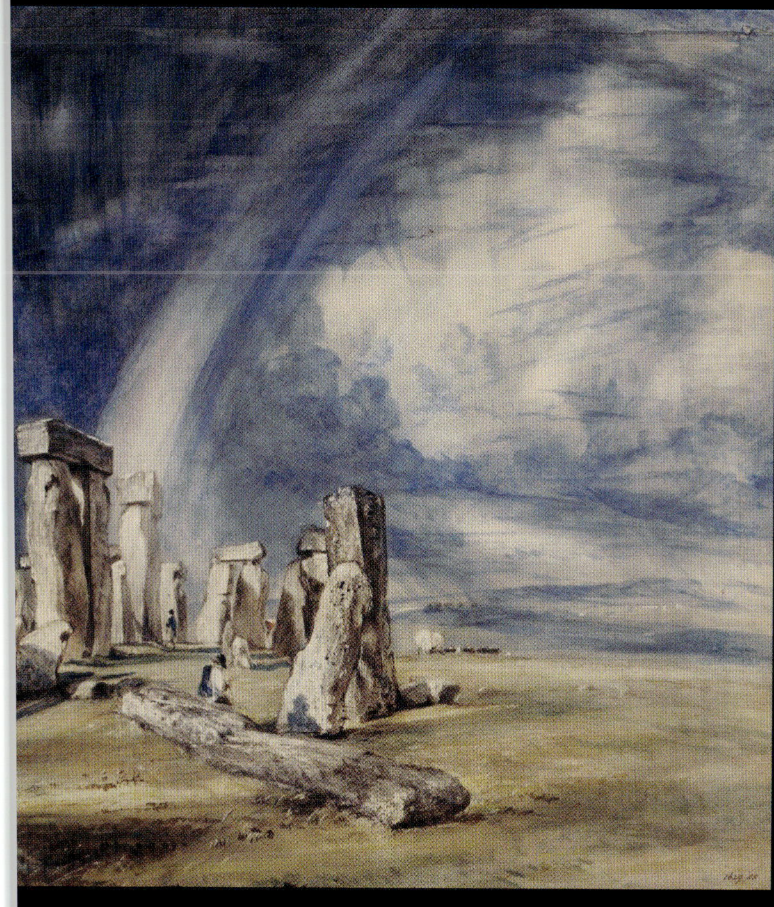

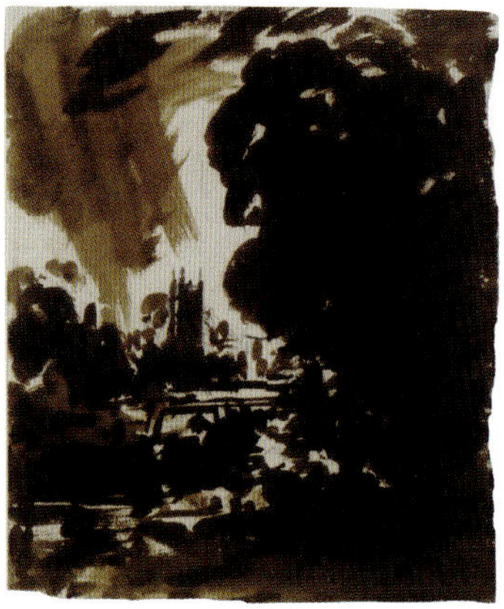

View on the Stour: Dedham Church in the distance, c. 1836

CONSTABLE TO WILLIAM WORDSWORTH
35 CHARLOTTE STREET, LONDON, 15 JUNE 1836

My dear Sir

May I beg as a mark of my sincere esteem that you will do me the honour to accept my little work – (on the Chiaroscuro [i.e. Constable's *English Landscape*]) – the subjects of which are for the most part in the neighbourhood of Dedham – in Essex – one of the early and favourite haunts of our valued friend the late Sir George Beaumont whom my mother knew as a little boy – I feel that I am indebted to him for what I am as an artist – and it was from his hands that I first saw a volume of your poems – how then can I can I [*sic*] ever be sufficiently grateful – my little work occupied me during a season of sadness – occasioned by the loss of the mother of my seven children –

I heard from Mr Judkin of your intended tour – I wish you every happy result from it –

I shall always reflect with pride that – you – was at one of my lectures – my last is tomorrow – but I fear I must not again flatter myself with the hope of seeing you there –

I am
my dear Sir
most truly your faithful
and obliged
John Constable

My friend Mr Spedding had offered to take my little book to you when he went into the north – had you not been here.

CONSTABLE TO C. R. LESLIE

35 CHARLOTTE STREET, LONDON, 30 DECEMBER, 1836

My dear Leslie

I am vexed with myself for having so long delayed to write to thank you for your kind invitation to these dear children.

This fearful weather intimidates me – but it seems little likely to change. In spite however of all my dreads, & of all I can say about the danger of such an 'excursion into the country,' in this most inclement time, I can only say that it makes no alarm whatever in the children, & they insist on my coming out of my lurking hole where I had laid up for the winter – & I must accompany them to your house on Monday the 2nd to keep the 1st, New Years Day.

Now all this I do and let them do, only on condition that you and Mrs Leslie dine with me on Wednesday. We have a small but pretty thigh of a doe – from my old friend the Countess – and we are almost alone, only our friends Mr & Miss Spedding – very old & much esteemed friends of my poor wife – & that is all. Our object is to get a long & quiet hour for the children & Miss Spedding, who is fond of Maria.

'Prithee come – life is short – friendship sweet.' These were the last words of poor Fisher to me, in his last invitation.

I hear the meetings of Council are frequent – I hope that no one will occur to prevent you from coming on Wednesday at 6.

My month with school [ie the Life Academy] is March. I have 3 men & *one woman* allotted to my share. I have concluded on the three figures in the 'Peter Martyr,' [by Titian, destroyed] for I am determined to sift that picture

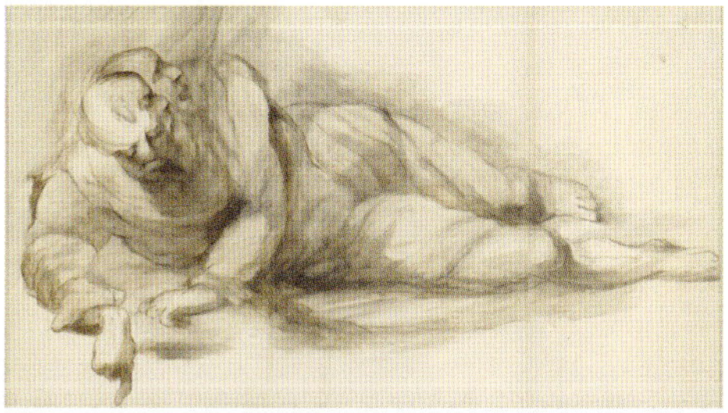

Study of the fallen figure of the saint in Titian's St Peter Martyr, 1836

to the bottom. I believe they will turn out admirably well, especially the 'flying monk.' I have by me a very old print of the subject 5 years before that of Titian, which is done from the picture when it occupied the same place in the Dominican church. The picture was by 'Jacobi Fiori' – Jacob of the flower, or in the cant way of the old Italian painters, 'Jemmy of the Flower'. The flower stands as his name in the print, forming a very conspicuous figure.

Yours truly, J. C.

Constable carried on working on Arundel Castle, *and attending to Academy business. He was suddenly taken ill on the night of 31 March 1837, and died early next morning*

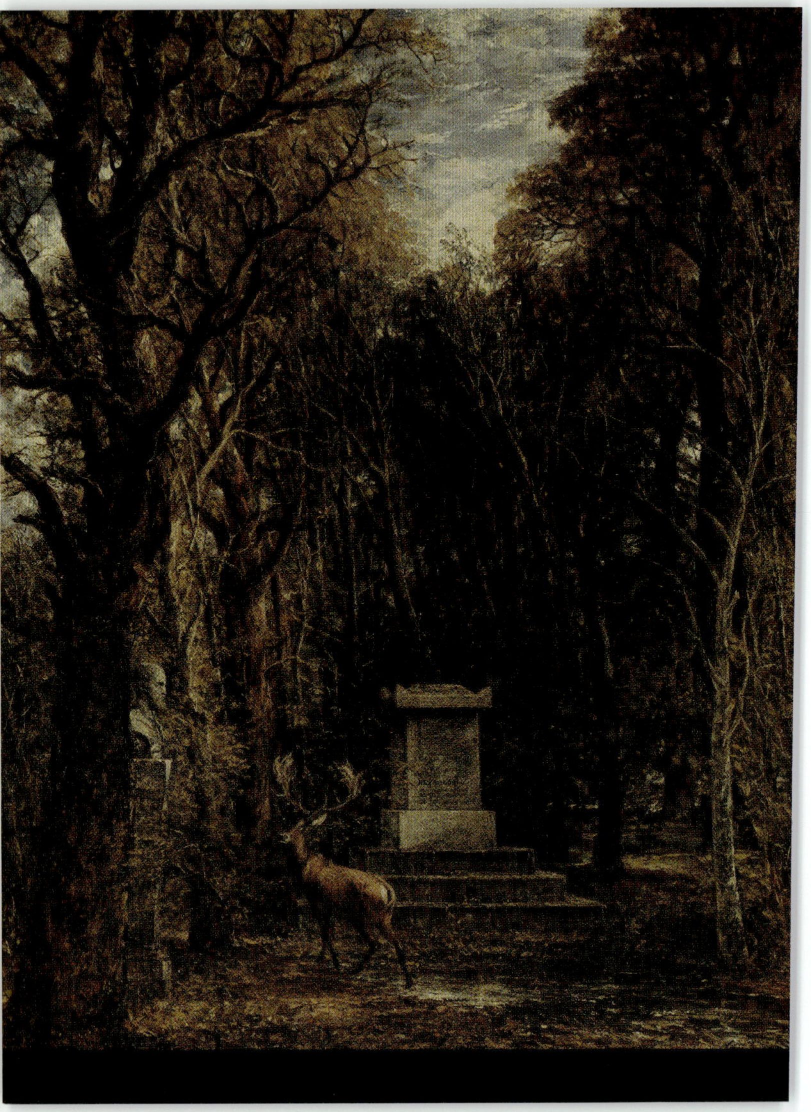

DEATH OF JOHN CONSTABLE, ESQ. R.A.

Bell's Weekly Messenger
9 April 1837

This melancholy and unexpected event took place at his house in Charlotte Street, Fitzroy Square, on Saturday, the 1st inst. about two o'clock in the morning. He had been occupied upon his picture intended for the ensuing exhibition at the Royal Academy, until a late hour on Friday, and about eleven o'clock that night he retired to bed, apparently in his usual good health. Shortly afterwards he complained of being unwell, and a servant was dispatched for a medical gentleman residing in the neighbourhood, who came immediately, but without avail, Mr. Constable expiring a few seconds after he arrived. He appears to have died of spasm at the heart. On the Saturday prior to his decease it fell to his lot, as visitor, to close the final session of the Royal Academy at Somerset House, previous to the establishment being removed to

Opposite: Cenotaph to the Memory of Sir Joshua Reynolds, 1836

the National Gallery at Charing Cross. On that occasion he addressed the students upon the rise and progress of the arts, pointing out to them the true method of study that leads to eminence, and expressing a hope that in taking their last farewell of the edifice which had been, as it were, the 'cradle of British art,' they would remember with grateful feelings the advantages they had derived from instruction within its walls. He then returned them his thanks for the constant attention they always paid to him, and the diligence with which they had attended to their studies during his Visitorship. At the close of his speech the students arose and cheered him heartily, little suspecting that this would be his last address.

Mr. Constable was in his 60th year, and was born at Bergholt, in Suffolk. In early life he evinced very strong natural talent for the arts, and his friends placed him under the tuition of a Royal Academician. At the commencement of his professional career he painted some few portraits, but his genius and taste were decidedly in favour of landscape, and he finally abandoned the uninteresting walk of portraiture for the more congenial one for which he was so eminently qualified. None but those intimately acquainted with him can form an adequate idea of his enthusiasm and diligence; scarcely a day passed without some valuable addition being made to his private collection of drawings and sketches, bearing evident marks that his natural perceptions of what was good were strong and original. He was an ardent and sincere worshipper of nature, moving, as it were, in a sphere of his own. His style was very peculiar, and that peculiarity will render his works lasting and valuable in the eyes of all true judges of art, when many of the commonplace productions of his cotemporaries are sunk in oblivion. Some of his pictures have been highly prized by French connoisseurs, and on the occasion of one* of them being exhibited in the Louvre, he received a medal from the late King of France, complimentary of his talent. His first landscape of note was a view of Dedham Vale, in Essex; his last is a scene near Arundel Castle, in Sussex, and intended by him, as before observed, for the exhibition. Mr. Constable married a daughter of the late Mr. Bicknell, formerly Solicitor to the Admiralty; she died about eight years since, and by her he had seven children, all of whom survive him. In private life Mr. Constable was much and deservedly esteemed. As an artist his place will not easily be supplied; as a parent, friend, and companion, his loss is irreparable.

* *In fact, two. See pp. 11 and 159.*

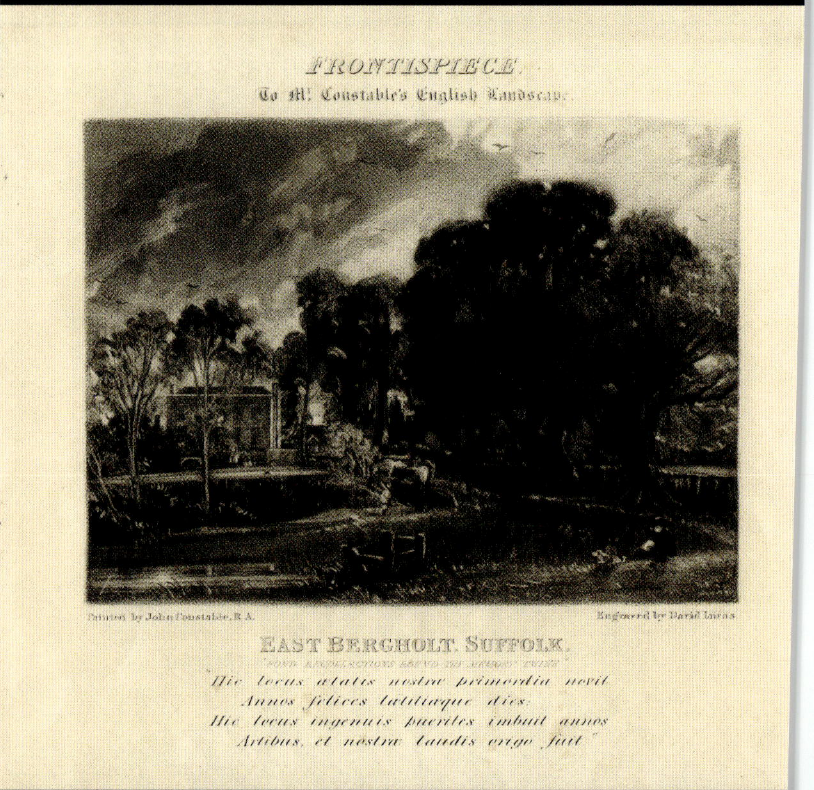

Frontispiece to English Landscape, 1831.
The image shows Constable's birthplace, East Bergholt House, with with the caption 'Fond recollections round thy memory twine.' (Mary Roberts). The Latin verse is by Alexander Neckham (1157-1217): 'This place knew the beginnings of our age/ Happy years and days of joy./ This place imbued our innocent boyhood years/ With the arts and was the origin of our fame.'

INTRODUCTION TO VARIOUS SUBJECTS OF LANDSCAPE, CHARACTERISTIC OF ENGLISH SCENERY, PRINCIPALLY INTENDED TO DISPLAY THE PHENOMENA OF THE CHIAROSCURO OF NATURE

Rura mihi, et rigui placeant in vallibus amnes,
Flumina amem, sylvasque, inglorius. – Virgil.*

* *Georgics* II, lines 485–6. 'Let my delight be the country, and the running streams amid the dells – may I love the waters and the woods, though I be unknown to fame' (trans H. Rushton Fairclough).

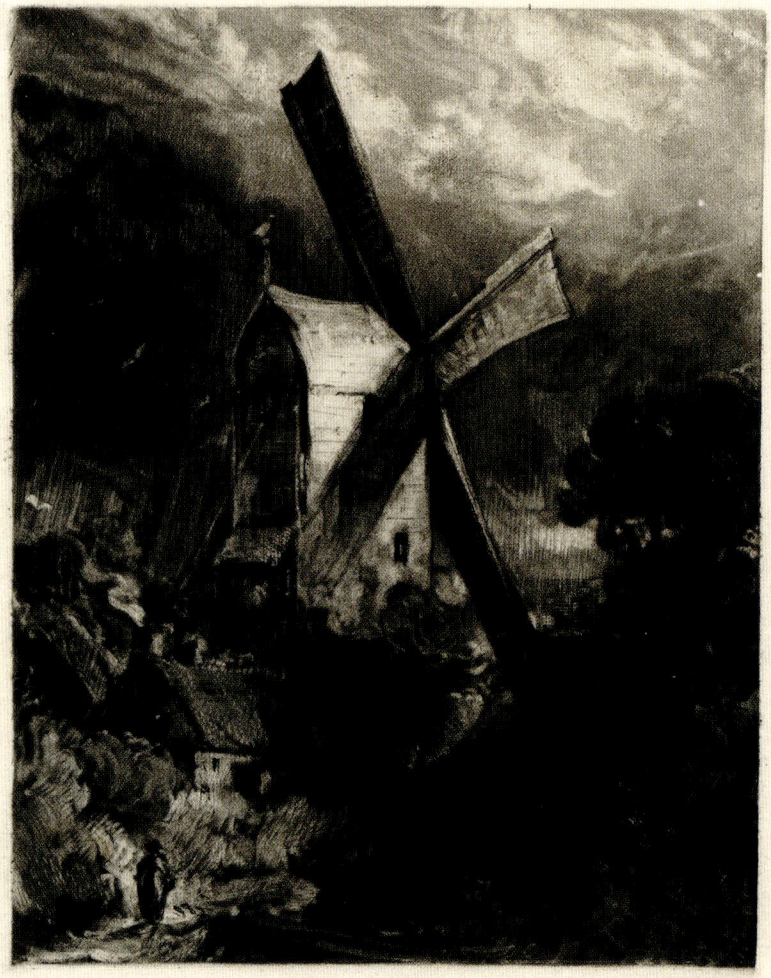

The author rests in the belief that the present collection of prints of rural landscape may not be found wholly unworthy of attention. It originated in no mercenary views, but merely as a pleasing professional occupation, and was continued with a hope of imparting pleasure and instruction to others. He had imagined to himself certain objects in art, and has always pursued them. Much of the landscape, forming the subject of these plates, going far to embody his ideas (owing perhaps to the rich and feeling manner in which they are engraved) he has been tempted to publish them, and offers them as the result of his own experience, founded as he conceives it to be in a just observation of natural scenery in its various aspects. From the almost universal esteem in which the arts are now held, the author is encouraged to hope that this work may not be found unacceptable, since perhaps no branch of the art offers a more inviting field of study than landscape.

> *Soul-soothing Art! whom morning, noon-tide, even,*
> *Do serve with all their fitful pageantry.* *

* Lines from William Wordsworth, 'Upon the Sight of a Beautiful Picture Painted by Sir G. H. Beaumont, Bt.' (1811).

Opposite: David Lucas after John Constable, Mill near Brighton: proof before letters, c. 1831

The immediate aim of the author in this publication is to increase the interest for, and promote the study of, the rural scenery of England, with all its endearing associations, its amenities, and even its most simple localities; abounding as it does in grandeur, and every description of pastoral beauty: England, with her climate of more than vernal freshness, and in whose summer skies, and rich autumnal clouds, 'with thousand liveries dight,'* the student of Nature may daily watch her endless varieties of effect, for by him it is, that these changes are particularly observed: "*Multa vident Pictores in imminentia et in umbris quae nos non videmus.*" – Cicero.†

It is therefore perhaps in its professional character that this work may be most considered, so far as it respects the ART; its aim being to direct attention to the source of one of its most efficient principles, the 'CHIAR'OSCURO OF NATURE,' to mark the influence of light and shadow upon landscape, not only in its general effect on the 'whole', and as a means of rendering a proper emphasis on the 'parts', in painting, but also to show its use and power as a medium of expression, so as to note 'the day, the hour, the sunshine, and the shade.' In some of these

* Approximate quotation from John Milton's *L'Allegro*. † Approximate quotation from Cicero's *Academica,* II, 7: 'How many things painters see in shadows and in the foreground which we do not see! (trans. H. Rackham).

subjects of landscape an attempt has been made to arrest the more abrupt and transient appearances of the CHIAR'OSCURO IN NATURE; to show its effect in the most striking manner, to give 'to one brief moment caught from fleeting time,'* a lasting and sober existence, and to render permanent many of those splendid but evanescent exhibitions, which are ever occurring in the changes of external Nature.

In the selection of these subjects, a partiality has perhaps been given to those of a particular neighbourhood: some of them, however, may be more generally interesting, as the scenes of many of the marked historical events of our middle ages. The most of these subjects, chiefly consisting of home scenery, are from the pictures exhibited by the author at the Royal Academy during the last few years; they are taken from real places, and are meant particularly to characterize the scenery of England; the effects of light and shadow being transcripts only of such as occurred at the time of being taken.

In art as in literature, however, there are two modes by which men endeavour to attain the same end, and seek distinction. In the one, the artist, intent only on the study of departed excellence, or on what others have

* Line from William Wordsworth, 'Upon the Sight of a Beautiful Picture Painted by Sir G. H. Beaumont, Bt.' (1811).

accomplished, becomes an imitator of their works, as he selects and combines their various beauties; in the other he seeks perfection at its PRIMITIVE SOURCE, NATURE. The one, forms a style upon the study of pictures, or the art alone; and produces, either 'imitative', 'scholastic', or that which has been termed the 'Eclectic Art. The other, by study equally legitimately founded in art, but further pursued in such a far more expansive field, soon finds for himself innumerable sources of study, hitherto unexplored, fertile in beauty, and by attempting to display them for the first time, forms a style which is original; thus adding to the art, qualities of Nature unknown to it before. The results of the one mode, as they merely repeat what has been done by others, and by having the appearance of that with which the eye is already familiar, can be easily comprehended, soon estimated, and are at once received. Thus the rise of an artist in a sphere of his own must almost certainly be delayed; it is to time generally that the justness of his claims to a lasting reputation will be left; so few appreciate any deviation from a beaten track, can trace the indications of talent in immaturity, or are qualified to judge of productions bearing an original cast of mind, of genuine study, and of consequent novelty of style in their mode of execution.

J. C.

35, Charlotte Street, Fitzroy Square, May, 1833.

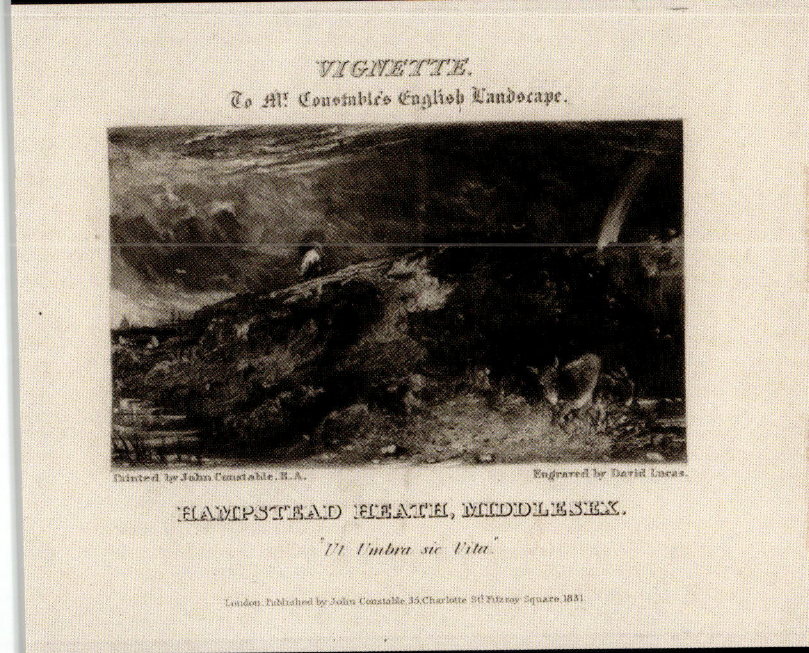

Vignette to English Landscape, 1831.
The image shows Hampstead Heath with St Paul's in the distance, with the Latin tag, 'Ut umbra sic vita', 'Life is a shadow', which was the motto on the sundial above the porch of St Mary's, East Bergholt

List of illustrations

All works are by John Constable and are oil on canvas unless stated otherwise. Measurements given height before width. Images from holding institutions unless noted.

Center for British Art, Paul Mellon Collection, New Haven, CT

p. 64 Ramsay Richard Reinagle, *Portrait of Constable*, *c.* 1799. 76 cm x 64 cm. National Portrait Gallery, London

p. 67 *The entrance to the village of Edensor, Derbyshire*, August 1801. Pencil and sepia wash on paper, 17 x 25.7 cm. Victoria and Albert Museum, London

p. 70 *A Stand of Elm Trees*, *c.* 1802. Black chalk on paper, 52 x 44.6 cm. The Art Institute of Chicago, Chicago, IL

pp. 72–3 *Dedham Vale*, 1802. 33 x 42 cm. Yale Center for British Art, Paul Mellon Collection

p. 74 (left) *Ann Constable*, *c.* 1815. 77 x 64 cm. Tate Britain, London

p. 74 (right) *Golding Constable*, 1815. 76 x 63 cm. Tate Britain, London

pp. 76–7 *Flatford Mill from the lock*, *c.* 1810. Oil on beige laid (?) paper, mounted on canvas, 19 x 24.1 cm. The Clark Art Institute, Williamstown, MA

p. 79 *View toward the Rectory, East Bergholt*, 1810. Oil on canvas laid on panel, 15.6 x 24.8 cm. Philadelphia Museum of Art, Philadelphia, PA

p. 80 *Maria Bicknell*, *c.* 1805–9. Graphite on paper, 48.8 x 34.8 cm. Tate Britain, London

pp. 86-7 *Autumnal Sunset near East Bergholt*, *c.* 1812. Oil on paper later laid down on canvas, 16 x 31.8 cm. Victoria and Albert Museum, London

p. 90 *Landscape with a double rainbow*, 28 July 1812. Oil on paper laid on canvas, 33.7 x 38.4 cm. Victoria and Albert Museum, London

p. 96 *Landscape – Boys Fishing*, 1813. 100-126 cm. Anglesey Abbey, Lode, Cambridgeshire, Fairhaven Collection (National Trust),

pp. 100-101 *Woodland Landscape*, 1815. Oil on board, 38 x 63 cm. With Christie's 7 December 2021

p. 105 *Maria Bicknell, Mrs. John Constable*, 1816. Oil on canvas, 31 x 25 cm. Tate Britain, London

p. 108 *Dog watching a rat, Dedham*, 1 August 1831. Pencil and watercolour on paper, 18.5 x 22.6 cm. Victoria and Albert Museum, London

p. 110-1 *Wivenhoe Park*, 1816. 56 x 101 cm. National Gallery of Art, Washington DC

p. 112 *The Fishing Lodge, Wivenhoe (also known as The Quarters behind Alresford Hall),* 1816. Oil on paper later laid down on canvas, 34 x 52 cm. National Gallery of Victoria, Melbourne

pp. 114–5 *The Beach at Weymouth*, 1816. 53 x 75 cm. National Gallery, London

p. 117 *One of the artist's sons with a dog*, *c.* 1821-3. Oil on board 28.9 x 24.5 cm. Private collection

pp. 118–9 *Stratford Mill ('The Young Waltonians)*, 1820. 127 x 182.9 cm.

National Gallery, London

p. 124 *The Grove, Hampstead*, 1821–2. 36 x 30 cm. Tate Britain, London

p. 126 *Cloud Study*, 1822. Oil on paper, 13.3 x 14.9 cm. Fitzwilliam Museum, Cambridge

pp. 128–9 *View on the Stour near Dedham* (full size study), *c.* 1821–2. 129 x 185 cm. Private collection with Christie's

p. 133 *Page from one of Constable's surviving sketchbooks*, used 1813–15. Pencil on paper, 9.6 x 12.4 cm (closed sketchbook). Victoria and Albert Museum, London

pp. 136–7 *Salisbury Cathedral from the Bishop's Grounds* (original version), 1823. 88 x 112 cm. Victoria and Albert Museum, London

p. 139 *Gillingham Mill*, 1823–7. 63 x 52 cm. Victoria and Albert Museum, London

p. 144 *Stone in the Grove of Coleorton Hall dedicated to Richard Wilson*, 28 November 1823. Pencil and grey wash on paper, 11.5 x 18.1 cm. Victoria and Albert Museum, London

pp. 146–7 *Scene on the Downs, near Brighton*, 1824. Oil on light card, 11.5 x 15.9 cm. With Christies 7 December 2010

pp. 152–3 *Sir Richard Steele's Cottage, Hampstead*, 1831–2. 21 x 29 cm. Yale Center for British Art, Paul Mellon Collection, New Haven, CT

p. 157 *Mouse with a piece of cheese*, 1824. Oil on grey paper, 10.1 x 13.3 cm. British Museum, London

pp. 160–1 *The Hay Wain*, 1831–2. 130 x 185 cm. National Gallery, London

pp. 164–5 *Scene on the beach at Brighton, c.* 1824. Pen, pencil and grey wash on paper, 18.1 x 26.4 cm. Victoria and Albert Museum, London

p. 167 *Brighton Beach with Colliers*, 19 July 1824. Oil on paper, 14.6 x 24.8 cm. Victoria and Albert Museum, London

pp. 174–5 *The Leaping Horse*, 1825. 129 cm x 188 cm. Royal Academy of Arts, London

pp. 180–1 *Branch Hill Pond, Hampstead*, 1824–5. 87 x 103 cm. Virginia Museum of Fine Arts, Richmond, VA

p. 186 *Mrs Treslove*, 1826, retouched 1829. 76 x 64 cm. Private collection

p. 188 *John Charles and Minna playing coach and horses, c.* 1822. Pencil and watercolour on paper, 8.4 x 18.9 cm. Private collection

p. 189 *Minna playing Bo-Peep, c.* 1822. Oil on millboard, 18 x 10 cm. Private collection

pp. 194–5 *A Boat passing a Lock*, 1826. 102 x 127 cm. Royal Academy of Arts, London

pp. 198–9 David Lucas after John Constable, *The Spring, c.* 1831, mezzotint on paper, progress proof with annotations and corrections by John Constable. Image size 155 x 215 cm. British Museum, London

p. 201 *Lord Brougham with coronet at*

First published 2026 by
Pallas Athene (Publishers) Limited
2 Birch Close, N19 5XD
Reprinted 2026

www.pallasathene.co.uk

ISBN 978 1 84368 287 5

Printed in China
through WorldPrint

Selection made, edited, introduced and annotated
by Anne Lyles,
with Alexander Fyjis-Walker
Series editor: Alexander Fyjis-Walker
Editorial assistant: Patrick Davies

This book is dedicated to the memory of
DICK HUMPHREYS
art historian, curator,
dear colleague and friend
AL & AFW